MEN AT WORK

GLENN KURTZ

MEN AT WORK

THE EMPIRE STATE BUILDING AND THE UNTOLD STORY OF THE CRAFTSMEN WHO BUILT IT

SEVEN STORIES PRESS
New York • Oakland • London

SEVEN STORIES PRESS
140 Watts Street New York, NY 10013
www.sevenstories.com

LIBRARY OF CONGRESS CATALOGING-IN-PUBLICATION DATA

Names: Kurtz, Glenn author
Title: Men at work : the Empire State Building and the untold story of the craftsmen who built it / Glenn Kurtz.
Description: New York City : Seven Stories Press, 2025. | Includes bibliographical references and index.
Identifiers: LCCN 2025008092 (print) | LCCN 2025008093 (ebook) | ISBN 9781644215029 hardcover | ISBN 9781644215036 ebook
Subjects: LCSH: Hine, Lewis Wickes, 1874-1940 | Empire State Building (New York, N.Y.)--History | Building trades--New York (State)--New York--History | Iron and steel workers--New York (State)--New York--History | Documentary photography--New York (State)--New York--History
Classification: LCC F128.8.E46 K87 2025 (print) | LCC F128.8.E46 (ebook)
LC record available at https://lccn.loc.gov/2025008092
LC ebook record available at https://lccn.loc.gov/2025008093

College professors and high school and middle school teachers
may order free examination copies of Seven Stories Press titles.
visit https://www.sevenstories.com/pg/resources-academics
or email academic@sevenstories.com.

Printed in the USA.

9 8 7 6 5 4 3 2 1

CONTENTS

For A.X. G. and Z. F. M. K.
and to the memory of my father,
whose office was all the way up
on the third floor.

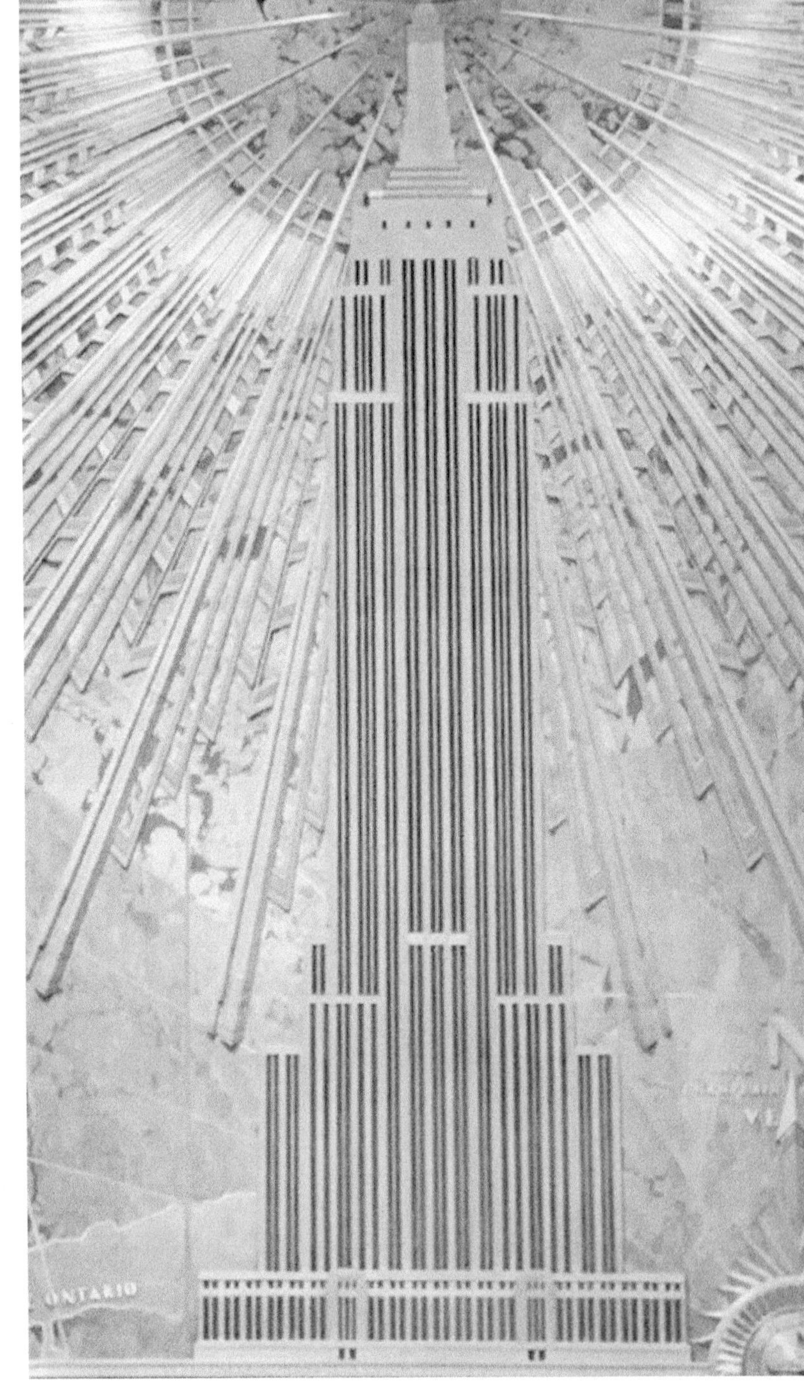
ONTARIO

ONE
THE NAMED AND THE UNNAMED

> "Those who conceived it, those who designed it, those who made it, all built into the very steel and stone of Empire State a spirit dedicating it to the service and the glory of man."
> —*Empire State: A History*

> "Pyramids, Empire State Building—these things just don't happen. There's hard work behind it. I would like to see a building, say, the Empire State, I would like to see on one side of it a foot-wide strip from top to bottom with the names of every bricklayer, the name of every electrician, with all the names. So when a guy walked by, he could take his son and say, 'See, that's me over there on the forty-fifth floor. I put the steel beam in.'"
> —Mike Lefevre, steelworker

The Empire State Building has always been more than an edifice of steel and stone. Since its conception, it has occupied a unique place in the American imagination. Unlike its immediate competitors, the Chrysler Building and 40 Wall Street, which briefly vied for the title of world's tallest office building in 1930, or the Woolworth Building, which held that title a generation earlier, from 1913 until 1930, the Empire State Building has always embodied something beyond a great skyscraper. The building's unprecedented height, its powerful, elegant lines crowned by a soaring mast, gave physical form to an ideal of America. In the words of John Jakob Raskob, its lead financier, the Empire State Building represented "a land which reached for the sky with its feet on the ground." A recent critic called it "a cathedral not merely of architecture, but of Americanness." And while the venture was explicitly commercial, celebrating America's arrival as an economic world leader, the "Americanness" of the Empire State was never circumscribed by its function as an office building. On the contrary, the building was, as its publicists ceaselessly repeated, a towering *human* achievement. It was "the tallest structure built by Man," "Man's greatest gesture skyward," "a supreme expression of Man the Builder." The business of America might be business, but the Empire State's construction signaled the nation's arrival on the grander stage of world civilization. In the phrase of a contemporary journalist, "it is the future, solid and tangible, there for you to stand on and touch." Even its name distinguished it. The Woolworth Building, the Chrysler Building, the Manhattan Company Building at 40 Wall Street, all celebrated the great men or great corporations that built them, lending their namesakes the monumental stature of the skyscrapers themselves. For this reason, the Chrysler Building might be derided as "the fulfillment in metal and masonry of a one-man dream," as one contemporary critic sneered. The Empire State Building, by contrast, seemed to encompass the *American* dream, something more dynamic, more abstract, than any individual or corporate striving. For almost one hundred years, it has seemed to embody our national character and our national aspirations. Perhaps only the Eiffel Tower in Paris—the world's tallest structure from 1889 until 1930, though notably not a useful structure—packs the same vital charge of technical virtuosity and transcendent national symbolism. Tall as it is, the Empire State Building has always pointed to something higher.

As a symbol of national, indeed of human aspiration, the Empire State Building was resilient enough to escape the circumstances of its birth. Built between October 1929 and May 1931, its construction coincided with the onset of the Great Depression. This almost doomed it as a commercial venture. On its opening day, the building was only 23 percent occupied. It would not become profitable for two decades, and until the Second World War, it earned as much from visits to the observation deck as it did from rent.

Yet the completion of the world's tallest skyscraper just eighteen months after the stock market crash of October 1929 only emphasized the qualities that made America great, our grit in the face of hard times, our undaunted optimism.

"The Empire State Building is a monumental proof of hopefulness," asserted *The New York Times* on May 1, 1931, the day of its grand opening. The economic downturn would not last, the editors assured their readers, and therefore, the building's "inspiring sweep" should "be thought of as having a significance which extends far beyond the corner of Fifth Avenue and Thirty-fourth Street." True, the economic collapse was shocking. "It seems scarcely possible that it is little over twelve months ago that New York was a riot of expenditure, luxury, wholesale gayety and almost drunken prosperity," marveled the Princeton, New Jersey, *Patriot*, in October 1930, just as steelwork on the Empire State was topping out. "Anyone who spends a larger part of their waking hours in the city of New York in the late autumn of this year cannot but admit the existence of a dull, heavy cloud of encircling gloom." For the New Jersey paper, just as for *The New York Times*, however, the new skyscraper pierced the gloom. "There are a few bright spots left. Hard times, apparently, cannot stem the day to day magically changing skyline. Where the old red brick Waldorf-Astoria of tarnished memory once raised its venerable head, the enormous Empire State Building now soars upward to a terrific height and dominates the city." While the moods of its symbolism have shifted with the times, as any enduring symbol's must, the Empire State's potency as a symbol has persisted or even increased over the years. When New York's Landmarks Preservation Commission declared it the city's "quintessential landmark" in 1981, therefore, I think they took a provincial view, understating the building's larger historic and cultural role. Since its opening, the Empire State Building has been a symbol of the American Century, a symbol of the rising, indomitable American spirit.

This symbolism defines the Empire State Building. It defines how we see it, how we understand and relate its history, how we grasp its architecture and interpret the images associated with it. And for the length of the Empire State's history, Lewis W. Hine's magnificent photographs of its construction

workers have provided the indispensable visual evidence for this definition, the Empire State as a grand, symbolic narrative. Of the hundreds of images Hine captured, one in particular has seemed to distill the structure's inspiring essence. Often called *Icarus* or *The Sky Boy*, it shows a lone worker reaching upward to tighten a bolt.

The man's handsome face is tensed in concentration. His muscular arms and precarious stance convey daring and grace. As he reaches upward, the Hudson River and the country's wide horizon fall away in the distance below him. "Lifted like Lindbergh in ecstatic solitude," in the words of a recent commentator, this one heroic worker, it seems, embodies everything the skyscraper stands for. In *The Sky Boy*, the great endeavor achieves a human face and a vigorous body. He, too, reaches beyond himself, expressing in a single gesture the nation's skill, strength, and determination. He, too, gives physical form to an American ideal. It would be beside the point to ask who he was. As much as the building itself, the Sky Boy captures the spirit of America rising.

Walk into the Empire State Building through its imposing Fifth Avenue portal today, and you will find the symbolic narrative built into the lobby architecture. As you emerge through the revolving doors, the first thing you see at the opposite end of the cathedral-like space, is a two-story, stainless-steel depiction of the monumental structure itself. Pause here for a moment. Feel how the design of this marble gallery propels you forward, toward the giant, illuminated representation. On the floor, three rows of alternating black-and-gray chevrons channel your steps, like strobing arrows set in stone. On either side, the three-story, gray marble walls, flickering with streaks of flaming red, rise to a heaven of Machine Age planets and stars. A gold-leaf Milky Way splashes across the ceiling mural, drawing your attention the length of the great hall. Near the end, floor and walls angle inward to converge on the stately, reeded columns that frame the silver profile of New York's most audacious marvel. In this depiction, the building rises in sharp, metallic lines over a marble map of New England. At its peak, the skyscraper's golden, Art Deco dirigible mooring mast—itself a striking

(Left) The Sky Boy.

EMPIRE STATE

gesture toward a future "when Zeppelins are expected to swarm on the New York horizon"—penetrates the sun, unleashing a blaze of stainless-steel rays that flash over the landscape. These rays—perhaps sunbeams, radio waves or, prophetically, television signals—broadcast an unmistakable message to the nation and to the Old World beyond. *This is the Empire State Building, tallest building in the world, bold, gleaming symbol of modern America.*

Standing at the foot of this haloed representation, you can take in the monumental structure at a glance, experiencing for yourself what John Jakob Raskob hoped the building would symbolize. With your feet on the ground, you feel drawn skyward by the structure's euphoric aspiration.

If your neck grows tired as you gaze upward, however, you might turn your glance to the right. There, ten steps beyond the black marble information desk, around a structural hump in the lobby design and perched inconspicuously above a radiator grille, you will discover a bronze plaque, mounted at eye level. Although not part of the architectural design, I think this plaque is symbolic, too. It measures thirty-two by twenty-six inches, tiny compared to the giant rendering of the building with which it shares the wall. Unadorned, it lists the names of thirty-two men, laborers who contributed to the building's construction and who received Certificates of Superior Craftsmanship, awarded by the New York Building Congress. The plaque is unlit, and the passageway where it hangs is dark. When I visited in March 2025, a posted sign, "Entry Beyond This Point Is Limited to Tenants and Their Invited Guests," warned visitors against approaching it. But if a guard doesn't stop you, you can still step up and read the names of these thirty-two men, recipients of Empire State Craftsmanship Awards, embossed in hand-drawn, Art Deco lettering against a plain black background. Among them are Michael Tierney, rock driller; Gus Comedeca, steam shovel operator; James P. Kerr, stone setter; Charles E. Sexton, bricklayer; James Irons, stonecutter; Frank Moeglin, sheet metal worker; Vladimir Kozloff, wrecker; Ferruccio Mariutto, terrazzo worker; Samuel Laginsky, glazier; Peter Madden, asbestos worker.

(Left) The grand entrance.

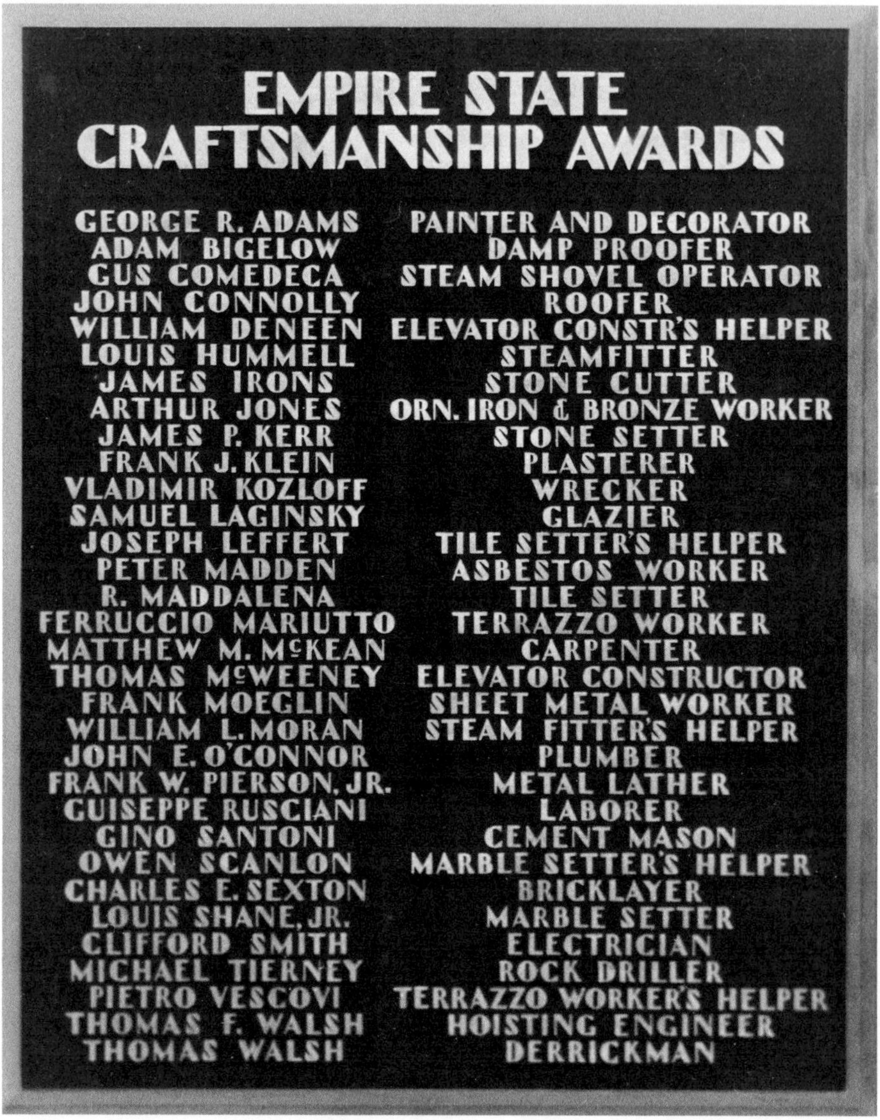

EMPIRE STATE
CRAFTSMANSHIP AWARDS

GEORGE R. ADAMS	PAINTER AND DECORATOR
ADAM BIGELOW	DAMP PROOFER
GUS COMEDECA	STEAM SHOVEL OPERATOR
JOHN CONNOLLY	ROOFER
WILLIAM DENEEN	ELEVATOR CONSTR'S HELPER
LOUIS HUMMELL	STEAMFITTER
JAMES IRONS	STONE CUTTER
ARTHUR JONES	ORN. IRON & BRONZE WORKER
JAMES P. KERR	STONE SETTER
FRANK J. KLEIN	PLASTERER
VLADIMIR KOZLOFF	WRECKER
SAMUEL LAGINSKY	GLAZIER
JOSEPH LEFFERT	TILE SETTER'S HELPER
PETER MADDEN	ASBESTOS WORKER
R. MADDALENA	TILE SETTER
FERRUCCIO MARIUTTO	TERRAZZO WORKER
MATTHEW M. McKEAN	CARPENTER
THOMAS McWEENEY	ELEVATOR CONSTRUCTOR
FRANK MOEGLIN	SHEET METAL WORKER
WILLIAM L. MORAN	STEAM FITTER'S HELPER
JOHN E. O'CONNOR	PLUMBER
FRANK W. PIERSON, JR.	METAL LATHER
GUISEPPE RUSCIANI	LABORER
GINO SANTONI	CEMENT MASON
OWEN SCANLON	MARBLE SETTER'S HELPER
CHARLES E. SEXTON	BRICKLAYER
LOUIS SHANE, JR.	MARBLE SETTER
CLIFFORD SMITH	ELECTRICIAN
MICHAEL TIERNEY	ROCK DRILLER
PIETRO VESCOVI	TERRAZZO WORKER'S HELPER
THOMAS F. WALSH	HOISTING ENGINEER
THOMAS WALSH	DERRICKMAN

The craftsmanship award plaque.

Here, within the lobby of the Empire State Building itself, are two competing symbols of the majestic skyscraper's history and significance, one familiar and one forgotten.

In the shining steel outline, you have the Empire State Building as the American superlative. The tallest man-made structure, built in record-breaking time, it towers as a beacon, radiating ambition, self-confidence, and modernity. "The skyscraper is the most distinctively American thing in the world," wrote Colonel William A. Starrett, one of the builders, "so far surpassing anything ever before undertaken in its vastness, swiftness, utility, and economy that it epitomizes American life and American civilization." As the loftiest skyscraper, the epitome of the epitome, the Empire State Building is the focal point, not just of the lobby, but of New York City and State, of the nation and nations overseas, of the solar system—perhaps, if we recall the ceiling mural awash with stars, the fulcrum of the whole galaxy. It's not too much to say that, in this wall relief, the Empire State—and with it, the rising American superpower—are imagined as the center of the universe. Civic and national pride, enthusiastic journalism and publicity, heroic images of the construction, and almost a century of popular culture all converge like the architecture on this central, symbolic representation of the structure.

When we think of the Empire State Building, this is what we think of, and not the office tower long since overshadowed by newer, taller competitors. There's a reason Tom Hanks and Meg Ryan meet there in the 1993 film *Sleepless in Seattle*, and not at Chicago's Willis Tower, formerly the Sears Tower, then the country's tallest building. Skyscrapers are "expressions in steel of the passion of the twentieth century," wrote critic Philip N. Youtz in 1929. No other peak in America attains the Empire State's height of passion, its emblematic grandeur and romance.

From the start, the romantic story of the building as the symbol of American ascent has been told in correspondingly impressive language. "Insofar as a single building may be said to typify and represent the progress and dignity of the great city, EMPIRE STATE is New York," claimed the owners in a *New Yorker* advertisement from April 1931, weeks before the building opened. Contemporary journalists went much farther. "As you shoot up and up, floor after floor, you are boosted straight into the future," wrote one. "The Empire State building pierces the clouds and goes beyond them. At the top you're just a little lower than the angels," wrote another.

To those engaged in creating and burnishing the grand story, the building is an "airy tower of limitless aspiration." It is "a temple of paralleled silver shimmering between earth and sky." It is "poetry, mysticism and inspiration," "the lantern of Manhattan," the "First Wonder of a New World." "The Empire State Building," concluded John Tauranac in his 1995 history of its construction, "is *the* twentieth-century New York building."

Innumerable books, films, cartoons, advertisements, photographs, and crystal, metal, wooden, and plastic souvenirs attest to and celebrate the potency and durability of this Empire State Building, proof of American hopefulness, vigor, achievement, and power.

I want to tell the other story, the forgotten story of the plaque with the workers' names, the story of the Empire State Building and the ordinary men who built it. Like the commemorative plaque itself, this history of the Empire State is off the main path, overlooked, and only dimly legible. And yet, as if hidden in plain sight, the story of the men named on the Craftsmanship Awards plaque offers a singular window onto a neglected dimension of the famous building. This neglect is not accidental. On the contrary, it betrays a pattern of selective attention that is as telling and definitive of American culture as the Empire State Building itself.

The thirty-two Craftsmanship Award winners intrigue me because they stand out against the black background of thousands of unknown and anonymous workers who contributed to the landmark building's creation. Astonishingly, no list of laborers was ever compiled. In contrast to the distinguished gentlemen who owned, designed, and managed construction of the Empire State, and whose names appear on a tablet at the base of the stainless-steel totem in the lobby, workers were plural, a group, not typically seen as individuals except as representatives. Like the Sky Boy and the other men who appear in Lewis Hine's famous photographs, when viewed from the perspective of the building's inspiring symbolism, it seemed beside the point to ask who the individual was. He was a worker. In this sense, it is surprising that the plaque exists at all. Indeed, the men listed on the Craftsmanship Awards plaque constitute the majority of those whom it is now possible to identify by name.

These two artifacts in the Empire State Building's entrance, therefore, represent two different kinds of history, different decisions about whose names and what information are considered important and worth preserving, two sets of values by which to measure the meaning of the building and the nation that built it. The stainless-steel depiction of the building represents history on the grand scale, the story of a handful of powerful men at the pinnacle of their careers, giving monumental form to their vision of the new, twentieth-century American civilization. Biographies of these men, often memoirs by them, are easy to find, and narratives of their achievements draw on well-curated archives. Most histories of the Empire State Building focus on these men, the owners and builders. The commemorative plaque, on the other hand, represents a different scale of history, history closer to the ground, often the history of a different class. This is the story of countless, ordinary individuals performing their jobs and seen, if at all, only fleetingly—from below as anonymous, heroic figures, or from above as an undifferentiated mass. In each case, the men are seen through the lens of other people's ideas about them. The histories of these ordinary lives are frequently impossible to reconstruct, and documentation, when it exists, is fragmentary and marred by unresolvable discrepancies. Yet history on the grand scale is no less partial and fragmentary. The celebrated story of the Empire State serves a national mythology; but it is incomplete, sanitized, simplified, a shorthand for the nation's greatness. Stories on the individual scale, by contrast, are incomplete for the opposite reason, because the documentation is haphazard, and the lives of the men were messy and often tragic. The grand symbol is brightly lit and theatrically staged, making its incompleteness harder to see. It replaces detail with the pomp and approbation of public culture. The symbol of ordinary lives is incomplete as if by design. It is an aside, unlit if not entirely hidden or lost, and what remains of it is hard to make out, full of gaps and mysteries.

I am a child of the Empire State Building. My father's office was located there, and I grew up visiting the structure, running through its marble hallways. I don't recall ever asking how the building had come to be. For me, visiting my father or spying the structure's silhouette from the Long Island Expressway as we drove into New York City from our suburban home, the Empire State Building was simply *there*, a central feature of the landscape, like a mountain peak, a straightforward fact. Only much later did I learn that there are no straightforward facts.

Let's start, then, with the simplest question: *Who built the Empire State Building?*

On the grand scale, the answer is clear. We know who paid to have the building built, the moneymen led by John Jakob Raskob, at the time one of the richest and most influential businessmen in the country, mastermind behind the spectacular growth of both DuPont and General Motors in the 1920s and one of the inventors of the consumer credit industry. Raskob was joined in the venture by the industrialist Pierre S. du Pont and the banker Louis G. Kaufman, among others. Alfred E. Smith, four-time governor of New York State and defeated 1928 Democratic presidential candidate, served as the president and garrulous public personification of Empire State Inc., the company that owned the building. While Raskob preferred to work behind the scenes, Al Smith was always in front of the newsmen and their cameras, one of the most prominent and admired public figures in New York and the nation in the 1920s and 1930s. Crowds greeted his comings and goings. It wasn't unheard of for him to have to dodge kisses when he strode through train stations in New York, Boston, and Washington, DC. His case of laryngitis in April 1931 was considered news fit to print. Though few recall his involvement now, in press accounts of the time the structure that would become the world's tallest skyscraper was known as "the house that Al built" or "Al's shack." The photographer Lewis Hine, who contributed more than anyone to the heroic aura of the building, referred to it as "Al's big shanty." One journalist predicted the future would dub the skyscraper's architectural style "Alsmithian." And a newspaper wit, astounded by the building's unequaled 102 stories, quipped, "If it was bein' put up by just a regular politician and not Al Smith, wouldn't any of us believe it. We would demand a recount."

We know the architectural firm that designed the building, Shreve, Lamb, and Harmon, led by Richmond Harold Shreve, head of business; William Frederick Lamb, chief designer; and Arthur Loomis Harmon. The firm is well represented by buildings in New York City and elsewhere, including 500 and 521 Fifth Avenue, Hunter College, the Joel W. Solomon Federal Building and United States Courthouse, in Chattanooga, Tennessee, and what is now the MIT Sloan School, in Cambridge, Massachusetts.

We know the names of the general contractors, the brothers Paul and Colonel William A. Starrett, and their partner, Andrew J. Eken, who headed one of the era's most prominent construction companies, responsible for many of New York's famous skyscrapers in addition to the Empire State: the New York Life Building at Madison Square, the McGraw-Hill Building on West Forty-Second Street, and 40 Wall Street, which lost the competition for world's tallest skyscraper to the Chrysler Building in 1930, before both were surpassed by the Empire State. William and Paul Starrett each published memoirs—William's *Skyscrapers and the Men Who Build Them* appeared in 1928, and Paul's *Changing the Skyline* in 1938—detailing their role in the creation of the modern American metropolis.

We know the name of the Empire State's structural engineer, Homer G. Balcom, a legendary figure in the construction trade, responsible for Rockefeller Center, among many other landmarks. We know the names of the men who designed the Empire State's elevator, plumbing, ventilation, electrical, and telephone installations, at the time the largest such jobs in history. Many of these men contributed articles to a twelve-part series published in *The Architectural Forum* in 1930 and 1931, providing the most comprehensive technical account of the construction to survive.

But as for the men who performed the labor, workers who held the tools and who assembled the enormous structure by hand, these names are for the most part lost. Their faces may appear in photos, but their identities were not considered noteworthy. Seen from their perspective, on this scale of history, we have no answer to the question. We don't know who built the Empire State Building.

To say the names of the workmen are lost gives the wrong impression. These names were never known, if by "known," we mean recorded for posterity, for the purpose of being remembered. In part, this has to do with labor practices of the 1920s and 1930s. Construction workers were day laborers, hired short-term and as needed. Paid an hourly wage, men frequently moved from job to job and city to city. Beyond this, even from the perspective of this historic job, laborers were considered something less than complete people. They were *hands*, skilled or unskilled, hired to perform a particular task on a specific day. The name of the individual was—and in most cases, is still—less important than the job itself. Of course, the men were known to their fellow workers and perhaps even to their bosses. Individual foremen might have favored workmen; subcontractors might have a dedicated roster of employees or regular laborers. But the line between personal identity and identity in the historical record has a distinct threshold. Above the line are employers and managers; below the line, their employees and workers.

As workers, the men who built the Empire State were subject to rigorous accounting. In addition to each foreman's daily report on the men working under him, detailing the tasks they performed, the Starrett Bros. and Eken's on-site Timekeeping Department, responsible for monitoring the labor force and for administering payroll, collected records with individual names and personal details. "The hiring of men for the different trades is done by the respective trade foreman," explained a member of the Starrett company's staff. "All hiring is done before 8 A.M. on the main floor in the direct vicinity of the timekeeper's office. Each man is given a hiring ticket, upon which is written his name, class, rate of pay and time and date hired. He presents this ticket to the timekeeper's office where a personnel card is filled in with his name, age, home address, and a notation if he is single or married—and the number of children in the latter case. There is also a record of earnings kept upon his personnel card for income tax record."

The information on these cards, rich and revealing as it might have been to later historians, was not considered worth preserving. Or perhaps this information, province of just one office within the Accounting Division of a massive and complex organization, was too specific, and therefore of no significance to the higher levels of project management. At upper levels of administration—the levels where decisions about what information is "important" are made—the names of the men were immaterial. What mattered was the number of men present at the site on any given day and the building trades they practiced.

The most detailed record of the construction of the Empire State Building is a notebook, composed anonymously in the office of Starrett Bros. and Eken, general contractors, in November or December 1930, apparently as an in-house keepsake. Buried for decades in corporate archives, it was rediscovered in the 1980s by architectural historian Carol Willis and published in 1998 as *Building the Empire State*. The notebook contains an organizational chart, listing the names and positions of the administrators of the project, led by Superintendent J. W. Bowser. There are eight levels of responsibility below Mr. Bowser, including the heads of production and cost distribution, accounting, engineering installation, and construction. The bottom layer of the Construction Division lists the names of the ten foremen who managed lathers, pipefitters, masonry, carpentry formwork, concrete, stonework, general labor, traffic, drillers and excavators, and watchmen and fire patrol, plus the master mechanic and the store keeper. Below this level of organization, the chart stops. Names are no longer recorded.

Instead, the notebook reproduces an exemplary Daily Job Report, the diary of activity scrupulously maintained by the contractor. The Job Report documents August 14, 1930, the date on which 3,439 workers were employed on the site, the highest number for any day during construction. Here, the men are listed by trade:

1 Carpenter Foreman
2 " Deputies
10 " Pushers
269 Carpenters
10 Carpenter Apprentices.

And so on, through thirty-two lathers, 281 bricklayers, 123 derrickmen, 243 elevator constructors, twenty-three asbestos pipe-covering mechanics—in all 1,928 men employed by Starrett Bros. and Eken, and 1,511 employed by the twenty-four listed subcontractors.

We know the names of many of these subcontractors, at least the men who owned the companies and the foremen who managed their work on this project. On April 16, 1931, Al Smith and the architectural firm Shreve, Lamb, and Harmon, hosted a "Dinner in Commemoration of the Completion of the Empire State." A program of the event was published, listing the names of the sixty guests. These are undeniably men who built the Empire State Building. But no workers were present.

Because the Empire State was a high-profile project, the general contractors were more conscientious than usual about documenting their team. The Starrett Corporation's notebook is supplemented by a scrapbook or photo

One of Al Smith's cats and her kittens.

album, entitled *Erection Views of Empire State Building*, including many labeled images that preserve the names and faces of the foremen, the surveyors, the job runners, material checkers, and timekeepers—second- and third-tier professionals who helped to manage the supremely efficient organization that erected the building in eighteen months, a record never equaled. Digging into these archives, we learn what was memorable about the project from the perspective of the corporate office. For example, here we discover that a Miss C. Lynch was the chief nurse at the construction site, one of the very few women whose contribution to the building is documented. We can learn the names of the accountants, the field distribution checkers, and those in charge of cost distribution and construction. We learn the names of the cats that inhabited the building during construction and that became mascots of the work and Al Smith's pets. Peggy and Isabella. In the ninety-five-page album created by the Starrett Corporation to commemorate their achievement, two full pages—ten photographs—are devoted to these cats and their kittens.

Below this threshold of official, corporate attention, however, beyond which names cease to be recorded, remain the thousands of individuals who may equally claim to have built the Empire State Building. These are not only construction workers, but also the men and women who labored in the architects' office; the drafters of architectural drawings; the calculators who performed intricate mathematics with slide rules to prove the soundness of the structural design; the stenographers and secretaries, who enabled the necessary correspondence and communication; the Black counter workers, who served lunch at the five on-site canteens provided for the construction workers. Their names were not recorded. Their identities are not known and cannot be recovered.

Today, more than ninety years after the completion of the Empire State Building, even the number of workers is impossible to determine. Newspapers of the day were uncertain how many men were employed or the number of trades they practiced. Published figures ranged wildly from 3,000 to 10,000 men and twenty-five to sixty-seven trades. The surviving Daily Job Report records 3,439 men—but that was just one day, August 14, 1930. Construction lasted from October 1, 1929, until May 1931. In a letter to *The New Republic*, Belle Moskowitz, director of publicity for Empire State Inc., insisted the number of workmen was 4,000. Colonel William A. Starrett himself asserted that, "in the course of its erection more than 10,000 workers will have contributed directly toward its creation."

Each of these figures may be correct, depending on how you count. Since workers were hired on daily or weekly pay cycles, the construction crew might remain consistent at three thousand men from week to week yet be composed of substantially different individuals. Three thousand men may have been *at work* on the building at any given time. But over the course of construction, perhaps five, ten, or fifteen thousand individuals may have *worked on* the building.

The line that divides the named from the unnamed, an individual from a number, and public from private identity, is like a threshold of visibility, a scale of resolution. Try to peer beyond it, and things grow blurry. At the scale of the ordinary individual, precise numbers, dates, and names—that is to say, basic "facts"—tend to break down, though you'd never know it from more general histories of the construction, which almost always favor the large-scale, corporate view.

For an individual worker's name to be recorded, resolving into visibility, something exceptional had to happen.

We know the names of the dead—at least some of them. Here, too, the details grow fuzzy if you inquire below the corporate perspective. Empire State Inc. maintained that five men were killed on the job. That number remains authoritative today, and it is cited by John Tauranac in *The Empire State Building: The Making of a Landmark*, and by Jim Rasenberger in *High Steel: The Daring Men Who Built the World's Greatest Skyline*. Other numbers are also in circulation. A cartoon drawn by Walter Steinhilber and published in June 1931 in the Marxist journal *New Masses*, pictured the building stuffed with corpses, with the caption, "42 men killed constructing the new Empire State Building." *The Daily Worker* alleged that 128 men had died, seventeen on a single day. As late as 1968, Frances Low, writing in *American Heritage* magazine, asserted fourteen men had died.

All these numbers are incorrect.

Tauranac and Rasenberger rely for their figure on a letter issued by Starrett Bros. and Eken in November 1930, intended to dispel rumors of a high death toll propagated by workers' rights advocates. In that letter, addressed to the Committee on Accident Prevention of the Building Trades Employers' Association of the City of New York, the contractors specifically contest claims of forty-four and sixty-three dead. They write: "For your information and in order that you may be advised of the actual situation in regard to the 'deaths' which have occurred from accidents, we beg to advise that the following 'deaths' have occurred and we are including a short description surrounding each case."

Perhaps we can read the contractors' discomfort with the subject in the fact that "deaths" is here twice placed in quotation marks. Putting "deaths" in quotation marks makes it seem as if they are alleged. But the stated purpose of the letter was to establish the official record of fatalities.

January 31, 1930—Laborer was sawing a plank when a truck struck the opposite end, causing the plank to hit him.
January 31, 1930—Laborer ran into blast area, against warning, was struck by falling bricks.
April 29, 1930—Ironworker.
July 14, 1930—Carpenter while working on shaft head fell down elevator shaft.
July 30, 1930—Carpenter adjusting a lead sheaf when he leaned into shaft and was struck by an ascending hoist.

In 1998, with the publication of the Starrett Corporation's in-house notebook, the names of these men came to light. Laborers Giuseppi Tedeschi and Luis De Dominichi, ironworker Reuben Brown, and carpenters Sigus Andreasen and Frank Sullivan. In the Starrett's notebook, the anonymous author compares the accident victims to the "war dead" and calls them "unsung heroes of peace." Apparently the Starretts considered commemorating them publicly. "It would be a thoughtful act to inscribe their names upon the bronze plaque which will bear the names of those other workers who were the recipients of the craftsmanship award certificates." But this thoughtful act was not performed. The names of the dead were not included on the plaque in the lobby. As a result, they disappeared from view. Publication of the Starrett's notebook allowed them to be recognized and remembered. Yet even here, looking more closely, there is uncertainty concerning their identities. According to an obituary published in the Brooklyn *Standard Union*, for instance, the notebook misidentifies the carpenter Andreasen, whose name was not Sigus but Peder Joachim. Genealogical databases enable me to sharpen the picture slightly. Peder Joachim Andreasen was forty-seven years old, a native of Bergen, Norway, and had emigrated to the US in 1909. He was married with one child and lived on Fifty-Eighth Street in Borough Park, Brooklyn. He is buried at the Evergreens Cemetery.

Mistakes like this notwithstanding, the Starrett's letter is still incomplete. At least two additional deaths occurred after the letter was published. They are not accounted for in the official record, and subsequent historians have overlooked them. In December 1930, according to multiple newspaper accounts, another carpenter, Albert Carlsen, a fifty-three-year-old native of Finland, was struck by a materials hoist. And in April 1931, just as work was winding down and the men faced almost certain unemployment in the depths of the Great Depression, a fourth carpenter, a thirty-year-old Norwegian immigrant, Finn Egeland, married and with a three-year-old child, fell or jumped from the building. Though reports describe him as a worker, and some provide details of his job on the building, his death was ruled a suicide. Does he count toward the number of deaths during construction? The contractors did not believe so, and his name is not included in the Starrett Corporation's in-house notebook.

Like so many facts, the number and names of the dead become less distinct upon closer inspection. Like the question of who built the building, the simple question, *How many men died during construction of the Empire State Building?*, is neither simple nor precise enough to account for the complexity of what happened.

At least one innocent passerby died during the construction, a woman named Elizabeth Eager. On July 11, 1930, the forty-five-year-old schoolteacher crossed Thirty-Fourth Street, west of Fifth Avenue, at the wrong moment. According to the Starrett's account, Eager "was struck on the ankle by a piece of broken ironworker's plank. She sustained a fractured ankle and it was reported to us that blood poisoning resulted in her death."

What information, whose life or death, is considered important? The answer depends on your perspective, on how you frame the question. Elizabeth Eager was not a man, and her death does not register in any official accounting of those who died during construction. Nevertheless, additional particulars surrounding her death can be found in a 1936 book, *Men of Danger*, by Lowell Thomas. As his title indicates, Thomas was interested in painting a romantic portrait of construction workers. Consequently, he does not mention Elizabeth Eager's name, and the circumstances of her death only serve to enhance the perilous nature of the male workers' job.

> One of the few casualties which occurred during the building of the Empire State was caused by the wind. A workman was carrying a plank along the edge of one of the upper floors. The wind struck the plank and it began to "get away" from him. To save himself he let go of the plank and fell flat on his stomach. The plank went bounding down toward the street. It crashed on the extension at the twenty-first floor and was partially splintered. One of the big twisted splinters flew across Thirty-fourth Street and struck a woman, breaking her leg. The wound became infected, and she died. But of course that was an exceptional kind of accident.

It is only by accident that an ordinary person's name becomes visible in the public record. History at the scale of the individual is composed of these accidents and exceptional moments—a death, an award, a chance encounter with a journalist or photographer—the ordinary person's fifteen minutes of fame. Only through these accidents can we begin to populate the roster of workers who built the Empire State.

Construction of the world's tallest skyscraper was a sensational event, extensively reported in the press. Workers were frequent subjects of human-interest stories, especially when their jobs were highly dangerous. Ironworkers were the particular favorites with journalists of the early twentieth century, and they remain our figureheads for that era. These men were portrayed as dashing characters, profiled in books and articles like Thomas's *Men of Danger* and John Cushman Fistere's "No Timid Man Could Hold This Job." From these accidents of a journalist's attention, we glean the names of seven additional ironworkers who helped to build the Empire State Building, including Sam Lowman, Slim Cooper, Dave Ricketts, and Paul Masey. Two more ironworkers, Carl Russell and Neil Doherty, were identified by name in photos published to illustrate their daring escapades in the high steel a quarter mile above New York City's streets. The ironworker Victor Gosselin, interviewed in John Cushman Fistere's article, appears in both text and photos. Captured in some of Lewis Hine's most exhilarating images, Gosselin is by far the best-known worker who contributed to the Empire State Building.

These brief glimpses of ordinary people were not meant as biographical sketches, as we might expect from the profile of a prominent man. Instead, they were published to offer a representative moment, a snapshot or slice of life. In a few rare cases, as we shall see, these snapshots may expand to become a window, providing clues we can follow to create a fuller picture of an individual worker, as through a combination of multiple exposures. Present in a variety of sources, as the prime example, the ironworker Victor Gosselin comes into much sharper focus. In conventional histories, therefore, he is frequently the only worker identified by name, where his charismatic personality provides a welcome human touch.

For the most part, however, men in journalists' reports and in photos of the construction remain anonymous. And even when a worker is mentioned by name in these glancing appearances, something odd almost always happens that again occludes his individual identity. In the passage into public visibility, the ordinary individual is transformed from a man into a symbol, his identity subsumed in a larger, more urgent cultural narrative. The ironworkers so celebrated then as now for their prowess on the high steel, even when named, were not lauded primarily as individuals performing a job but as romantic heroes, symbols of the mammoth enterprise, its audacity and modernity, archetypes of virility, daring, skill, and pride, the essential characteristics of the triumphant, modern American spirit.

Nowhere is this more evident than in Lewis Wickes Hine's iconic photographs of the Empire State's workers. Hired by Empire State Inc. in 1930 to publicize the building during its construction, the pioneering documentary photographer took almost a thousand photos of the workmen. There are dozens of formal portraits of individual workers, and hundreds of photos of the men performing their jobs: drilling the foundations, wrestling with pipes and cables, laying brick, walking the narrow steel beams. Some of these images, like *The Sky Boy*, count among the most influential photos in the history of American photography. Hine's original prints now routinely sell for tens, sometimes hundreds of thousands of dollars.

Lewis Hine was an inspired choice to document the men who performed the construction. By the time he was hired by Empire State Inc. he had been publishing photographic studies of workers and artisans, so-called work portraits, for a decade. Born in 1874 and trained as a teacher and sociological researcher, Hine began his photographic career in the early 1900s, recording immigrants at Ellis Island. He made his name as the staff photographer for the National Child Labor Committee in the 1910s, talking his way into factories, mines, and workers' homes to document the extensive use of children in unregulated industrial production. A lifelong believer in the democratic ideals championed by the early twentieth-century Progressive movement, Hine had a deep, personal sympathy for laborers and for the members of the working classes, many of them immigrants. His work studies in the 1920s included railroad engineers, workers at power plants, machine shops, harbor workers, truck drivers, men and women in print shops, candy stores, operating a telegraph or typewriter. Hine's *Mechanic at Steam Pump in Electric Power House*, sometimes called *Man with Wrench*, shows a young man taut with effort, haloed by a gear, his wrench apparently tightening a bolt. Reproduced widely in textbooks, this image has become synonymous with America in the Machine Age.

On the job at the Empire State, Hine was enthralled by the construction workers he encountered. He photographed men in many trades—carpenters, bricklayers, stone setters, plumbers. But like his contemporaries, Hine was particularly drawn to ironworkers. Hine included twenty-eight photographs from the Empire State job in his 1932 book, *Men at Work: Photographic Studies of Modern Men and Machines*. Through these spectacular images, workers like the Sky Boy became the iconic figures we know, men "like spiders spinning a fabric of steel against the sky," as the photographer writes in a caption.

In Hine's engaged and sympathetic portraits, something revealing and ineffable of the workers' personalities emerges. Yet while Hine is rightly celebrated as a defender of the individual in the face of industrialization and an overbearing mass culture, his attitudes toward the subjects of his photographs were also complex. In his published images, if the men are identified at all, it is by profession: foundation man, ironworker, pipefitter, hoist engineer. Like journalists of his time, Hine suppresses the identities of his subjects, using these anonymous individuals to illustrate a larger, abstract story—"The Spirit of Industry," as he writes in the preface to *Men at Work*, or "the Human Side of The System," as he calls it elsewhere. Although known as a father of American documentary photography, instead of straightforwardly documenting individuals, in his accompanying texts, Hine self-consciously transformed the workers into symbols.

Since that time, Hine's photos have given human faces to the grand story of American ascent. His images secured the Empire State Building as the era's defining symbol of the nation and established the daredevil ironworker as the embodiment of the American character. Taking their cues from him, art historians have viewed his images through this thematic lens. "The hundreds of photographs he took during the construction of the Empire State Building in 1932 [*sic*] must rank as an American epic," wrote Beaumont Newhall, curator of photography for the Museum of Modern Art in New York, in a 1938 article credited with establishing Hine's place in the history of American photography. Newhall's vivid account of Hine at the site describes him, like the workers and the building project itself, in the heroic language still conventional today.

> Day by day, floor by floor, he followed the steel work upwards. With the workmen he toasted sandwiches over the forges that heat the rivets; he walked the girders at dizzying heights, carrying over his shoulder not a pocket-size miniature camera, but a five by seven inch view camera complete with tripod, or a four by five Graflex. When he reached, with the workmen, the very pinnacle of the world's tallest building, he had them swing him out over the microcosm of New York from a crane, so that he might photograph in midair the moment they had all been striving for—the driving of the final rivet at the very top of the so-called mooring mast on the skyscraper.

In subsequent decades, Hine's Empire State images have been understood as touchstone representations, not only of the structure, or of the workers seen building it, but by extension of American culture as a whole in the years before World War II. In this view, as Kate Sampsell-Willmann writes, "the images are not of men at work; rather they are of Hine's version of American *virtue* manifested in the faces of American workers."

For almost a century, then, Hine's photographs—and the workers pictured—have been understood in mythic terms. Introducing his 1998 collection of Hine's Empire State images, Freddy Langer pushes this tendency to its extreme, setting these images in their most dazzling and grandiose rhetorical frame. "Hine shows men in heroic poses, often stripped of their shirts, recalling the heroes depicted in Classical Greek statues," he begins. "Some stand with steel cables in hand, pulling them taut, as though they were holding the globe in place. Others grapple with wrenches so large that they look as though they could set the clockwork of the earth's orbit in motion. Those wielding spirit levels look as though they were working to put life straight, while engineers using surveying equipment peer into the future." On this scale, not only the men, but their labor is rendered mythical. "Men holding welds, whose gas flames splinter into a thousand sparks, repelled by the iron they seek to master, create a veritable fireworks display as though rejoicing in work, the greatest of all celebrations."

Like Newhall, like almost every other writer on Hine before and since—perhaps even like Lewis Hine himself—Langer views the images in abstract, conceptual terms. Art history, like history in general, has its grand and its personal scales. Writers define their subject with their attention, and peering at Hine's images, historians have universally seen a myth. Reaching so extravagantly for the largest possible frame of reference—the globe, the Earth's orbit, life itself—these promoters of the mythic view aim to convey in their prose the millennial achievement of American ascendance, for which the skyscraper is the dominant symbol. But approaching Hine's images on the mythical scale distorts the content of the images. We do not see what is in the photograph, but instead what the writer imagines the photographs represent.

To illustrate his flamboyant text, Langer reproduces Hine's photo of the bronze plaque that hangs in the Empire State Building's lobby. He comments, "This, perhaps more than any other photograph taken by Hine, clearly demonstrates the photographer's attitude toward the workers." But Langer's perspective blinds him to what Hine photographed. He understands "work" and "workers" purely as tokens. His myth-infused language raises the men in these

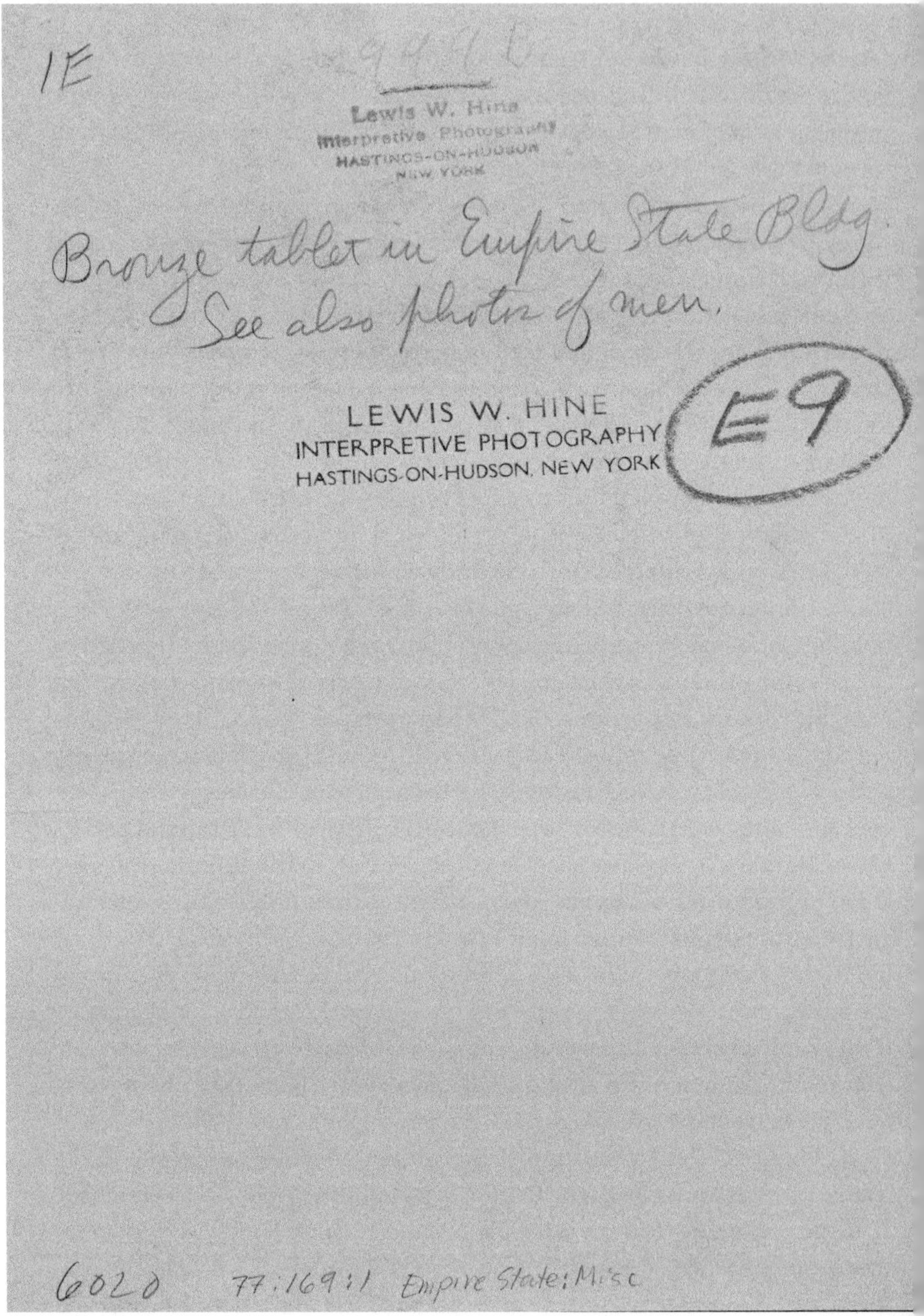

1E

Lewis W. Hine
Interpretive Photography
HASTINGS-ON-HUDSON
NEW YORK

Bronze tablet in Empire State Bldg.
See also photos of men.

LEWIS W. HINE
INTERPRETIVE PHOTOGRAPHY
HASTINGS-ON-HUDSON, NEW YORK

E9

6020 77:169:1 Empire State: Misc

Lewis Hine's handwritten note, "See also photos of men."

photos above any distasteful individuality and into the realm of metaphysics. Only on this scale is their labor considered significant. Far from a peculiarity of Langer's, this approach is the common thread in almost all descriptions of Hine's Empire State photographs. Just as the building itself seems to transcend its commercial function to become symbolic of the American spirit, these men, as well, are understood as ideals incarnated. Seen on the grand scale of American myth, therefore, the images' very content evaporates. In the eyes of these historians, individual men are replaced by concepts, and Hine's photographs are not documentation, but conceptual illustration. Thus, noted historian and Yale professor Alan Trachtenberg may conclude, "These are not 'portraits.' They are pictures of the work itself."

This mythical perspective falsifies Hine's photographs. It falsifies the men, and it falsifies the history of the Empire State Building. It imagines greatness only in grandeur and so skews both the historical record and the cultural imagination, directing the narrative of American achievement toward concepts and capital and away from labor and lived experience. To understand what Hine photographed beyond the mythic scale, we must look at his work more closely, with greater attentiveness to what we see. Viewed instead on the scale of the individual, rather than as examples of American mythology, Hine's evocative images are also "snapshots" as I have described, exceptional moments in which an individual appears in the public record. They are portraits of *particular* workers, unique documents, offering a momentary glimpse into the lives of otherwise invisible people. Indeed, on the back of a working print of Hine's photo of the Empire State Craftsmanship Awards plaque, now housed at the George Eastman Museum in Rochester, New York, we can read Hine's own handwritten directive: "See also photos of men."

This is an extraordinary clue, missed until now because its information fell below the threshold of attention for historians interested primarily in concepts, symbols, and myths. Its preservation is one of those accidents that allows individuals to rise to visibility.

While it has been noted that several of Hine's images identify their subject as a "superior craftsman," it seems no one has fully appreciated the significance of this description. Hine's world-renowned images are not abstract portraits of "workers." They are portraits of specific men. In fact, most of Hine's portraits show the winners of Certificates of Superior Craftsmanship, the same men whose names appear on the overlooked bronze plaque in the Empire State Building's lobby.

This remarkable, unnoticed convergence makes it possible to view the Empire State Building from a new perspective, shifting from the grand scale of myth to that of the ordinary worker. Hine's perceptive portraits put faces to the names on the bronze plaque. And the inconspicuous plaque in the lobby helps to restore names and in some instances personal details to the previously unknown men in Hine's acclaimed photographs, men who, until now, have been used solely as the embodiments of generalities and abstract ideals.

Seen from this perspective, Hine's images, the building's history, and the Empire State Building itself become something different than they are in the grand, symbolic narrative.

As famous as Hine's Empire State images have become, they have never been seen in this context. Understood now for the first time as the documentation of specific men, the images' content—what they *show*—changes. From the mythological perspective, the men's identities are inconsequential. What matters is what they represent. The grand story achieves its inspiring grandeur at the cost of the reality of the people pictured. The workers' individuality and the gritty details of their lives and work are sacrificed to the needs of a larger, conceptual narrative. This in part explains why the men's faces were separated from their names in the first place, leaving them to float anonymously through almost a century of fanciful interpretation.

From the individual perspective, by contrast, who the men are is the essential question, and every attempt to make them represent something else forces us to look away from the reality of their lives toward some airy abstraction. The story of the Empire State Building on the scale of the individual may sacrifice the "grandeur" and rhetorical consistency of the mythological narrative, but it makes visible a previously hidden dimension of lived experience, exposed in accidents and exceptional moments, easily overlooked or dismissed. Yet these fleeting, tentative clues have the power to transform what we see.

There are no archives dedicated to the workers. Information about these ordinary men resides solely in public sources, with all their sprawl, gaps, mistakes, and inconsistencies, or in private collections buried in a descendant's closet or passed down informally through family lore. For these reasons, I have not been able to identify some men at all. For others, traces of a life emerge piecemeal, in scattered flashes. For a few workers, an isolated recollection or stray reference in a newspaper provides just enough to glimpse the personality of an otherwise unknown man.

In each case, Hine's masterful portraits serve as evidence that these were living men, not abstract figures who merely represented "workers." Pursuing the surviving documentation as far as it will lead, therefore, offers an alternative to the conventional, corporate history of the famous structure, since each scrap of information provides a new, specific answer to the question, *Who built the Empire State Building?*

Perhaps reconsidering this question from the perspective of these ordinary individuals will enable us to reimagine the Empire State Building's history on the grand scale, too, changing what we see when we look at it. By revising our conception of what this enduring symbol stands for, we might arrive at a fuller appreciation of the everyday, human sources of its greatness.

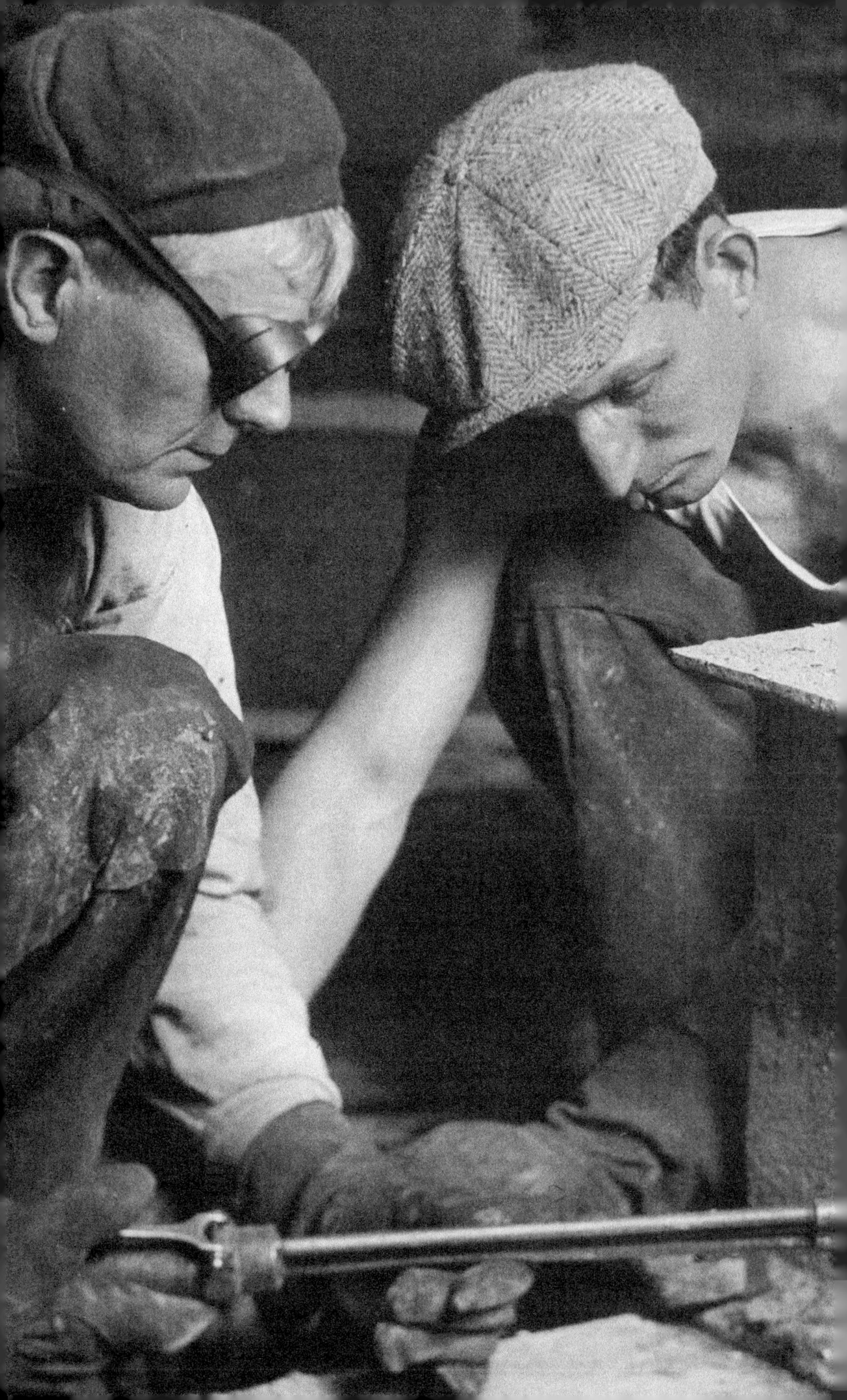

TWO

MEN WHO MAKE OUR MODERN WORLD SAFE

When your gaze is trained on Man in his glory, it can be difficult to discern actual men. The conflict between the skyscraper as a grand symbol and the building as the labor of individual workmen is present everywhere in the history of the Empire State Building. In contemporary accounts, the workers were not forgotten as individuals so much as never clearly seen. Journalists of the era, our eyewitnesses and reporters, had a hard time with the transition from the lofty view to the close-up and often failed to distinguish between individual men or even recognize the distinctions between different trades. Consequently, the historical sources, consulted for generations to flesh out with colorful detail the technocratic story of the Empire State's construction, tend instead to generalize the men rather than focusing specific attention on them, perpetuating clichés and cultural stereotypes of "workers."

In the eyes of journalists, the men are an army, crusaders, pioneers. They are children, monkeys, Tarzans, mountain goats, trapeze artists, puppets on a string. Above all, they are a *type*, referred to as a group, a mass, occasionally as a special and separate breed. And of all the different trades active in the work, almost always, the men who appear in the newspapers are ironworkers, the representative type, the men who set the columns and beams of the steel structure in place, the builders of modern America.

Ironworkers are "the human army that attacks the sky above," in Gilbert Swan's "Sidelights of New York." They are a "grimy, sweaty, stop-at-nothing army" in the series "Men and Steel" by William Engle in the *New York World-Telegram*. To *The Christian Science Monitor* in March 1931, they are "acrobats of the girders." To Roderick Morison, New York correspondent for the London *Daily Mail*, ironworkers standing around the coke furnace that heated the rivets recall "pioneers huddled round their camp fire."

Ironworkers are heroes, not individuals but symbolic figures, clothed in the garb of their ancestors. Some critics, reviewing this tendency, assert that the glorification of the anonymous individual was a response to trends in Soviet iconography. Melissa Dabakis, in "The Individual vs. the Collective: Images of the American Worker in the 1920s," contends that, during that decade, "the role of the American worker was elevated to a heroic stature, at least in part to compete with the glorified role of the worker in Soviet society. Thus, American workers, portrayed as free and independent within the capitalist system, served as happy and satisfied counterparts to workers in a socialist economy." But this treatment of workers as heroes of American mythology long predates the Russian Revolution. At the dawn of the skyscraping era, in 1908, Ernest Poole gave the figure its distinctive American twist in *Everybody's Magazine*. "Rough pioneers are these men of the steel, pushing each year their frontier line up toward the clouds. Wanderers living for their jobs alone. Reckless, generous, cool-headed, brave, shaken only by that grim power of Fate, living their lives fast and free, the cowboys of the skies."

These representative men, "the boys with the big muscley arms," are admired for the feats they perform, and above all, for the coolness of their temperament and the masculinity of their bodies. "You do not search musty libraries for stories of classical heroes any more [*sic*]; they are here to-day in the flesh, outwardly prosaic, incredibly nonchalant, crawling, climbing, walking, swinging, swooping on gigantic steel frames as they build the Babel Towers of Manhattan. Hairy-chested huskies, strapping youths, clean-limbed, clear-eyed men who tread, sure-footed, on steel girders hundreds of feet above the city streets." Marked by the danger and physical extremity of their jobs, they face their fate with equanimity. They are "a race of brawny men whose hands are rough and gnarled, whose shoulders are leather muscle, whose wind-lashed faces are calm and unemotional." In their climb to the heavens, they may absorb into themselves something of the quality of that lofty upper realm. "The ironworker heaves himself from one beam to another, upward, always upward—his shoulders bulging, his knees tense, but his face as placid as the blue sky only an arm's reach beyond him." Seen from afar, they might almost be gods. "For the men who appear tiny as flies to the spectators in the streets beneath are shown here as muscular, clear-eyed, poised, and self-confident creatures whom Lysippus or Phidias would have delighted to model in imperishable marble."

Yet to encounter the men in person is a disappointment. They have no conception of how others see them, little idea how to comport themselves as heroes. In September 1930, Gilbert Swan observed the Empire State's ironworkers lounging on the sidewalk, and not in the heights above:

> The human side of a great skyscraper may be studied almost any day between the hours of 12 and 1 o'clock. In that period the blasé gentlemen who seem to be hanging by their toe on a steel girder, who wield a triphammer while straddling a plank at a dizzy height, who toss crimson-hot rivets to one another, who send steel giants into the Manhattan skies, can be observed in their leisure moments. Sitting single file and double file in a half square centering on Fifth Ave at 34th or 33rd streets you'll find them behaving just about the same as any workman during his noon lunch hour.

It is *distance* that matters, distance that creates the hero. Up close, "these workers are merely lusty humans who meet their girl friends [*sic*] at the corner and make a date for the coming evening. Or, minus such social engagements, they make remarks about the pretty stenographers and clerks who go by." Swan emphasizes the irony. The great symbol they are creating stands beside them. "Flanking them is a glittering masterpiece of skyscraper art—the Empire State Building, which steadily rises to an eventual height greater than ever before attained by man." On the sidewalk, however, hardly heroes or even adult men anymore, the workers sit by, oblivious. "But the men who put the pieces together, like children making a jigsaw puzzle, seem quite unaware that they are actors in a metropolitan drama."

"How could mere toil align thy choiring strings!" rhapsodized the poet Hart Crane in 1930, contemplating the transcendent beauty of the Brooklyn Bridge. The real story, the journalists of the time almost always imply, is not the work of men but the Works of Man. It is a mystery, then, how mere toil—"the *human* side of a great skyscraper"—transforms into something greater. At a loss to articulate this seemingly inconceivable alchemy, writers of every grade turned, like Hart Crane, to poetry. The very consistency with which writers and journalists described ironworkers using figurative or mythological language, while failing to describe the actual men standing in front of them, provides insight into unconscious habits of perception, the ways ubiquitous yet unexamined clichés not only reflected but also created the era's social texture.

For the metamorphosis from man to hero to occur, ordinary workers must be seen from far away, both physically and rhetorically, not as men but as metaphors. "When the whistle blows," Gilbert Swan continued, describing the workers now at the end of their lunch hour, "they disappear through the heavy boards that slide back and forth. Soon far above the throng, higher than any trapeze artist in a circus, one of them suddenly appears swinging out on a steel girder, or poised against the clouds." Elevated and distant and no longer distinguishable as individuals, the men may once again serve as symbolic representations of Man, embodying the ideal without any distracting ordinariness.

From this perspective, in the grand view, the ironworker becomes the definition of American heroism, as he has been since his image first burst upon philosopher William James in 1899, "a workman doing something on the dizzy edge of a sky-scaling iron construction," the finest modern example, James said, of "human nature *in extremis*."

The archives of Empire State Inc. are now housed at the Avery Architectural and Fine Arts Library of Columbia University in New York. The bulk of these archives consists of twenty-three oversize scrapbooks, compiled for the corporation's publicity office by two clipping agencies, which collected every mention of the building in the newspapers, magazines, and trade journals of the time. These crumbling black pages with their pasted montages of yellowing newsprint now reside in archival boxes. It's an invaluable resource, granting an overview of how contemporaries, witnessing the construction of the world's tallest building, understood the historical event. Two additional boxes hold Empire State Inc.'s collection of more than 250 working prints by Lewis W. Hine.

The sheer scale of the project attracted the most attention. Hundreds of the clippings repeat the sensational statistics circulated by Empire State's publicity office. If all the materials had been transported to the site on a single train, it would be fifty-seven miles long, hauling fifty-seven thousand tons of steel, ten million bricks, two hundred thousand cubic feet of stone, 6,400 windows. The train arriving at Fifth Avenue would end in Bridgeport, Connecticut. The steel itself was enough to lay a double-track railroad from New York to Montreal. The Empire State had the largest, fastest, most automated elevators of its time, the heaviest pipes, the largest telephone and telegraph installations. Excitement over the building's size occupies most of the column inches devoted to the building, all but overwhelming mention of the people who installed these materials. The quantity and size of the materials were themselves the news. The steel frame's heaviest column warranted its own headline in *The New York Times*. This was not a peculiarity of the Empire State Building. The same fascination with materials can be seen in the coverage of the Woolworth Building, in its time the engineering marvel of the New World. "There are 87 miles of electric wiring in the Woolworth Building—sufficient to extend from New York to Philadelphia. The electric current outlets, strung less than three feet apart, would light the entire 23 miles of water-front around Manhattan."

When workmen are mentioned, we rarely encounter individuals. Instead, most commonly, we meet caricatures shaped according to prevailing cultural ideals of Man. In the American context, this regularly shades into comments about ethnicity and a reliance on social hierarchies based on racial and class stereotypes.

Observing the clientele at the lunch counters installed by the contractors within the Empire State Building, journalist Richard Massock notes, "The dinner pail has almost disappeared with the Irishman's hod, both converted into curios by the skyscraper age. Only the Italians bring home-prepared lunches. The American mechanic eats a hot noon-day meal." This tendency was characteristic. Again, similar coverage was given to the ironworkers who built the Woolworth Building. "Most of the structural ironworkers, the men who put up steel spider webs and then nonchalantly stroll around on the lofty threads, are Irish. A fair proportion of them are Swedes, 'Squareheads' their fellow workers call them. It's a toss up as to which of the nationalities is more daring, but on the whole the Irish are more inclined to take chances."

By the 1930s, after a decade of increasingly restrictive immigration legislation, a degree of anxiety about the fitness of these men as symbols of America rings out clearly. In April 1931, Margaret Norris and Brenda Ueland published an article about workers on the Empire State Building,

"Riding the Girders," which Norris included the following year in her elaborately titled book, *Heroes and Hazards: Talks with the Daredevils of To-day; True Stories of the Careers of the Men Who Make Our Modern World Safe by Their Courage.* There, she betrays her cultural preferences and prejudices. "Ironworkers are recruited from all over our own country and most parts of Europe," Norris proclaims, "though one rarely finds a Jew or an Italian or a Pole among them and never a negro." If we are to rely on these men for our safety, Norris implies, it's important they be of the right type. In fact, Jews, Italians, Poles, and Black Americans were restricted from many trade unions. They were not ironworkers, not due to an incapacity for the job, but because they were actively excluded by union bylaws and by management. The journalist's breezy description betrays a deeper, pervasive cultural racism.

The men Norris admires include "a big husky fellow with a twinkle in his eye"; "a red-headed foreman"; "a jolly, swaggering Irishman who worked on the Empire State Building"; "a handsome dark young ironworker whose slow drawl explained his nickname, 'Alabama.'" Describing ironworkers as a class, Norris reiterates the mythological characteristics ubiquitous since Ernest Poole's "cowboys of the skies." In Norris's words, they are "a devil-may-care, fiery, light-hearted lot, the men who put up steel." And when Norris describes the ideal ironworker, she clearly has a preferred type in mind. "The Scandinavian countries furnish many men of this trade. Their adaptability for the work is explained by the fact that many of them have been sailors or are the sons or grandsons of sailors, accustomed to working in rigging and at the top of the mast. Big, strapping Swedes, Norwegians, Danes, Finns—'squareheads,' they are called—are always among the best on the job. Even the Irish admit it. They are tireless, courageous, nimble, and yet strong as an ox."

Uncharacteristically for journalists of her era, however, Norris names a few of the men she profiles—not workers, but managers—and allows them to speak. She introduces Owen Eachus, superintendent of steel construction on the new Waldorf Astoria Hotel, built in 1931. While his prejudices are also on display, the picture he paints is more diverse than either he or Norris seems to recognize. Nevertheless, describing what kind of man makes a good ironworker, both Norris and Eachus answer with a list of ethnicities.

"It's hard to beat the Americans," Owen Eachus insists; "and the majority of them come from the South: you can tell it by their drawl. Wages in the South are low. When a bridge or a building goes up there, the men follow the contractor up North, East, or West—wherever he goes. The Southerner may be lazy, but up North he has to buy his own meal ticket; and he does it, too. We also have lots of Canucks (French Canadians), half-breed Indians, and Irishmen. One of the cleverest men, physically speaking, I ever had in my outfit was a Frenchman."

The "half-breed Indians" Eachus mentions were likely among a small number of Mohawk ironworkers, members of the Caughnawaga or Kahnawake tribe, whose reservation lies south of Montreal along the St. Lawrence River. Kahnawake Mohawks had been involved in ironworking since 1886, when the Dominion Bridge Company began a project for the Canadian Pacific Railway, just south of Kahnawake village. Mohawk ironworkers were active on most of the major American skyscrapers of the twentieth century. But specific interest in them as an ethnic category did not appear until the decades after the Empire State Building was completed. Joseph Mitchell's 1949 profile, "The Mohawks in High Steel," published in *The New Yorker*, was the first to single out their contributions to American construction. Even then, however, while Mitchell quotes recollections from individual workers, his article, like the earlier attention to ironworkers in the 1920s, is concerned with the men as a group. He, too, is interested in characterizing this *type* of worker, this cultural or ethnic type, not any particular man. And once again, the description confirms the cultural stereotype, now not only of the ironworker, but also of the Indian. "They roam from coast to coast, usually by automobile, seeking rush jobs that offer unlimited overtime work at double pay . . . Occasionally, between jobs, they return to Brooklyn to see their families. Now and then, after long jobs, they pick up their families and go up to the reservation for a vacation." Always described collectively as "they," the men are treated as an indistinguishable group, best understood by those who employ them. "Several foremen who have had years of experience with Caughnawagas believe that they roam because they can't help doing so, it is a passion, and that their search for overtime is only an excuse." In 1930, when the Empire State Building was under construction, perhaps two hundred Mohawk ironworkers were active throughout the United States. A small number worked on the Empire State. But today, thanks to Mitchell, they are the most famous group of skyscraper workers.

If the men are not identified by ethnicity, still, in the eyes of journalists and managers, their very identity as members of the working class lends them certain characteristics that also serve symbolic purposes within the cultural typology of the nation. In his review of the Empire State for *The New Republic*, critic Edmund Wilson decried the monstrous building's purposelessness and futility, opening just as the Great Depression rendered its office space superfluous. Concluding his analysis of the architecture and recounting his tour of the structure, Wilson writes:

> This big loft is absolutely empty, there is nothing to look at in it—or rather there is only one thing: a crude but genial mural drawn in pencil by, presumably, one of the plasterers or electricians, which, all unknown to the management, confronts every visitor to the fifty-fifth floor. A large male figure is seen standing upright and fornicating, *Venus aversa*, with a stooping female figure, who has no arms but pendulous breasts. The man is saying, "O, man!" Further along is a gigantic vagina with its name in four large letters written under it. One is grateful to the man who drew these pictures: he is a public benefactor. He has done something to take the curse off the opening of the Empire State Building.

Wilson's observation provoked a sharp, arguably Freudian, response from Empire State Inc.'s publicist, Belle Moskowitz. In her letter to the editor, "Cave Drawings in the Empire State," Moskowitz responds, "We naturally have no bone to pick with any conclusions Edmund Wilson or any other writers wish to reach. The thing that got under the skin of ourselves and the Empire State executives, was the reference to the pornographic art work on the walls of the fifty-fifth floor. It is natural when some 4,000 workmen are employed in the construction of a building such as this, that some small mind should exhibit its pornographic urge on the walls."

While Wilson and Moskowitz dispute how to interpret the drawings, they agree that workers represent the earthier qualities of civilization. The workmen—"presumably, one of the plasterers or electricians"—"naturally" display the genial or small-minded characteristics of their class. That's to be expected, says Moskowitz, and "lest Mr. Wilson think this unusual, however, we wish to refer him to any subway lavatory." But that's precisely why the graffiti is refreshing! Wilson retorts. The lower classes add life. They belie the stuffiness of the upper classes. In Wilson's response to Moskowitz, he puts a fine point on the distinction. "I didn't mean to criticize the building for the existence of the drawings: I merely meant to contrast its essentially anti-social character with their all-too-human humanity." As ideals, the workers are stereotypes or metaphors, not men. But as men, "the human side" of the Empire State, they are all too human.

Not all journalists were content to view the structure and the men who built it from afar. Some daring reporters took a closer look for themselves. And yet the journalists who ventured to the heights to visit workers in their native element were often so impressed by their own adventure they only dimly perceived the men they met along the way.

Typical was Edmund M. Littell, who published an account of his excursion in an article entitled "Men Wanted" in April 1930. "To understand the story of the Battle of the Skyscrapers which is related farther on, you must understand the story of the ironworker, for his are the arms that bring every beam to beam. And to understand him, you must call upon him in his habitation of height and steel. I have done this."

Littell climbed the Chrysler Building and the Bank of Manhattan Company Building at 40 Wall Street, then in a race for the title of tallest skyscraper. "As I moved up in the elevator in the unfinished [Chrysler] building, steel beams flashed past as telegraph poles do when you're riding in a train. Fifty-three, fifty-four, fifty-five, fifty-six! At the fifty-sixth floor the elevator came to a creaking stop. Clutching a cold, black column of steel with a grasp that well-nigh snapped my fingers, I clambered out. I was nine hundred feet above the sidewalk." Arriving at the job site, Littell again reaches for metaphor to describe the men at work. "From this point I could watch the ironworkers above me scramble like monkeys among the branches of the building." And even when he encounters an individual worker, Littell recounts his own impression of him, not anything about the man himself. "As I was in the midst of these reflections, an ironworker, whose name should have been Jake even if it wasn't, ambled down a beam toward me. A kind of morning constitutional, I suppose. He and his fellows seemed so much like aviators up here that I told him they ought to be equipped with parachutes. He grinned, verifying my observation that his name must have been Jake."

We never learn anything about "Jake," except that he smokes a corncob pipe, nor about any of the other workers, whom Littell can't quite acknowledge as people. But we learn how an ordinary reporter feels when subjected to the rigors of the ironworker's life. At 40 Wall Street, Littell climbs a wooden ladder to the top. "My knees begged me to edge back down. My lungs burned, my heart sounded like the 'put-put-put' of a motorboat, and my hands were numb. I had to use this ladder to get up with the riveters. It was only ten feet high, but beneath were nine hundred feet of the most insubstantial kind of air. Yet the ironworker—placid and imperturbable above me—moved lightly and surely; as safely, I thought, as a puppet on a string."

Lowell Thomas, author of *Men of Danger*, appears to have gone farther than any other journalist in his quest to show us the life of these men. He doesn't interview a worker or relate a worker's life story. Instead, Thomas impersonates a worker. Disguised, he is smuggled into the site of the Empire State Building by a complicit workman. "You get here about 8:30 tomorrow morning, and just walk in that shanty there," the man tells Thomas, "just don't say nothing to anybody." Thomas's inside connection leaves work clothes for him in a locker and instructs him how to behave. "Don't bother to shave; and rub some dirt on your hands after you get your clothes changed."

Arriving in the morning, Thomas finds a heavy black sweater, a pair of khaki overalls, a greasy cap, gloves and thick-soled shoes stashed for him in the locker. Properly costumed, he follows his guide, "Mike," up the temporary elevators that carry workers to the worksite.

> "We'll have to walk from here up," said Mike. "Now you'll see why the boys like to ride the ball." He started up an iron ladder which was resting on the girder of the floor above. It swayed a little under our weight and it seemed almost perpendicular to me. But that was only the first one. We went up five or six of these. And it seemed that the breeze grew stronger, fresher, with every floor. We were up where the riveters were at work. It was a machine-gun battle. There would be a lone *at-at-at-at-b-r-r-r-up*! Stopping suddenly. Then another would start. And another. Then it seemed as if the racket with them all going at once struck my face with physical force.

Up another series of ladders, they arrive at last at the very top, where the newest beams are being put in place. Thomas, unlike Littell, understands that these are mortal men. "There I saw the 'connectors' up close. Two columns reared themselves still higher towards the sky. A man sat on each one. They were looking down as the quivering cable came up—up with the beam they were waiting to set." Yet the experience of their shared mortality seems to exhaust his interest in them. He does not attempt to speak to or describe the men, but rather to put himself in their place. Thomas is convinced to walk across a beam. "At about the halfway point the trivial, but paralyzing, thought crossed my mind: 'Suppose my hat should blow off!' [T]he only other sensation I can remember was one of incredible loneliness."

Perhaps the most egregious usurpation of the ironworker's identity was perpetrated by Earl Sparling, who published a "dialogue" with an iron-worker, musing on his accomplishment while visiting the observation deck of the Empire State Building shortly after its opening on May 1, 1931. "It seems a long time now, that day when the forge fire glowed right in the middle of the eighty-sixth floor and the tower was still just a mass of steel girding against a rainy sky. It's different now." Published without quotation marks or any indication of its source, the dialogue, I suppose, was a literary fantasy, a chance for the journalist to demonstrate his writing skill.

> Up here, 102 stories high, a quarter of a mile above the side-walks, you really can't see very much.
>
> That, Joe, is the joke of it.
>
> Remember, we talked about that months ago, when you and the rest of the gang were topping out on the eighty-sixth floor.
>
> You said, "We'll build them higher than this some day [*sic*]." And you added, "But what's the use? When you get up this high, all you get is rain and fog."
>
> It was cold and raw that day and the wind was howling. You and the rest of them were anxious to get the job done. You wanted to stay on the good ground for a while and get acquainted with the kids.

“Character—An Empire State Craftsman.” Hine’s portrait of Arthur Jones.

The piece goes on like this in its strangely stilted language. Yet Sparling was clearly well informed. Some of his details can be verified. When the workers completed the final rivets in the steel structure on September 16, 1930, the weather was foggy and hazy, as it was on the first days the observation deck was open in early May 1931, impeding the vaunted view. Sparling's character also recalls one of the deaths at the site with specific detail. "I got to thinking to-day and I tried to pick out the shaft that carpenter went down. I couldn't find it. All the shafts look alike now, and the elevator operators are dressed up in swell uniforms, and when the elevators go up and down the men in the spats complain that their ears buzz."

Perhaps self-conscious about his technique, however, Sparling includes himself and his purpose in the story. The two men joke about publicity that celebrates the "character" of the workers. "Well, you're a character, too, Joe. And I guess you get the idea of all this. It's a nutty way to write a story, but it's the only way I can write it and talk about characters instead of directors and architects."

Of course, creating a character to be your mouthpiece and pretending this is the authentic voice of a workman was not the only way to write a story that did not focus on directors and architects. But it is revealing that this was how Earl Sparling chose to do so. Despite his apparent admiration for the worker and his work, Sparling continues to respect the seemingly inviolable boundary that separates the figure of the worker as an idealized character from the reality of the actual men.

Nevertheless, Earl Sparling's "dialogue," though easy to criticize in retrospect, provides the first clue that will allow me to connect a face in one of Lewis Hine's worker portraits with a name engraved on the bronze plaque in the Empire State's lobby. The joke Sparling imagines his worker making about "character" refers to a tourist brochure for sale at the observation deck gift shop. "I got a copy of a handsome pamphlet at the souvenir counter," Sparling writes. "It was filled with swell language and photographs. There was a big picture of Al Smith, and a couple of pages of officers and directors, all looking very proud indeed. Then came the architects and the contractors. And on page 16 there was a picture of an old bird, with a pipe in his mouth. The cutlines read, 'Character—An Empire State Craftsman.'"

This brochure is not included in the scrapbook pages held in the Avery Library archive. However, after a few weeks of searching, I found a copy of the "handsome pamphlet" on eBay. Published by Empire State Inc.'s publicity office to celebrate the building's opening, it is entitled *Empire State: A History*. On its cover, the forty-eight-page booklet bears a silver, black, and gold reproduction of the stainless-steel icon that dominates the building's lobby, boldly announcing it as a contribution to the grand history of the building. The text is suitably orotund. "From the swarming sidewalks, the impatient traffic of motor cars and people afoot, Empire State lifts itself to superb isolation, unbroken quiet, serene aloofness." There is a full-page photograph of Alfred E. Smith, and four pages of officers, directors, and builders, looking very proud indeed, just as Sparling says. And on page sixteen there is a portrait of a worker with a pipe in his mouth. He has goggles on his forehead, heavy gloves on his hands, and a concentrated, determined expression.

A copy of this photo, published in the tourist brochure, is mixed in with hundreds of other images of workers, stored in the archival boxes that hold Lewis Hine's working prints from the Empire State job. Hine submitted these prints to the publicity office of Empire State Inc., in fulfillment of his assignment, and so they have ended up here, in the basement of the library at Columbia University. This copy bears Hine's handwritten note on the back. He writes "burner," indicating the worker's profession, and he adds, "the man received an award for super craftsmanship."

If this man received an award for craftsmanship, then his name must appear on the bronze plaque in the building's lobby. But who was he? Hine scrawled different captions on his prints of this portrait. On another copy, held in the collection of the George Eastman Museum, Hine characterizes him by his notable accessory, "A burner takes his noon pipe seriously." Searching more carefully for this man, I noticed he also appears in another photo, which shows him kneeling before a steel beam, an acetylene torch in his hand.

Hine captioned this photo: "Burning hole in beam so it will fit." But neither Hine nor the publicity office recorded the man's name, and "burner" is not one of the professions honored on the Craftsmanship Awards plaque.

Ultimately, it would take months to identify the "old bird," using clues in the photograph itself and through a process of elimination. The man's goggles and heavy gloves are not generic workmen's clothing but specific tools of his trade. He works with metal. Among the award winners, there were only a few possibilities. As I connected other portraits with names on the plaque in the Empire State's lobby, the options narrowed to one.

The names of the corporation's officers and directors appear beneath their portraits in *Empire State: A History*, the tourist brochure Earl Sparling gently mocked for using an anonymous worker's portrait to illustrate the grand concept of "character." Now, the name of the worker may also be added to this history. This is a portrait of Arthur Jones, Craftsmanship Award winner for ornamental iron and bronze.

Arthur Jones at work, award winner for ornamental iron and bronze.

THREE

"WHO IS THE CRAFTSMAN?"

The Lewis Hine photographs of Empire State workers preserved at the Avery Architectural and Fine Arts Library are not in order, but have been shuffled according to the needs or whims of the previous researchers to access them. The photographic paper is curling a little with age, and despite the best conservation practices, some prints have creases, folds, or missing corners, damage they might have sustained when still in the files of Empire State Inc.

By themselves, the photos offer little direction to discover their origin or purpose beyond documenting the building's construction. In contrast to other projects in Hine's large body of work, any notes he made about this job, as well as any office memoranda from Empire State Inc. regarding his assignment, appear to be lost. More puzzling still, as Judith Mara Gutman observes in *Lewis W. Hine and the American Social Conscience*, half of the one thousand images Hine is thought to have created have never been found. A cache of previously unknown images may lie buried in a basement somewhere, an archive, a file cabinet, or a junk shop, waiting to be discovered. Formal prints of a few particularly striking images, enlarged and mounted for display, are held by many museums—including the J. Paul Getty Museum and the Museum of Modern Art in New York—and the New York Public Library. Others are in private collections scattered around the world. But the majority of the approximately five hundred known working prints, made during Hine's one-year employment by Empire State Inc. reside at Columbia University and at the George Eastman Museum in Rochester, New York. Those at the Avery Library come from the files of Empire State Inc. Those at the George Eastman Museum were a gift of the New York Photo League, an organization of socially conscious photographers, founded in 1936, that Hine joined late in his life and that acquired much of his archive when he died in poverty in 1940.

The images that survive in accessible archives fall into five general categories: portraits of individual workmen; images of workers at their jobs; photos of ironworkers during tower construction; ironworkers completing the Empire State's peak, the so-called mooring mast; and shots of the building itself, seen from various vantage points around New York City.

The two archives hold multiple copies of many of these working prints and frequently several versions of the individual portraits, with the men in different poses or captured from different angles. Frequently, a man's portrait resides in one archive, while the photo of him at his job is in the other. Almost all the prints bear the stamp of Hine's photographic studio on the back, "Lewis W. Hine, Interpretive Photography, Hastings-on-Hudson, New York." Some have numbers, referring to Hine's catalog of images available for licensing. Others have cryptic notations that may reflect Empire State Inc.'s use of them. Perhaps a quarter of the images, both at Avery and at the George Eastman Museum, have something written in Hine's handwriting on the back pertaining to the image itself. This is the only documentation from Hine to survive. Among these handwritten notes, a handful mention the workers' names.

As with the print of the pipe-smoking "burner," published in the publicity brochure, a few of Hine's notes are quite specific about the reason he photographed a particular man. One photo identifies Michael Tierney, rock driller. A variant of the same image adds, "a rock-driller who received a diploma for craftsmanship." Another photograph names Peter Madden, asbestos worker. A duplicate of that image explains, "Workman, Empire State. Received 'Award' for Craftsmanship." Sorting through the stacks of unorganized photographs in the basement of the Avery Library and in the George Eastman Museum's study room, I recognized that almost all the men whose names are written on the back of their portraits were winners of Empire State Craftsmanship Awards. Another photograph identifies James P. Kerr, award-winning stone setter. Another, Matthew M. McKean, award-winning carpenter. And several images, housed at the George Eastman Museum, identify Charles E. Sexton, award-winning bricklayer, according to one note, the "best bricklayer in N.Y."

Solely from these notes, it becomes evident that Lewis Hine's work at the Empire State Building has been mischaracterized by art historians since the photographs came to public notice. Empire State Inc. may have hired

Lewis Hine to create artistic impressions of "work" or to "celebrate labor," as critics have assumed since the 1930s. Based on the evidence of the existing photographs, however, it is clear that Hine's assignment explicitly included making portraits of the individual winners of Empire State Craftsmanship Awards. The portraits are not a random selection of workers Hine admired or found picturesque. Instead, Hine photographed at least twenty-five of the thirty-two award winners. These "superior craftsmen" account for most of the formal worker portraits he produced at the Empire State Building.

Each of these portraits therefore gives a face to a name on the bronze plaque in the Empire State's lobby. For figures who have been used symbolically for so long, even this moment of identification is significant. At the most basic level, associating a name and a face helps to focus the question of a man's distinctive life. Simply asking this question opens a new dimension in the history of these photos—new not because it was never there before, but because it was never considered worthy of historical attention. The men in their actual lives are too "ordinary." And their lives as individuals too often contradict the heroic, mythological depiction of them as gods, as "devil-may-care" cowboys who work for the love of adventure, not because it is their job. Investigating the history of these men as individuals, we find them struggling to make a living, to support their families, to navigate the contentious, sometimes violent relationship between labor and management that marked the building trades in the first half of the twentieth century. We find them confronted by the irresistible transformation of their jobs by machinery, struggling to be craftsmen in the Machine Age. Most decisively, from a historical perspective, we find the men confined by the views of them held by the upper and educated classes, the pen-wielding classes, which saw and defined them, as we have seen, according to racist, classist prejudices and the needs of national boosterism.

But where do we find these men as individuals, and what can we know of them? Construction workers frequently led itinerant lives, in this way escaping the coarse grain of official attention. Employment records from the era are rarely preserved, and the private lives of ordinary people are sparsely documented. The Great Depression induced many families to relocate in search of improved prospects or cheaper housing. Family names change through the generations. With no other starting point, the only way I could locate the men who built the Empire State Building was to follow the ninety-year-old paper trail—the brief appearances dispersed in newspapers, genealogical databases, military and union records, all the official forms and documents, the stray references and random "snapshots," which momentarily catch ordinary people as they pass through daily life. Yet here I encountered another barrier, the standardization of these forms, their rampant inaccuracies and inherent ambiguities. Even with better access to these sources than has ever been possible before, still, there are many different degrees of "identification." In rare instances, an identification provides a glimpse sharp enough to lead up to the present day, where a man survives in living memory. In other cases, associating a face and a name will be all I can do. Ordinary people surface only briefly in the public record before sinking back into obscurity. Undoubtedly, someone, somewhere, could once have recognized each of the men in Hine's portraits, a relative or descendant. But that knowledge is private and seldom survives more than a generation or two. In some cases, the outlines of a man's life emerge from the documents. Most identifications quickly trail off into mystery.

In each case, however, the paper trail leads us back to Lewis Hine's portraits, though now seen through a changed lens. No longer abstract or solely artistic impressions, Hine's photographs are the most explicit and expressive surviving documentation of these workers. Even in the absence of further information, when seen as the portrait of a specific individual, Hine's images emerge as profound studies of each man's character.

Let's begin with the portrait of carpenter Matthew McKean.

Matthew M. McKean's identity in Hine's portrait is confirmed by an inscription on the back of a working print. But his identity in the historical record is merely a collection of tantalizing hints. A Matthew McKean, carpenter, submitted a Declaration of Intention to become a US citizen on January 22, 1942. According to this document, he was born on September 8, 1882, in Irvine, North Ayrshire, Scotland, and arrived at Ellis Island from Glasgow aboard the SS Columbia on May 7, 1923. The ship's manifest, which can be found in the Ellis Island database, corroborates these details. At the time of his arrival, this Matthew McKean had been married for eleven years to a woman named Elizabeth (the Declaration of Intention contains the typo, "Eliabeth"). But Elizabeth and the couple's two children remained in Scotland and never emigrated. Instead, Matthew traveled with another man, Joseph McKean, likely his brother. Both men were "joiners" or carpenters. They were

Matthew M. McKean, carpenter.

headed for the home of a cousin, John Raeside, a plasterer, likewise born in Irvine, Scotland, who had emigrated a decade earlier, in 1913. Joseph McKean appears to have returned to Scotland in the 1930s, and he died there in 1958. But Matthew remained in the US. A draft registration card, also from 1942, confirms that Matthew Methieson McKean lived at 11 West 65th Street in Manhattan and specifies that he was employed by Beekman Builders, Inc. A Social Security claim provides his date of death, November 14, 1946. The only other personal details these documents contain is that he had varicose veins and a tattoo on his left forearm.

If this is the right man—and I could find no one else with this name whose profile seemed to fit—Matthew M. McKean would be forty-eight in Hine's portrait. His head is cocked slightly to one side. He wears a large, cloth cap that accentuates the delicacy of his features. Hine captures him bent slightly forward. His lips are compressed, and he gazes intently but softly beyond the frame. At the very center of the portrait, Hine emphasizes the sharp crease that runs down Matthew McKean's cheek to his jawline, care etched into his face. If these few details are all we can learn of the man who received the Empire State Craftsmanship Award for carpentry, they still add a poignant depth to a name on the bronze plaque.

For the rock driller Michael Tierney, instead of tantalizing hints, the public record presents a bewildering abundance of information, none of it specific enough to provide certainty that I've found the right man.

A Michael Tierney is listed as a boarder at a rooming house on 184 East Ninety-Sixth Street, Manhattan, in the 1930 US census. He's thirty-seven years old, an immigrant from the Irish Free State, who arrived in the US in 1909. He is employed as a "laborer" for "construction," which, while too vague to pinpoint him as the man in Hine's photo, distinguishes him from the seventy-seven other Michael Tierneys who lived in the New York City area at the time and who appear in the US census. The other Michael Tierneys are policemen, firemen, railroad men; there is an attorney, a supervisor at the Federal Reserve Bank.

According to the records at Ellis Island, only one Michael Tierney immigrated in 1909. On September 22, a twenty-one-year-old, single man arrived from Cootehill, Ireland, aboard the ship *Caronia*. This would make him forty-two in 1930, not thirty-seven as stated in the census, a discrepancy not unusual in genealogical records, but casting doubt on the identification. More than 140 other Michael Tierneys arrived in the years surrounding 1909. One emigrated in 1907 from Meelish, Ireland, age twenty-two; another on December 8, from Kilmacreeva aboard the *Lusitania*. In 1908, a twenty-one-year-old Michael Tierney, a laborer from Shinrone, Ireland, arrived with his mother, Annie, and another arrived on the ship *Saxonia* from Dunmore, Ireland, on May 28, 1908. Any or none of these could be the man in Hine's photo.

In July 1934, a Michael Tierney, former construction worker, caught the eye of a journalist, and a brief interview with him appeared in *The Brooklyn Daily Eagle*. "Mike was a steamfitter before the Big Blow," the article says, referring to the 1929 stock market crash. Like many men in those first, desperate years, this Michael Tierney took to selling apples on the street. "He has made a real go of the apple business, likes it better than fitting pipes—although it doesn't pay nearly as well. 'But,' he says, 'it gives you more time to study people—and by the way, you'd be surprised to know the people I sell apples to.'"

Is this the right man? Steam fitting is a construction trade distinct from rock drilling. But construction workers often changed jobs, and journalists have been known to get their details wrong before. Without more specific information, it's impossible to know if this is the man who appears in Lewis Hine's photograph and who won an Empire State Craftsmanship Award. With no other definite information to go on, Hine's portrait of Michael Tierney is the best surviving documentation.

The portrait of Tierney at his job shows him leaning on his drill, excavating the pit, which extended forty feet below street level, in which the foundations for the Empire State Building were laid. In *Men at Work*, Hine published a work photo almost identical to this one, but showing a different rock driller. Tierney's portrait and his work portrait are reunited here for the first time. These were probably among the earliest photographs Hine took at the construction site. General excavation commenced on January 22, 1930, and was completed on March 17, the day before erection of the steel frame began. Although their work was extremely hazardous, excavators were among the lowest-paid workers on the site, earning just over one dollar an hour. In the work portraits, they operate without goggles or ear protection and without a mask. Yet Hine's formal portrait of Michael Tierney

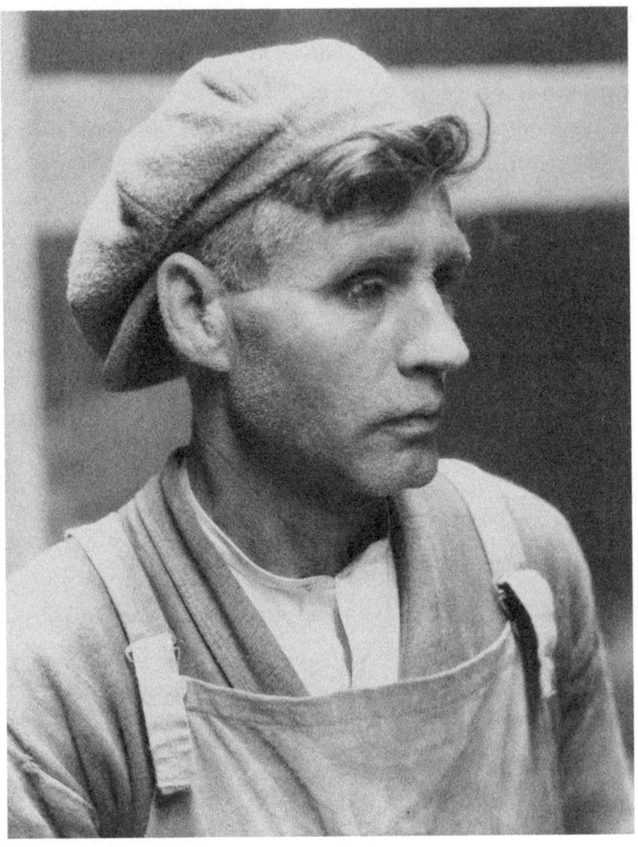

Michael Tierney, rock driller.

shows a man with a surprisingly thoughtful, vulnerable expression gazing pensively past the frame of the photo. Dust cakes his hair and eyelashes.

Although I have not been able to identify Michael Tierney further, his identity in Hine's photo was never really a mystery. Bearing the title *Foundation Men*, this portrait of Michael Tierney appears on the first page of Hine's *Men at Work*. The photographer provides this caption: "Their noisy pneumatic drills break up the bed rock where a new building is to stand. They work in a haze of rock dust which they know will shorten their lives. The man above received an award for craftsmanship."

For anyone examining Hine's 1932 book, the name of the award-winning rock driller should have been easy to deduce. It was engraved on a plaque in the building's lobby. Yet in reading the images with this caption, critics have instead sought their symbolic content. For Kate Sampsell-Willmann, in her fine study, *Lewis Hine as Social Critic*, the "nameless, and therefore abstract 'foundation' man was not only digging the foundation of a building; his virtue assured the foundation of American society in such uncertain times." Sampsell-Willmann discerns a larger, thematic message in Hine's decision to begin his book with this portrait. "These men are the true 'spirit of industry,' not the owners, the mortgagors, or the capitalists." Analyzing the portrait, she concludes, "Hine clearly appealed to the American mystical belief in the inherent worthiness of work as an end in itself."

James P. Kerr, stone setter.

Because she views the photograph as symbolic, Sampsell-Willmann misses the specific information Hine provided in his caption. Michael Tierney is not nameless or abstract, nor was his work an end in itself. He was a man, most likely an Irish immigrant, who performed a dangerous, life-threatening job to earn a living, one of three hundred excavators who labored in alternating day and night shifts to complete the removal of nine thousand cubic yards of earth and 17,398 cubic yards of rock in less than eight weeks. But here, as elsewhere, the worker's individual identity has been sacrificed to the needs of a generalized, theoretical narrative. Tierney's supposed anonymity is the prerequisite for his use as a symbol.

My inability to identify Michael Tierney more precisely in the historical record therefore calls attention to a gap in our knowledge. Highlighting this gap is fundamentally distinct from ignoring it or glossing over it with conceptual analysis or mythology. Again and again, critics will gaze at these "documentary" images and see something abstract, without questioning their own vision, as if it were natural to ignore the photograph's manifest

content, natural to see the representation of an idea, not the likeness of a man. In this way, the tension between the documentary and mythical dimensions in Hine's photograph collapses, and with it the space within which the worker might appear as an individual. The assumption of anonymity thus reinforces the larger cultural preference for nameless workers and for rendering invisible the personal cost of their labor. In fact, Michael Tierney is not anonymous. We just don't know much about him.

Sometimes, identifying a man in the public record yields an oblique glance at the circumstances of his life.

Stone setter James Patrick Kerr was twenty-two years old in 1930, when Lewis Hine photographed him. He lived at 583 Tenth Avenue, Manhattan, in a rented apartment he shared with his mother, Mary King, and his sister, also named Mary. Mrs. King, of Irish ancestry, was a homemaker; Mary was an operator for the telephone company. The family paid seventeen dollars a month for their flat. By this standard, James made a good living as long as he had a job. According to the contract for the Contracting Stone Setters Association and the Journeyman Stone Masons and Setters Union, the wage for a stone setter in 1930 was $1.92½ per hour, or $15.40 a day.

Public records allow me to assemble a brief sketch of James Kerr's family history. In 1910, the family had lived around the corner, on West Fifty-Third Street, Manhattan. The father, Patrick Kerr, then twenty-three years old, had immigrated in 1890. Although the 1910 census gives his birthplace as Scotland, an 1890 ship's manifest shows Patrick Kerr, age three, departing Londonderry, Northern Ireland, with three other children younger than ten and no apparent adult guardian, aboard the *Ethiopia*. They arrived in New York on September 30, 1890. In the 1910 census, Patrick J. Kerr's profession is bricklayer. He was killed in a street accident on February 9, 1911, when his son James was three. By 1920, Patrick's widow, Mary Kerr, had remarried. Her new husband, Joseph King, was a twenty-eight-year-old dock laborer. With her new husband, Mary and her two children moved to the apartment on Tenth Avenue where they remained through James's employment at the Empire State Building, ten years later. A 1927 photo in the collection of the New York Public Library shows the back of the five-story brick tenement building in which they lived. Their apartment would have been filled with the sound of building construction. The entire block east of the Kerr's home was being demolished to make room for the thirty-five-story American Women's Association Building, a project financed by Anne Morgan, daughter of J. Pierpont Morgan, who devoted much of her inheritance to improving the lives of working-class women. That building opened in 1929, just as demolition work on the Waldorf-Astoria Hotel at the corner of Fifth Avenue and Thirty-Fourth Street began, clearing the ground for construction of the Empire State Building.

Lewis Hine made several portraits of James Kerr. In some, he demonstrates an element of his job, using a level to ensure that the limestone blocks that form the Empire State's facade stand straight. In another, he relaxes on the scaffold suspended outside the building, called a "duck walk," leaning inward against a steel column. His arm rests on a pressed aluminum spandrel panel, installed below an empty window opening. He holds his cap in his hand and offers the camera a shy smile.

*

The identification of a worker is itself a window onto the culture beyond, which sometimes elucidates additional pressures that shaped how the men were seen. For some reason, the award of a Certificate of Superior Craftsmanship to bricklayer Charles E. Sexton provoked the ire of Maurice Heaton, a professor of fine arts at Teachers College, Columbia University. In the article "Who Is the Craftsman?" published in the 1938 edition of *Art Education Today*, Professor Heaton felt moved to question whether a bricklayer deserved the title of "craftsman" at all. According to Heaton, Sexton "did his job well, conscientiously, with an easy and even beautiful swing; just fast enough to please both the boss and his union. He represents labor at its best. He is happy at his work, but nobody can point to his brickwork between the thirty-third and thirty-fourth stories and feel that he has done something fine." In the professor's view, within the realm of building construction, the title of craftsman should be reserved solely for architects or builders, not tradesmen. "He is not given a chance to develop his imagination, and there you are. From a creative and artistic point of view carpenters, masons, and mechanics are not craftsmen." It's not clear how Heaton happened upon Charles E. Sexton's name, nor why he selected bricklaying among the professions represented on the Empire State Building plaque to illustrate his opinions regarding craftsmanship.

In contrast to Heaton, Lewis Hine was particularly drawn to Charles E. Sexton. Hine made numerous portraits of him, and the prints frequently have descriptive notes on the back, for example, "Charlie Sexton. Craftsman Bricklayer on the Empire State Building."

Charles Eugene Sexton was born in Albany, New York, on August 2, 1873, to parents also born in New York. His father, Eugene, was a mason. In 1900, Charles married Emilie Urbach, a German immigrant who had arrived in the US in 1883. Initially the couple lived in the working-class Hell's Kitchen neighborhood of Manhattan, like many of Empire State's other workers, but by 1920, they and their four daughters had left Manhattan for Bay Ridge Avenue, Brooklyn. Charles was by then a bricklaying foreman. His 1918 draft registration specifies that he is superintendent of building construction for a contractor located on East Forty-Second Street. By 1925, the Sextons had relocated to Putnam Valley, New York, where they remained for the rest of their lives. Charles Sexton built a family compound on Tinker Hill

Charles E. Sexton, bricklayer.

in Adams Corners, about fifty miles north of the Empire State Building. In the 1930 census, taken on April 10, 1930, five months before he received his Craftsmanship Award, Sexton and his wife, Emilie, lived with a married daughter and her husband in a home they owned worth $10,000. Charles Sexton seems to have been a respected neighbor. Alone among the Empire State craftsmen, as far as I have been able to determine, his award received notice in his hometown paper. The *Haverstraw-Rockland County Times* observed simply that he "received a gold medal and a certificate of excellence for work done on the new Empire State Building." Charles Sexton was fifty-seven years old when Lewis Hine photographed him at the construction site. He died at age seventy-three on April 4, 1947.

Three of Sexton's four daughters remained in Putnam Valley, but the following generations scattered, and eventually the property was sold. His great-great-granddaughter, Karen Tompkins, recalls that one of these daughters, her great-grandmother, told her about Charles's work on the Empire State Building when she was a child. But, like the family, over time

that history, too, had dispersed. "I honestly don't remember anyone else talking about it," she said.

Most American families can reconstruct this kind of genealogical sketch from records held in the National Archives, if buried by the enormous quantity of data and the mistakes and contingencies of record-keeping and indexing. Yet the more intimate notion of an ancestor's personality is preserved over time, if at all, solely in a few anecdotes or photographs, passed down to their descendants. Like the names of a few workers in the broader context of history, these few private recollections stand out against—and eventually, stand in for—the living detail that has been lost.

We come closest to rejoining the disparate elements—recovering not only a name and a face, but the rough contours of an individual identity—with the asbestos worker Peter Madden.

Peter Madden, asbestos worker.

Using genealogical resources, I can trace Madden's family to Friday, December 23, 1870. On that day, when *The New York Times* reported the sudden, unexplained collapse of an eight-story brick building on West Thirty-Fifth Street, just a block from where the Empire State Building would one day stand, a census taker visited Peter Madden Sr., his wife, Ellen, both Irish immigrants, and their first child, Mary, age two, at their home in the nineteenth ward of Manhattan. Their apartment was located in the blocks between East Fifty-Ninth and East Sixty-First Streets, bordered by Second Avenue and the East River, where today the Queensboro Bridge and the Roosevelt Island Tramway arrive in Manhattan. Peter Sr. was a railroad clerk. By 1880, the household was busy with seven children under the age of twelve. Peter Madden Jr., the fourth child, was born on July 6, 1873. He was an exact contemporary of the bricklayer Charles Sexton, the "vital records" of his life—birth, marriage, death—all falling in the same years. He died in the Bronx on March 23, 1947.

Peter Madden Jr. married Katherine O'Donnell in 1900. Following state and federal census records, we catch glimpses of the family in five- or ten-year intervals. By 1905, Peter has become a pipe insulator. The family lived on Pleasant Avenue, Manhattan, on the far eastern edge of the island, near 117th Street. They remained in this neighborhood for ten years, through the births of their three children. In the 1920 US census, Peter Madden appears among numerous other Peter Maddens—a longshoreman; an insurance agent; a shipyard driller; a bartender; a driver for Standard Oil—distinguished by his profession, "Insulator," in the industry "Asbestos Co." When Lewis Hine took his portrait in 1930, Peter Madden was fifty-seven years old.

By then he lived on East 138th Street in the Bronx with his wife and youngest son, also a pipe coverer, who may also have worked on the Empire State Building. The apartment was just one block from the 138th Street station of the IRT subway line known as the Third Avenue Elevated or "the El," which would have provided easy access to the construction site. A contemporary photograph of the neighborhood shows handsome four- and five-story brick buildings, some with window awnings, and the Romanesque facade of St. Luke's Catholic Church. The Madden's neighbors were mostly first- and second-generation Americans, born in New York to immigrant parents from England, Scotland, Ireland, Germany, Russia, and Romania.

Peter Madden's great-grandson, the writer James McManus, has no personal recollections of his great-grandfather. When I contacted him, he reached out to his extended family and gathered the few remaining impressions of Peter that have survived the seventy-five years since his death. James's cousin, Daniel Madden, recalled, "after Grand Pa Pete finished the Empire State he got a letter of reference from Alfred E. Smith of NYC. My Mom kept it all this time and handed it down to me." The letter is on the stationary of Empire State Inc., dated November 26, 1932. Addressed to Mr. Roy Scott, Chief Engineer of the State Hospital in Central Islip, Long Island, it reads: "This will introduce you to Mr. Peter Madden who was an asbestos worker on the Empire State Building during its construction. His name is listed on the plaque in the lobby of this building as being the best man in his line of work. I am glad to recommend him to you and if there is anything you can do to assist him, it will be appreciated." It is unknown whether Al Smith's recommendation yielded work for Madden. The hospital, more formally known as the State Hospital for the Insane, had opened in 1889. A sister institution, the Pilgrim State Hospital, designed to relieve overcrowding at the older facility, opened a few miles away in 1931, and this may have been where Madden sought work.

James McManus also related an anecdote from his sister, Ellen. She recalled hearing her grandmother, Betsy, wife of Peter's oldest son, describe how the men would bring home canvas scraps left over from their work, still covered with asbestos. Betsy used them as dishrags. "It's a wonder anyone survived!" Ellen wrote. Indeed, the dangerous consequences of prolonged exposure to asbestos fibers had been noted since the early 1900s, and on March 24, 1930, two weeks before Peter Madden appeared in the US census, a report was submitted to the British Parliament, which concluded that 66 percent of those working with asbestos for twenty years or more suffered from asbestosis, a chronic lung condition. But the use of asbestos in pipe covering and insulation was not banned in the US until 1973. The substance was declared a human carcinogen in 1975.

Terry Madden Best, Peter's great-granddaughter, forwarded me a recollection in the form of a short story, written by her father, Peter's grandson, Joseph F. Madden. The story takes place at their house in upstate New York, sometime in the mid-1930s. It offers a brief glimpse of Peter Madden and his family through the eyes of a young grandson, recalled many years later. It's the sort of history preserved in private family archives, kept in a shoebox in a closet.

In these stories, Peter Madden comes across as a strict but kindly man. "Saturday night was game time. Pete surreptitiously gave us some pocket money. The chips and cards were out on the table in the back porch. Poker lessons were about to begin. If I lost all my money Pete would again surreptitiously restore it accompanied by a stern look. Pete detested 'punks' even if they were his own grandchildren—as a matter of fact them even more so."

Peter's son, Thomas—Tom or Tommy, as his son, Joseph, called him—became a building inspector for New York City. During the summers, the men were at their jobs in the city, while the rest of the family stayed at the bungalow upstate. "On Friday evening they would arrive bearing civilized bakery food and other luxuries," Joseph recalled. "Tommy and Pete did not envision the weekends as a time of gentlemanly leisure. Eighteen holes of golf were not on the agenda. Saturday and Sunday were home improvement days punctuated by Mass on Sunday morning. Attending Mass was not optional." The home improvement projects gave the young grandson an opportunity to observe the men. "Tommy and Pete were not all that compatible in work methods. Tommy was a squarer and measurer. Pete was a 'by the eye' craftsman. Pete would take a costly piece of pine and saw it into two exact halves without benefit of a tape measure or right angle square. Tommy would fume at this cavalier style."

The heart of Joseph Madden's recollection concerns digging a well. In the story, the men employ a dowsing rod to locate water. They settle on a spot to dig, directly beneath a large rock. Some comedy ensues. When Tom ties a rope around the rock and attempts to drag it from the ground with the family flivver, the result is a dislocated drive shaft. Eventually, however, the rock is removed, the hole dug, and at about fourteen feet, they strike water. They then brace the hole with flat stones. "It was during this final phase that my grandfather and I reached a new level of understanding," Joseph writes. "Pete was at the top of the hole. I was at the bottom. Pete selected a flat rock and began tying it to the rope. His old hands miscued and the rock plummeted into the well. It whizzed past my nose and plunged into the water. We both fell silent for a brief time that seemed like an hour." Suddenly realizing a power he had never suspected, Joseph commands Pete to lower the ladder, which his grandfather does, silently. "I climbed out unceremoniously and went into the bungalow and put on my bathing suit. To my recollection there was no further discussion of the incident."

It's little enough, a charming anecdote like any family might preserve. And yet, if we look again at Lewis Hine's portrait of Peter Madden with these stories in mind, I think they shift a sensitive balance within the photograph, changing it, and allowing us to see the image anew.

There is a tension inherent in any photograph between the general and the specific, and the precise balance of it depends on how much you know about the subject. To a family member, the portrait of a loved one is a picture of that person. The expressiveness of the face characterizes a known personality, the way his eyes and the lines in his face embody his bearing and his life. It's difficult to see beyond the specific. The more you look, the more you see Peter. By contrast, with no knowledge of its subject beyond the appellation "worker," a portrait is a formal composition, available for any signification. It is not the man, Peter Madden, we see, but instead an example of a *kind* of man. The specificity of his expression then does not characterize him personally but characterizes a type. Viewers then fill in the contours of this type with their own impressions, ideas, and assumptions. In this case, it's equally difficult to see beyond the general.

This tension between the general and the specific gives Hine's portraits, indeed, all symbols, their power. The specific anchors the image in reality, while the general provides its beguiling, symbolic aura. But art history and the culture at large consistently reduce this tension to something simpler. The specific individual is forgotten, and only the beguiling type, the ideal, remains. Then, the significance of the photograph consists in how well the man represents the ideal. Each feature, each subtle nuance of his expression, is reflected outward, toward the definition of an abstraction, rather than inward, toward the definition of a man. To ask who he was, or to probe beneath this symbolic surface, appears pointless. It merely confirms an ordinary man in his ordinariness. Indeed, accustomed to the grand perspective of symbolism, we may feel that anecdotes about Peter Madden's life only diminish the evocative image of him Lewis Hine created, as if the ideal were more real than the man.

For the construction workers Hine photographed, the very quality of the images encouraged this attitude. Lewis Hine's genius so exceeded the mundane requirements of his assignment that the men disappeared beneath his art. For Hine, for Empire State Inc.'s publicity office, and for art historians since, the weight of the image as an abstraction overwhelmed the workmen and the circumstances and purpose of their portraits. Yet recognizing these men as individuals is the only way we grasp the actual, historical content of Lewis Hine's work.

I've sought to rejoin the elements of these men's identities not to elevate them above their ordinary lives. On the contrary, the pressure to make them seem more than ordinary leads to the mythological caricatures ubiquitous in the journalism of the era and sadly still conventional today. Instead, I wish to hold the tension between the specific and the general as clearly as possible before our eyes, to preserve a space in which to recognize these men, even if we know little about them. Hine's magisterial portraits are the rarest kind of historical record, offering a momentary glimpse into the lives of otherwise unknown people. These lives may appear as mere wisps against the grandeur of the Empire State Building. But for this very reason it is necessary to preserve them. Because it is *these* men who built the great American landmark. Recognizing them as individuals, rather than as heroic caricatures, reminds us this extraordinary building was constructed by ordinary men, and this is what makes it a fitting symbol for America.

FOUR

"THE MAN ON THE JOB"

Lewis Hine was hired by Empire State Inc. to produce portraits of the men who won Empire State Craftsmanship Awards. However, because this fact about his employment has never been recognized until now, other dimensions of Hine's job at the Empire State have also been lost or misconstrued, the gaps filled in with speculation. In the absence of sources, authors have ventured various explanations for how Lewis Hine came to photograph the construction of the Empire State Building in the first place.

In her collection of Hine's letters, *Photo Story*, Daile Kaplan suggests that "Hine apparently made contact with the building's publicity firm through John Shreve, one of his Hastings-on-Hudson neighbors." It is true that Richmond (not John) Shreve was a resident of Hastings-on-Hudson, the New York suburb where Hine lived, as were several other men associated with the building, including the consulting structural engineer, Homer G. Balcom, and Charles E. Andres, whose company supplied the building's 6,400 window frames. However, there is no evidence that Hine knew or moved in the same social circles as these men, despite living in the same upstate town. David Farber, author of a biography of John Jakob Raskob, the building's chief financier, follows Neal Bascomb's *Higher: A Historic Race to the Sky and the Making of a City* in the far-fetched assertion that Hine was hired at the instigation of the millionaire corporate manager. There is no evidence for this claim, either.

Employing a photographer to document construction of a major skyscraper was a common practice. Walter Chrysler had engaged Margaret Bourke-White to illustrate his building's most eye-catching decorative features. And Frank W. Woolworth had hired Irving Underhill to show the progress of his building during construction, with regular photographic updates appearing in Woolworth stores across the country. While the idea of hiring a photographer may have been raised by the directors of Empire State Inc., still, the task of carrying it out would fall to the publicity office. Publicity for Empire State was run by Belle Moskowitz and her son, Josef Israels II, through their public relations firm, Publicity Associates. Both Jim Rasenberger and Elisabeth Israels Perry, author of a biography of Belle Moskowitz, identify her as the source of the commission. While little hard evidence has yet surfaced to substantiate this claim either, it is almost certainly correct. In a letter from 1938, Hine refers to Israels as "my mentor on [the] Empire State job." Yet Hine's connection with Belle Moskowitz goes much farther back, and it uncovers another dimension of the Empire State portraits and the building's cultural history that is generally unrecognized or recognized only generally.

Belle Moskowitz had known or known of Lewis Hine since at least 1909. It is possible they had met in 1906 or even earlier. While their lives and careers followed very different paths, both Moskowitz and Hine were rooted in the same vibrant world of early twentieth-century progressive social work.

Belle Lindner Israels Moskowitz had been personal secretary to Al Smith during his four terms as governor of New York State, and she headed the publicity campaign during his failed 1928 run for US president. In this capacity, as historian Robert A. Caro describes her, "all but unknown to the public but an almost legendary figure among politicians, she would be possessed of more power and influence than any woman in the United States." Detail-oriented, politically incisive, and a pioneer in public relations, Moskowitz was the force behind Smith's legislative agenda as well as his public image. In an unlikely partnership, she had helped to make the Tammany-bred Smith—the "red-faced, jut-nosed, gold-toothed, harsh-voiced smoker of big cigars"—into America's most effective leader of progressive reform. During Smith's governorship, New York State passed laws strengthening worker compensation and restricting child labor and abusive labor practices. Smith fought for low-income housing and higher teacher salaries; created public parks; and reorganized state government—initiatives all quietly coordinated and publicized by Belle Moskowitz. The governor rarely made a decision without first consulting "Mrs. M.," as he affectionately called her. When Smith sought the Democratic Party's nomination to run for president, Belle Moskowitz worked as director of publicity for the Democratic State Committee. In 1926, *The New Yorker* summarized their relationship, and the daunting challenges it faced during Prohibition, in these concise terms: "a stout Jewish woman working herself close to a physical breakdown in the belief she can make a wet Roman Catholic President of a dry, Protestant country." When Smith lost the 1928 election to Herbert Hoover in a landslide, he became instead president of Empire State Inc. Belle Moskowitz followed him into this new endeavor and became the skyscraper's director of publicity. In his eulogy after her sudden death in 1933, Smith, brokenhearted, said, "She had the greatest brain of anybody I ever knew."

Born in 1877, the daughter of German-Jewish immigrants, Belle Lindner had left school at age eighteen to work at the Educational Alliance, a settlement house for new immigrants in New York's Lower East Side. Aimed at integrating the predominantly Eastern-European Jewish immigrants into American society, the Alliance offered a range of social programs, including education, health services, childcare, legal aid, and employment training. In her three years there, Belle Lindner's work concentrated on the Alliance's entertainment and exhibitions, roles in which her sensitivity to the immigrants' social concerns and her genius for organization began to emerge.

According to Elisabeth Israels Perry's biography, *Belle Moskowitz: Feminine Politics and the Exercise of Power in the Age of Alfred E. Smith*, Moskowitz got her start in politics with the Council of Jewish Women. The Council, Perry writes, worked within a larger network of organizations like the Educational Alliance, creating a scientific basis for social reform. "They took surveys, collected statistics, and presented graphic conclusions to potential supporters. Next, they mounted publicity and lobbying campaigns to get laws passed. Even then their job was not finished: the enforcement and social consequences of the laws had to be closely monitored." After her marriage to the architect and painter Charles Henry Israels in 1903, Belle Israels quickly became a prominent figure in the Council, campaigning for tuberculosis prevention, improved housing codes, anti-prostitution measures ("dance hall" reform), mental health reform, and child welfare.

In 1909, Belle Israels published an article in one of the leading sociological journals of the era, *The Survey*, until that year known as *Charities and The Commons*, edited by the brothers Arthur P. and Paul U. Kellogg. Lewis

Hine was *The Survey*'s staff photographer. Belle Israels's article, "The Way of the Girl," appeared in *The Survey* on July 3, 1909, with illustrations by Hine. This is their first documented connection. Three years earlier, however, in 1906, Belle Israels had organized an exhibition on child labor at the New York State Conference of Charities and Correction, an annual forum focused on social work and prison reform. Perhaps instructed by her work with non-English-speaking populations, Israels was an early and savvy adopter of visual, as well as textual, presentation of information. Her exhibit, Perry writes, featured "a hundred photographs, probably taken by Lewis Hine."

Lewis Wickes Hine had come to the cause of social reform along a different path. A native of Wisconsin, he was born in 1874, three years before Belle Moskowitz, and one year after Al Smith. As a young man, he attended the State Normal School in Oshkosh, Wisconsin, where he met Frank Manny, a progressive pedagogue and student of educational philosopher John Dewey. In 1901, Manny became superintendent of the Felix Adler School of Ethical Culture in Manhattan, and he recruited Lewis Hine to teach there.

The Society for Ethical Culture, founded by Felix Adler in 1876, promoted a vision of social justice and social reform through education and good works. The Society was actively involved in issues of workers' rights, housing, health, and education on a practical rather than legislative level, and it sponsored clubs, libraries, gymnasiums, job-training programs, employment bureaus, and the first free kindergarten in the United States. Belle Israels and her first husband, Charles Henry Israels, had been involved in the Society for Ethical Culture since the early years of the century. The Society operated another Lower East side Settlement, Madison House, founded in 1898, and located two blocks from the Educational Alliance, where Belle Lindner had worked. By 1907, Belle Lindner Israels was a member of the Ethical Culture Women's Conference, and she served on its executive committee. It's possible she had first encountered Louis Hine here, through the Society for Ethical Culture. While the precise origin of their connection cannot be established, Lewis Hine and Belle Lindner both came up in the same small circle of professional social work. In 1914, after the death of her first husband, Belle Israels married Dr. Henry Moskowitz, also a social reformer. Together with Felix Adler, Henry Moskowitz was a cofounder of the National Association for the Advancement of Colored People. Eventually, he wrote Al Smith's 1928 campaign biography, *Up from the City Streets*.

Lewis Hine taught at the School of Ethical Culture from 1901 to 1908. It was there, as a teacher, that he first took up photography, encouraged by Frank Manny to explore the medium as a pedagogical tool. By 1904, Hine was the school photographer. Beginning in 1906, he published articles and photographs in several journals devoted to pedagogy, as well as in Gustav Stickley's *The Craftsman*, the magazine of the American Arts and Crafts movement.

As Belle Moskowitz was learning to promote social justice through politics, Hine pursued the Ethical Culture vision as an educator. He received a Master of Pedagogy from New York University in 1905, and he also attended the Columbia School of Social Work, where he met Arthur Kellogg in 1904. Kellogg and his younger brother Paul invited Hine to provide photographs for their journal, and his first great images, documenting immigrants arriving at Ellis Island, were published in *Charities and The Commons* in June 1908. Belle Lindner Israels's name appears on the masthead of that issue as a member of the journal's staff.

Arthur and Paul Kellogg remained Hine's lifelong friends and supporters. It was under their influence that he became a "sociological photographer," employing photography to further the cause of social reform. In 1908, Hine left the Ethical Culture School and began to work full-time for the National Child Labor Committee, which Felix Adler had also helped to found. For the next ten years, Hine devoted himself to the cause of ending child labor in the United States, creating his second body of great work, after the Ellis Island immigrant photos of the early 1900s. He traveled around the country, documenting the working and living conditions of the poor, mostly immigrant children employed in mines, textile mills, and factories by unregulated American industry. In Daile Kaplan's words, "Hine helped redefine the role of photography to encompass social images and reformulate the field of social work, where the emphasis shifted from issues to individuals." His images were pivotal in helping to create public consensus for the passage of anti-child labor laws.

In 1918, Lewis Hine embarked for Europe with the Red Cross. He spent a year and a half photographing the consequences of World War I on civilian populations in Greece, Serbia, Italy, Belgium, and France. He returned to the US in May 1919. In the immediate postwar period, public attitudes in America toward immigrants, labor, and progressive politics had hardened, and Hine's previous emphasis seemed incompatible with the new climate. Having spent two decades immersed in the world of social welfare and reform, Hine therefore sought a new direction for his photographic work. In an interview from 1938, he recalled this decision. "In Paris, after the armistice, I thought I had done my share of negative documentation. I wanted to do something positive. So I said to myself, 'Why not do the worker at work? The man on the job?'"

Hine's first series of work portraits, "The Railroaders," featuring engineers and machinists on the Pennsylvania Railroad, was published in Arthur and Paul Kellogg's journal, by then renamed *The Survey Graphic*, in October 1921. In his first excitement at discovering work and workers as a subject for his photographic investigation, Hine had written Paul Kellogg, "I have just finished a series of photographs showing the Human Side of The System, (Pennsylvania),—the very best thing I have ever done. The industrial lead I have been following is tremendous and virgin soil." Paul and Arthur Kellogg were equally enthusiastic. Over the next ten years, *The Survey Graphic* regularly published these studies of laborers and craftsmen at their jobs in power plants and machine shops, in offices, kitchens, and stores. Like the portraits Hine would later make of Empire State workers, these images feature ordinary men and women and explore the physical relationship between the worker and the work, the exchange between labor and life. Hine emphasizes expressions of concentration. He focuses on arms and hands, on the engagement with tools and machines, and the effect these have on the bodies and faces of those who tend and direct them. The work portraits include some of Hine's most widely reproduced images and represent his third body of historically significant photographic documentation.

No letter of employment has surfaced to prove it, but the circumstantial evidence is compelling that, in 1930, when she needed a photographer to publicize the construction of the Empire State Building, Belle Moskowitz turned to someone she had known and trusted since her early days as a social reformer. Unlike the building's architect or its corporate directors, Belle Moskowitz would have known Hine and seen his work portraits, published in *The Survey Graphic*. She would have known he was ideally suited to the task. Indeed, Hine's previous work portraits may have served as a model for his images of the Empire State's construction workers. Five years earlier, in 1925, Hine had photographed a pair of riveters, a lone ironworker walking a beam, and a young ironworker gleefully "riding the ball" for an article in *The American Magazine*, entitled

"It's a Tough Job, but Somebody's Got to Swing It," an early contribution to the heroic depiction of skyscraper workers. In Belle Moskowitz, Hine had a powerful ally and supporter, and the early fame of his Empire State images undoubtedly derives in part from her effectiveness as a publicist. As one newspaper comic joked, "Thanks to its engineering, the Empire State Building has 102 stories in it. And thanks to its press agent, it has had 1,002 stories about it."

Critics have suggested that the Empire State portraits represent a break in Hine's social engagement, showing him celebrating corporate power rather than critiquing it. But the portraits themselves show little of this, focused as they are on individual men and their labor. Instead, in the relationship between Hine and Moskowitz, his employer, we see a divergence in the contexts that give meaning to the photographs, a divergence between how Lewis Hine understood his work and how Belle Moskowitz and Publicity Associates made use of it. I believe the deployment of these images to further a corporate message should be attributed to Belle Moskowitz, not confused with Hine's artistic or sociological goal. While she may have shared Hine's progressive political orientation, nevertheless, as the Empire State's director of publicity, Moskowitz had more practical requirements for the photographs. Moskowitz used Hine's individual portraits extensively, both during construction and after the opening, to create a heroic, Everyman image for the building and its workers—for example, in the souvenir pamphlet mentioned by Earl Sparling in his "dialogue" with an ironworker.

Without documentation, it is impossible to know the precise terms of Hine's employment. The only surviving source is a letter on the stationary of Empire State Inc. signed by Belle Moskowitz's son, Josef Israels II, naming Hine the building's official photographer and granting him unfettered access to the construction site. Yet Hine's hiring coincided with the selection of Craftsmanship Award winners, who were named in two groups during the summer and fall of 1930. Further, Hine's photos clearly demonstrate that part of his job was specifically to create portraits of these men. Hine photographed all the men in the first group of Craftsmanship Award winners, who were honored at a ceremony held on the fourth floor of the unfinished building on October 8, 1930. He produced portraits of at least half of the sixteen winners in the second group, who received their awards at a similar ceremony on February 11, 1931. Publicity Associates integrated these photos in its larger campaign to publicize and characterize the Empire State Building as the epitome of American achievement. Whatever Hine may have thought he was photographing, and whatever sociological interest Belle Moskowitz may have had in representing working men, the images—these probing impressions of the men's faces—were delivered as work for hire, and as such, they were props in the service of Moskowitz's expansive publicity campaign.

Now, however, almost one hundred years later, the use of the men's faces for publicity counts as another accident of attention, which helps restore the forgotten connections. During construction, Belle Moskowitz and Publicity Associates published an internal newsletter, circulated among the managers of the project. Called *Empire Statements*, the newsletter ran for six undated issues. Copies are in the scrapbooks collected by Empire State Inc. and held at the Avery Library archive. A page in volume 1, no. 2, published before October 1930, features six of Hine's portraits of the Craftsmanship Award winners. This confirms the identities of five more men whose names appear on the commemorative plaque in the building's lobby. Strangely, one man featured in the newsletter, although named an award winner and photographed by Hine, later disappeared. Thirty-two names are engraved on the plaque. Apparently, however, there were thirty-three award winners.

Steven or Stephen Coons, structural ironworker, presents a mystery. His name and portrait are included in *Empire Statements*, and he is listed among the award winners in press releases (where his last name, however, is garbled into "Orens"). Additionally, he can be seen standing next to a hat-waving Al Smith in a photo syndicated in numerous newspapers in October 1930 to publicize the first Craftsmanship Award ceremony. However, his name does not appear on the bronze plaque in the Empire State Building's lobby.

Indeed, quite peculiarly considering the attention paid to ironworkers in the press, the plaque does not recognize any structural ironworkers at all. It is not possible to determine whether Coons in fact received the award, or whether he was excluded for some reason after being chosen. Newspaper accounts fluctuate between announcing sixteen or seventeen names belonging to the first group of award winners in October 1930. *The New York Times* published both figures: seventeen on October 8, 1930, reflecting the names

Empire State Craftsmen Honored

Six of the EMPIRE STATE craftsmen who will receive medals and certificates of their skill from the New York Building Trades Congress

JAMES IRONS
Stonecutter

THOMAS F. WALSH
Hoisting Engineer

VLADIMIR KOZLOFF
Wrecker

FRANK A. MOEGLIN
Sheet Metal Worker

GIUSSEPPE RUSCIANI
Laborer

STEVEN COONS
Structural Iron Worker

EMPIRE STATE—The world's greatest office building

Photos by Wurts Bros. and Lewis W. Hine

Empire Statements, volume 1, no. 2.

Miami Daily News
FLORIDA
DATE OCT 26 1930

SURROUNDED BY A GROUP of workmen, Alfred Smith, former governor of New York, gazes upward f[rom] the 81st story of the Empire State building, under constr[uc]tion in New York. He presented certificates of craftsm[an]ship to the workers on what is to be the world's tal[lest] structure.

Steven or Stephen Coons, structural ironworker.

(*right*) "One of the Boys." Steven Coons in white hat and shirt stands next to Al Smith, bottom center, October 26, 1930.

in the press release and including Coons, and sixteen on October 9, 1930, excluding Coons, listing the men recognized at the ceremony itself.

In Hine's 1930 photo, Coons is forty-seven years old. He lived with his wife, Margaret, and two teenage children, Iroquois and Hugh, on Tenth Avenue in Brooklyn. His parents were both born in Pennsylvania. The name of his son indicates Native American ancestry, at least on his wife's side of the family, as subsequent documents confirm.

Shortly after Steven or Stephen Coons appears and disappears as a winner of an Empire State Craftsmanship Award, tragedy struck the family.

On August 19, 1931, *The Brooklyn Daily Eagle* reported that Margaret Coons, wife of Stephen A. Coons, died suddenly at the home of her brother, Iroquois Irwin, where she had gone "to recuperate from a stroke she suffered recently." One year later, on September 9, 1932, the older son, Iroquois Coons, would also die. By 1940, Stephen, then fifty-nine, and his son Hugh, twenty-five, are living together in Millville, New Jersey. Stephen is still an ironworker. His 1942 draft registration card shows the same residence. By this time, however, at age sixty-one or sixty-two, Stephen is unemployed. His death certificate gives his birth date as September 12, 1880. He died of carcinoma of the liver on July 26, 1955. He is buried at Oakwood Cemetery, Richmond, Virginia.

A similar biographical sketch is possible for Frank A. Moeglin, sheet metal worker, another man featured in Belle Moskowitz's *Empire Statements*.

Frank A. Moeglin, sheet metal worker.

He appears at age twenty-one in the 1910 census, living in Canton Township, Stark County, Ohio. He is the middle child of Elizabeth Moeglin, forty-eight, a native of Indiana. The household also includes an older son and a daughter. Frank's occupation is "catcher" at a rolling mill; his brother is "rougher" at the same mill. Their sister, Effie, is a "watch timer" at the water works.

A notice in *The Richmond Palladium and Sun-Telegram*, dated June 1, 1916, may give a clue to his activities at the time. The article reads: "All sheet metal workers in Richmond have been invited to attend the meeting of the newly organized Amalgamated Sheet Metal Workers' union at the Socialist Hall tonight." Charter members of the newly formed union, which would become Local No. 192, included Frank Moeglin.

On July 7, 1919, Frank A. Moeglin, then in the US Navy, married Anna C. Strack. He had enlisted in May 1917 and served as a coppersmith aboard the USS *Von Steuben* from September 1917 until his discharge two years later. After World War I, the Moeglins settled in Brooklyn, where Frank pursued his profession as a sheet metal worker. In the portrait by Lewis Hine, Frank Moeglin is forty-one years old. He died three years later, on May 24, 1934, though the cause of death is unknown. An article in the November 14, 1934, edition of *The Brooklyn Daily Eagle* notes a memorial service, held at the VFW Porter Post, to honor "departed Comrades." Frank Moeglin is buried at Cypress Hills National Cemetery in Brooklyn.

Of the six men named in *Empire Statements*, Vladimir Kozloff is the best documented in public sources. His professional history intersects with a number of other strands of American social and labor history, which gives us a more detailed, if still highly filtered, portrait of the man.

Vladimir Kozloff's naturalization papers, issued in 1926, indicate he was born on July 15, 1893, in Kamen, Russia. He writes that he has resided in the US since 1912, and in New York since April 1, 1919. One peculiarity of his naturalization application concerns his name. In addition to Vladimir Kozloff, he writes, he is "also known as Vladimir Koziol." It's possible Kozloff had already visited the US prior to his arrival as an immigrant. At Ellis Island, there is a 1910 ship's manifest with a "Wladimir Koziol" from "Biensnice, Wolhyn, Russia" that matches details in other documents. Wolhyn means the Volhynia Gubernia district, then part of the Russian Empire, now in the

Ukraine. There is no town, "Biensnice." There is also no Kamen, Russia. But there is a Kamin Kashirsky, part of the Volhynia Gubernia, and about 120 miles away, lies a small town called Berezhnitsa.

Another manifest for the same ship, dated October 31, 1912, two years later, also shows the arrival of "Wladimir Koziol," age nineteen, from Kamen, Russia. There are discrepancies between the two documents and no way to confirm whether this is the same man.

Kozloff comes into sharper focus briefly on June 15, 1917. A Vladimir Koziol, born in Kamen, Pinsk, Russia on the correct birthdate, registers for the draft. By this time, he is living in Bath, Maine, at 209 Water Street, where he works for the Texas Shipbuilding Co. as a reamer, someone who drills holes in the steel plates. Then he disappears again. I was unable to find other genealogical documents for this man until the 1940 federal census. There, Vladimir Kozloff, now forty-six, is living on Avenue A at the intersection of Fourteenth Street in Manhattan, with Charlson or Charlton Schrechovich. Both men are housewreckers. In 1942, Kozloff again

Vladimir Kozloff, wrecker.

registers for the draft. His employer is Bethlehem Steel, and he works at the Brooklyn Navy Yard. He's five feet eleven, with brown hair and brown eyes. By the 1950 census, he had resumed work as a demolition laborer, but by this time he has married. He lived on North Eighth Street, Brooklyn, with his wife Mary, an immigrant from Czechoslovakia. Vladimir Kozloff died on August 10, 1956, age sixty-five, and is buried in Saint Vladimir's Russian Orthodox Cemetery, Jackson, New Jersey. His grave is viewable online.

In addition to the last names Kozloff and Koziol, Vladimir Kozloff apparently used a variety of first names. Under these appellations, it's possible to gain further insight into his life, as well as to obtain the rare chance to hear a worker speak for himself, though again through the gauze of a journalist's cultural prejudices.

A 1937 article in *The American Magazine* describes a visit to the headquarters of House Wreckers' Union, Local 95, the only union in New York City representing workers in this specialized trade. There, the journalist William Seabrook conducts a brief chat with "F." Kozloff, "the secretary of the amazing all-Russian Local." Seabrook reports: "I asked him why so many Russians had gone into that queer trade. He said, 'There are a lot of jokes about us, of course, that Russians are no good except as destroyers, but the truth is, the White Russian peasant is strong as an ox and loves danger. Also, he is fatalistic, like the Oriental, and his humor is tinged with gloom. Hardly a week passes,' he added, with a cheerful smile, 'that somebody doesn't break his leg—or his neck. They love it. It keeps the work from being dull.'"

Is this an accurate representation of Kozloff's words? It's impossible to say, although the urgency given, once again, to ethnic stereotypes argues for caution. Indeed, conforming to the general pattern for journalists, publicists, and photographers of the era, Seabrook uses Kozloff and the scene at the union's headquarters at 15 East Third Street to paint a thoroughly clichéd ethnographic portrait. "It was more delightful and more completely Russian than any evening you could spend in the big restaurants where they serve borsch, blintzes, or pancakes, with caviar and sour cream, have countesses for hat-check girls, generals for head waiters, and balalaika orchestras in blouses playing the Volga Boat Song." Like many journalists of the time, Seabrook was more interested in depicting what he felt were the exotic characters and locale than in analyzing the conditions of the union members' lives: "Nine tenths of the house wreckers you see leaping out from under crashing tons of stone and steel in New York are White Russian peasants having the time of their fatalistic lives. This Local holds all its meetings in Russian, and they sound and look like a lot of Red anarchist plotters. As a matter of fact, they are not even radical. They are too busy fighting the laws of gravitation and sudden death to bother about fighting any man-made laws or governments."

In fact, Vladimir Kozloff and the members of the House Wreckers' Union were deeply involved in struggles against man-made laws and business practices. Eleven years earlier, on April 4, 1926, at the conclusion of a brief strike by members of the union, Kozloff is quoted in the newspaper, describing the reasons for the labor action. "We have been trying for some time to limit the work of our men to eight hours a day," he says. "Our experience is that most of the accidents in our business, which is very hazardous, occur after the eighth hour. The men are tired and should not expose themselves to danger beyond the eighth hour." According to Kozloff, there were seventeen deaths and two hundred injuries among the 2,700 men in the union in 1925, a very high percentage. In addition to limiting overtime, therefore, the union was demanding that only union foremen be assigned to direct the workers. "The union men have great interest, as you can well understand, in seeing that those under them have the best possible protection," Kozloff said, in what seems a more authentic representation of his voice.

Kozloff's employment on the Empire State coincided with the greatest challenge to organized labor in the interwar period. Tons of stone and steel were not the only things that came crashing down that fall. Demolition of the Waldorf-Astoria Hotel, which occupied the future site of the Empire State Building, began on September 24, 1929, just three weeks after the stock market reached its Roaring Twenties peak on September 3, with the average of twenty-five industrial stocks reaching 452.14. By March 5, 1930, the old hotel—it was thirty-six years old—had disappeared "down to the very last stone buried below the old machinery foundations," as architectural historian Carol Willis writes. On that day, the average for the twenty-five tracked industrial stocks closed at 318.43, a decline of 29.57 percent in six months. The market had lost more than $26 billion in value. By the end of 1930, when steelwork on the new skyscraper was complete, the loss would amount to $40,648,308,395—a sum that would have bought 739 Empire State Buildings, as one journalist calculated, "and leave $3,398,395 for incidental expenses."

Employment in the building trades, including demolition, therefore, was highly competitive, which put intense pressure on wages as well as on building practices, what the contractors called "efficiency."

At the peak of demolition, on November 22, 1929, 719 wreckers worked on the site of the future Empire State. Their work was not simply jumping gleefully from under falling debris, as implied by William Seabrook. A few lines from the Starrett's Empire State notebook hint at the violence of the process. "The brick and sandstone masonry of the exterior walls were drilled with 7/8 inch hollow drill steel in Ingersoll-Rand Pneumatic Rotary Jackhammers, the holes afterwards plugged and feathered, and pieces of masonry wedged out and dropped in small sections to the floor inside the buildings. The floor arches, which were of terra cotta construction, were broken down using Ingersoll-Rand Concrete Breakers, which were equipped with a special shoe shaped steel to break the terra cotta floor arch down to the floor below. All of the massive inside walls and machinery foundations had to be drilled and blasted with dynamite."

In all, a total of 24,321 loads of debris were removed. Another contemporary account of the demolition, full of nostalgia not only for the Gilded Age that gave birth to the grand hotel but also for the prosperous, jazzy decade that had sealed its fate, also incidentally paints a vivid picture of the hazardous work performed by Vladimir Kozloff and his fellow wreckers. "Few realize the extent of the devastation that wreckers have already wrought within. The hotel is a ruin," the author begins. "One comes away with many pictures in mind. One is of men standing upon a movable scaffold 33 feet high in the grand ballroom, intent upon peeling from the majestic ceiling a great mural painting. Another is of strong, large-mouth chutes, eleven of them, through which debris tumbles to the ground. The thud of the pounding material reverberating like the rising sounds of a mighty bowling game." Throughout the demolition site, the author, Gustav Zismer notes, one feels the "throbbing 225-horse-power air compressors which pump 2,500 cubic feet of air a minute so that seventy-five hammers and drills may continue their steady destruction of floors and walls." Exiting this scene of devastation, Zismer seeks to conclude his tour on a hopeful note, though not one relating to the workers. He observes "a cat and four kittens, snugly housed in one of the street floor show windows. Mascots are this mother and her babies. The rumble and the roar of operations reaches throughout the empty spaces. The cats peer bright-eyed, play, drowse." It's unclear whether these are the same cats that Al Smith later adopted.

Another article from this same moment, February 1930, also features statements by Vladimir Kozloff, though this time his first name is Americanized as "Walter." "A strike for 'safe conditions' and embodying no demands for higher wages or shorter hours was authorized yesterday by the House Wreckers' Union against the Albert A. Volk company," the article begins. "The union alleged that the 'break through' method employed by that company was extra hazardous and that twenty deaths had occurred last year where the method prevailed." The Volk company denied the charges, claiming the method, which involved breaking holes in the floor and dumping debris through to the basement, was "scientific, saving one-half to one-third the time in demolishing buildings." Walter Kozloff, identified as the business agent for the union, countered that workers were more likely to fall using this method, compared with demolishing one floor at a time. He noted that "there are no city or State laws controlling demolition work or prescribing safeguards." Therefore, it was incumbent upon the union to protect its workers. The Albert A. Volk company was one of the leading demolition experts in New York City at the time. Another was the Jacob Volk Company, founded by Albert's brother. The Jacob Volk Company, Kozloff stated, had recently signed a pledge to refrain from using the "break through" method, bringing the total number of employers who had agreed up to seventy. Starrett Bros. and Eken also adhered to the pledge, performing demolition of the Waldorf-Astoria one floor at a time.

Five months after he was awarded a Certificate of Superior Craftsmanship by the New York Building Congress for his work on the Empire State Building, Vladimir Kozloff is once more mentioned in the context of a labor conflict, this time over the issue of "open shop," the use of both union and nonunion workers on a job. On March 30, 1931, Kozloff and the president of the union, Leo Ross, charged that "a group of small contractors have employed racketeers to intimidate union men" and that the leaders of Local 95 had been compelled to hire private detectives for protection. The union's contract with employers was set to expire on March 31, 1931, and the union was engaged in contentious negotiations to raise wages for helpers and for "bar men," who performed the most dangerous work. The strike was settled with a compromise on April 9, 1931, by mediators in the State Labor Department. Instead of hourly wages of $1.20, as demanded, the bar men would receive $1.17½, and instead of $1.10, helpers received $1.05.

One week later, on April 16, 1931—coincidentally, the same day the owners and architects of Empire State held a gala dinner for the contractors and subcontractors to celebrate completion of construction—Kozloff's name again appears in a *New York Times* article, "Labor Men Indicted in Racketeer Case." "Vladimir Kozloff, 37 years old, of 535 East Thirteenth Street, business agent of Local 95 of the House Wreckers' Union, and Browak Pohorodny, 48, of 142 Suffolk Street, surrendered at District Attorney Crain's office yesterday on felonious assault indictments returned against them by the grand jury Tuesday on the complaint of Frank Silverman of 15 Sunswick Street, Long Island City, a non-union worker."

According to the complaint, Silverman, foreman of a demolition gang razing two houses at 423 West Twenty-Fifth Street, was attacked by six men, including Kozloff, "with bricks and fists." Kozloff is alleged to have previously "urged" Silverman to hire only union workers. Silverman refused, claiming his employers could not afford union wages. Kozloff is then alleged to have responded, "You'll get yours."

Kozloff's bail was set high, at $2,500, because according to the prosecutor, he had been charged in another, similar incident on March 20, 1930. Both men pleaded not guilty. There is no record of a trial, which means the charges were probably dismissed.

Although two laborers were killed while tearing down the Waldorf-Astoria, Starrett Bros. and Eken appear to have observed demolition practices approved by the House Wreckers' Union. Nevertheless, labor disputes surrounded the construction of the Empire State Building, which was also an open-shop job. Despite a promise by Al Smith to employ only union workers, the contractors, Starrett Bros. and Eken, accepted bids from nonunion subcontractors to keep construction costs down. The most significant case of nonunion labor concerned steel erection, which was subcontracted to the firm of Post & McCord, then celebrating its fiftieth anniversary in business. As Paul Starrett explained, "The steel mills, led by United States Steel and Bethlehem Corporation, had organized the Iron League, a group of subcontractors to whom they sold steel at prices much lower than nonmembers could obtain. In this way, the union men had generally been defeated. Post & McCord, who belonged to the Iron League, could purchase and erect the steel for a quarter of a million dollars less than we could, ourselves. In the interests of our clients, we were forced to accept their bid." The New York–based Structural Steel Board of Trade, representing eighteen of New York City's largest steel contractors, including Post & McCord, had refused to recognize the Iron Workers Union since 1905, making New York an open-shop state. The International Association of Bridge, Structural, and Ornamental Iron Workers therefore retaliated by calling strikes against Starrett Bros. and Eken on other projects in Cincinnati and Newark, in an effort to force the builders to abrogate the contract with Post & McCord. At the same time, rumors of a strike by other union workers on the Empire State Building circulated. Negotiations between the Structural Steel Board of Trade and the Iron Workers Union continued throughout the spring of 1930, as steelwork on the Empire State Building proceeded at its record-setting pace. Former Governor Al Smith offered to serve as mediator, seeking to avert a strike on the Empire State and to end the twenty-five-year standoff in New York over open-shop hiring in the steel trade. His offer was ultimately rejected by the Board of Trade, which walked out of negotiations just when an agreement seemed within reach, citing the strikes as proof of the union's bad faith. In May, following a tentative compromise, which divided steelwork in New York between open- and closed-shop jobs according to specified percentages, the union ordered the striking ironworkers back to work on the Starrett's out-of-town projects. This agreement fell apart in March 1931, and the open shop for steelwork in New York prevailed.

"Now a group of workmen is silhouetted against the dim sky," intoned T. S. Eliot in his 1934 poem, "Choruses from *The Rock*." "From farther away, they are answered by voices of the unemployed." For the construction trade workers at the Empire State Building, the issue of union labor was vitally significant. As unemployment across the country worsened, thousands of laborers arrived in New York City seeking jobs, often willing to accept wages considerably below those negotiated by the trade unions. According to one report, nonunion skilled laborers could be hired for six and seven dollars a day, instead of the union scale of between $13.20 and $15.40. Sidestepping the central issue of union pay, the administration of New York Governor Franklin D. Roosevelt passed a law, effective July 1, 1930, requiring all state, county or municipal building operations to employ only New York State residents. Private builders were urged to follow suit voluntarily. Thus, on August 15, 1930, at the height of construction work, *The New York Times* reported that "the 3,000 workers on the new Empire State Building, of which former Gov. Smith is the head, were recently checked over at Mr. Smith's request and 165 artisans from out of town were replaced by local heads of families." While assisting New York residents, at the expense of out-of-towners, this solution did little to address the severe pressure on wages caused by widespread unemployment. According to *The Daily Worker*, which was critical of both the national union leaders and building trade employers, "the union scale is paid, nominally, on union jobs but actually workers have take [*sic*] a discount in many cases and always are outrageously speeded. No pretense at paying a union scale is made on non-union jobs."

Starrett Bros. and Eken were not accused of evading union wages for union workers. Nevertheless, the stock market crash had significantly altered the projected costs for construction. In an article published in the *Building Congress News* in May 1930, Andrew J. Eken, vice-president of Starrett Bros., noted that material costs had declined significantly since work on the Empire State Building began. "Brick is now selling at the lowest price in ten years, steel shapes are likewise lower, the base price having dropped $1.00 a ton. Lumber supplies, influenced by intense competition, are also at low levels." Eken continued that he did not expect labor costs to decline. Still, from the builder's perspective, he acknowledged the effect of the worsening Depression on wages. "Some savings may develop in sub-contracting as recent contracts show a willingness to take work at lower figures."

In September 1929, the cost estimate for construction of the Empire State Building had been $43 million. The final figure was $24.7 million, representing both decreased materials costs and "savings" on labor. This difference is often celebrated, rightly from a corporate perspective, as a sign of Starrett Bros. and Eken's efficiency. At the same time, it should also be seen in the social context of the Depression. The 42.5 percent savings reflects a corresponding decline in employment prospects for construction workers, who were vulnerable on a daily basis to the ruthless economic forces that Vladimir Kozloff spent his life fighting.

Visually, the identification of Thomas F. Walsh, hoisting engineer, is simple. He is named in *Empire Statements* as well as in a widely published image from the October 8, 1930, Craftsmanship Award ceremony. In that photo, he is seen shaking the hand of New York's Lieutenant Governor Herbert H. Lehman. In the Starrett Corporation's in-house photo album, which includes a variant of this image, he is the only worker identified, there as "Tom Walsh." But several other award winners, whom it is now possible to reunite with their names, can also be seen in the photo, including Gus Comedeca, Giuseppe Rusciani, Samuel Laginsky, Vladimir Kozloff, James Kerr, and Charles E. Sexton, standing between Lieutenant Governor Lehman and Al Smith.

Recognizing Thomas F. Walsh visually, however, does not help to disentangle his biography. Indeed, not only are there numerous Thomas

Walshes in the public record, but two Thomas Walshes were awarded Empire State Craftsmanship Awards. One was the hoisting engineer seen in these photos. The other was a "derrickman" or a "bellman," according to inscriptions that Hine made on the back of photographs. This means that derrickman Thomas Walsh stood at the base of the derrick situated on an upper story and, using two cords, actuated bells located above the hoisting engine, which sat on a floor far below, out of sight of the derrick. The bells indicated how the derrick's boom and fall line were to move, up or down. Hoisting engineer Thomas F. Walsh received these signals and tended the engine that wound or unwound the cable, which ran through

RAFTSMEN REWARDED—
tificates attesting a job well done are
sented to seventeen workers on the
pire State Building by Lieut. Governor Herbert H. Lehman on behalf of t
New York Building Congress at a cer
mony yesterday. Former Governor Smi
was present, as you see.—N. Y. American Staff Ph

"Craftsmen Rewarded." The first award ceremony, October 8, 1930. From left to right, Gus Comedeca, Giuseppe Rusciani, Samuel Laginsky, Vladimir Kozloff, James Kerr, Thomas F. Walsh, James Irons? (partially hidden), unknown, Lt. Gov. Herbert Lehman, Charles E. Sexton, Alfred E. Smith.

Thomas F. Walsh, hoisting engineer.

holes left in the concrete slabs of the intervening floors. The difficulty of discerning the correct Thomas F. Walsh in the mass of men with the same name is therefore compounded by the necessity of distinguishing Thomas F. Walsh, hoisting engineer, from Thomas Walsh, bellman.

One could write a social history of New York City in 1930 based solely on its Thomas Walshes. One Thomas F. Walsh, age thirty-six in the 1930 census, was a timekeeper for the subway. Another was an officer on passenger ships. A Thomas F. Walsh was an inspector for the Brooklyn Police Department. Another Thomas F. Walsh was a racehorse jockey.

The most promising candidate in the public record that I could find is a fifty-eight-year-old Thomas F. Walsh, who in 1930 lived on Decatur Avenue in the Bronx with his wife Delia and their three children. Both Thomas and Delia are Irish immigrants. Thomas arrived in the US in 1887, when he was fifteen years old. In 1930, this Thomas's profession is "Engineer" for the industry "Stationary," which would be accurate. The term indicates a man who drove an engine that was not for transportation, in this case, a hoisting engine.

Twenty-five years earlier, in 1905, the family lived on Second Avenue in the Bronx, although in this document, the 1905 New York State census, Thomas Walsh's profession is fireman. But the same family is living on Thieriot Avenue, the Bronx, in 1920, and by then Thomas's profession has become "stationary engineer." Unfortunately, based solely on public records, it is not possible to sharpen this picture or to write a personal history of this one, particular Thomas F. Walsh who helped to build the Empire State Building.

Lewis Hine's photograph of Tom Walsh at his job, however, helps give some greater definition to the description of his job at the Empire State Building, which appeared in a technical article published in the *Engineering News-Record* in January 1931. "Experience on this building indicated that 400 ft. was near the economic maximum distance that steel should be raised with present hoisting equipment." The hoist drum that Tom Walsh is tending in Hine's photo was powered by an eighty- or one-hundred-horsepower electrical engine. It held a three-quarter-inch cable approximately three thousand feet long, which gave it a range of less than six hundred feet, since the cable was wound five times through sheaves forming the pulley system. "The most important factor limiting the hoisting distance on the Empire State Building, however, was the heating of the hoist drums and snatch blocks, particularly the latter. Sheave bushings, burned out by the long-continued operation during each hoisting of a load, had to be replaced every few days." The hoisting engineer was responsible for keeping the engine running smoothly. As seen in Hine's photo, the hoisting engineer worked alone in a small shed, which housed the engine, often eighteen or twenty stories below where the derrick was positioned. He was among the highest-paid workers on the site, earning $2.31 an hour, while the daredevil connectors sitting on the beams he hoisted earned $1.92.

Giuseppe Rusciani's identity in Lewis Hine's portrait is also confirmed by his presence in Belle Moskowitz's publicity newsletter. Additionally, he can be seen in the newspaper photo of the first award ceremony, published on October 9, 1930, in which Thomas F. Walsh stands front and center. At first, it seemed that the grain of information collected by the US government was not fine enough to distinguish the Giuseppe Rusciani who contributed to building the Empire State. Two Giuseppe Ruscianis arrive at Ellis Island from Italy, the first in 1913, an eighteen-year-old who was initially detained for medical reasons, and the second, a twenty-seven-year-old farm laborer, who arrived in 1923. Neither left any subsequent record that I could find. No Giuseppe Rusciani appears in US census records in the following decades, but many *Ruscianos*. One Giuseppe Rusciano arrived in the US on November 23, 1900, from Castroregio. Two Giuseppe Ruscianos arrived in 1901: a fifty-four year old from Naples on October 4, and a twelve year old on October 28, also from Castroregio. Three Giuseppe Ruscianos immigrated in 1913, and several more landed in the years after World War I. There was no way to tell if any of these was the man who would win a Craftsmanship Award for his work on New York City's most famous building. The problem was not an absence of documentation, but the impossibility of determining a pattern that would lead to one, particular man. While essential for compiling a statistical snapshot of the nation, the information in the census, in ship manifests, and in similar documentation, preserves the lives of individuals only incidentally. When it cannot return a specific answer, the data produces a blur.

But sometimes the image is blurry because the subject has shifted. While I could find no Giuseppe Rusciani whose profile seemed to fit, the 1930 census contained a *John* Rusciani, age thirty-five, living in the New Dorp neighborhood of Staten Island with his wife, Carmela, and their two young

Giuseppe Rusciani, laborer.

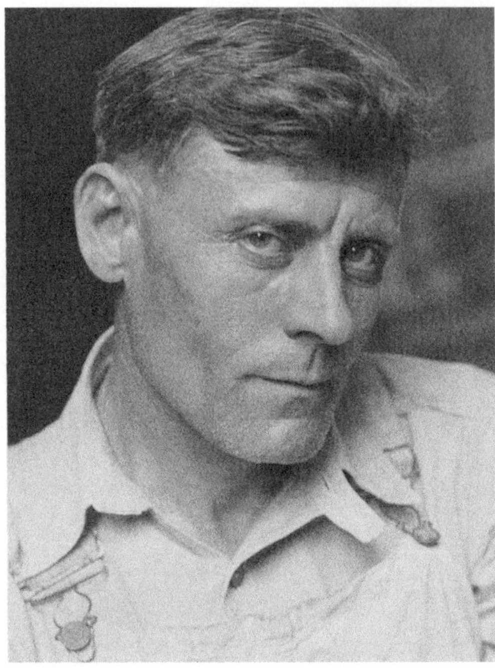

James Irons, stonecutter.

children. His profession is listed as "laborer" in the industry "concrete." This alone would not have been enough to identify him with certainty, though, as with many of the other award winners, it might have been as close as we could come to an identification. But after tracing the family through the 1940 and 1950 censuses, among numerous other documents, I found his 1985 obituary. "John Rusciani, a retired cement and concrete worker who help construct some of the greatest buildings in New York City, died Monday at Kennedy Memorial Hospital, Stratford. He was 91." The Empire State Building is named among the famous projects on which he worked. According to his obituary, John Rusciani was born in 1894 and came to the US in 1909, though I could find no record of his arrival at Ellis Island. He served in the US Army in France during World War I. After the war, he helped to organize Local 20 of the Cement and Concrete Workers Union of New York. He remained a union member for thirty-five years. The 1930 census, taken on April 8, six months before the craftsmanship award ceremony and just a few months before Lewis Hine would have created this portrait, indicates that John Rusciani owned his own home, worth $1000, and that his annual income for 1929 was $1,415. These documents offer no explanation for why

his name would appear on the commemorative plaque as Giuseppe, rather than with his adopted, Americanized name, John.

The award-winning stonecutter James Irons was born in Scotland in 1883, 1884, or 1885, depending on which document you believe, and he arrived in the US as a child with his parents in 1887. By 1930, now age forty-five, he lived at 4220 Seventy-Seventh Street, Queens, with his wife and their three children.

The documentation of the Irons family in America goes back to 1900. At that time, James, age fourteen, lived on Bodine Street, Queens, with his mother and two younger sisters. In December 1907 he married Violet Wood and, by 1910, they had a one-year-old daughter. They lived on Mott Avenue, Queens. James's profession was stone setter in the terra-cotta industry.

For some reason, there are two 1920 census records for the family, the first from January 4, the second from January 13. Both show them living on Van Alst Avenue, Queens. In the first, James's age is thirty-six; in the second, he has lost three years and now registers thirty-three. There are other discrepancies between the two census records. In the first, James's year of immigration and naturalization are both 1886; in the second, his immigration is 1900 and his naturalization 1910. In the first, his profession is "stone-cutter," in the second, "house decorator." There is no indication that two men with the same name lived at the residence. Perhaps different census takers spoke to different members of the family, one of whom had a looser grasp on James's history and profession.

It should not be a surprise, then, that official records sometimes produce a blurry impression of an individual. Even during his lifetime, even within his own family, the details of James Irons's biography—precise dates of birth or immigration, the contingencies of employment or residences—may have been unclear. But of course these statistics are not what matter most in the private context of a man's life or in the recollections of those who cared about him.

In October 2019, I spoke with James Irons's grandson, also named James Irons, who shared his impressions of his grandfather.

"He was a tough old coot," he recalled. "He used to tell me how he trained with Willie Pep, who was a boxer. James wasn't a boxer, but he'd bicycle with them. At that time, they did their swimming in the East River. He was a tough guy. Not a big man, but a tough man."

James Irons must have been especially tough, because he was more than thirty-five years older than his boxer friend. Guglielmo Papaleo or Willie Pep, as he was known, was born in 1922 and was perhaps the greatest featherweight champion of all time, winning the title twice, first in 1942 and again in 1949. He had two of the longest winning streaks in boxing history, undefeated in sixty-two and then in seventy-two bouts.

As a child, the younger James Irons used to visit his grandfather on the weekend.

"He would tell me stories about it, how it was being up on the girders and stuff like that," he said.

But he could not recall any specific stories of his grandfather's labor or the circumstances of his life at the time of the Empire State's construction. What remained instead was a general impression of the man.

"I do appreciate what he did," his grandson said. "I've always been very proud of him."

James Irons, stonecutter, died in March 1975, around age ninety.

FIVE

SPLENDID IDEALS

At noon on Friday, May 1, 1931, Alfred E. Smith tore the red-, white-, and blue-striped ribbon that stretched across the entrance to the world's tallest skyscraper. He tore the ribbon by hand, impatient with his two small grandchildren, who had attempted unsuccessfully to cut it with ceremonial scissors. The children, not yet competent with their tools, had "scarcely the proper understanding of just what was going on," as Smith said. They were there "to symbolize for all time to come that this building is to be a monument for generations to come." Flashbulbs flashed, newsreel cameras rolled, and the newsmen present noted the remarks, gestures, and clothing of the buoyant former governor. A few moments later, President Herbert Hoover, Smith's victorious rival in the 1928 presidential election, pressed a special button in his office at the White House, turning on the lights in the Empire State Building.

"Come on, everybody!" Al Smith called to his 250 invited guests, waving a formal, black derby hat, instead of his usual, signature brown derby. He turned a key and theatrically threw open the doors. Ebullient and animated, the president of Empire State Inc. led the distinguished party, which included Walter Chrysler among the many business leaders, into the pristine lobby. Outside, thousands of spectators surged against police lines, so great was the anticipation to enter the new building. As mounted policemen held the crowds on the street in check, Smith and his friends made their way to the elevators, where they ascended in stages to an exclusive celebratory luncheon on the eighty-sixth floor.

"You are eating higher up in the sky than any human being has ever eaten," Smith told his audience. "There may have been loftier meals on mountain tops or in airplanes. But not in buildings."

In the grand history of the Empire State Building, its triumphant opening day ceremony is the culmination. The event dominated the news and was amply documented, though it was not the only thing happening in New York City that day. *The New York Times'* list of What Is Going On This Week included the eighty-fifth convention of the New York Federation of Women's Clubs; a lecture, "Spring Bird Visitors," at the American Museum of Natural History; a meeting of the Interplanetary Society; a lecture, "Radio and Television as Conditions of Fine Art," at the New School for Social Research; and a luncheon of the Mount Vernon chapter of Hadassah at the Ritz-Carlton Hotel. But the opening of the Empire State Building was the best publicized event. Congratulatory speeches by Smith, Paul Starrett, Governor Franklin D. Roosevelt, New York City Mayor Jimmy Walker, and others were broadcast over the NBC and Columbia radio networks, allowing listeners at home to picture the scene for themselves. Subsequent front-page newspaper reports and newsreels shown in movie theaters brought images of the opening to audiences around the world. Today, this documentation constitutes a rich resource for those who wish to relive that moment in vivid detail.

Viewed from the perspective of the men who built the building, however, Smith's speech and the opening ceremony manifested a different story. Their work was done, and their association with the building from now on would be anecdotal. Like Lewis Hine's photos, which capture a transient expression and hold it still for our consideration, therefore, I want to pause the scene here for a moment at the formal end of the job to consider Smith's words from the workers' point of view.

"There may have been loftier meals on mountain tops or in airplanes. But not in buildings," the former governor had exclaimed. But Smith was exaggerating. Months before, the people who built the structure in which Smith and his guests were comfortably being served had eaten lunch that high and higher. Lewis Hine had even documented the meal, photographing men clustered around rivet heaters, eating their sandwiches on planked-over beams. A few seconds later in his speech, as we will hear, Smith would praise the workers for their role in making the celebratory meal possible. The president of Empire State Inc. had not *forgotten* the workers when he spoke to those enjoying this formal luncheon. Like

Smith's grandchildren, the workers make a symbolic appearance at the structure's opening, enhancing the greater symbolism of the building itself. But again, like the children, when it came to marking the significance of the occasion, the workers who had built the spot where Smith was standing did not quite count as full participants. Perhaps, as in the newspaper coverage of workers, it is a question of distance. Looking up at them during construction, the workers might seem larger than life to the journalists and businessmen on the street. Once their job creating this high platform was done, however, their relative positions would be reversed. The workers returned to ground level, and those who felt or found themselves higher up on the social scale might again comfortably look down on them.

Former Governor Smith, now formally occupying the building on behalf of the owners and speaking from its commanding perch, would be gracious toward the men in his words. His singular political gift was charm. Indeed, to his contemporaries, what distinguished Smith from other politicians and public figures of the day was his sincerity. "He is just a natural man with an abounding love in his heart for his fellows," wrote one admirer. "He treats everyone with the greatest respect. A man is a man to him always—no matter what his station in life." Even so, Smith surveyed the various stations in life from an exclusive position, and his expressions of respect for the workers at this stage of his career were often issued from on high. As one fawning journalist speculated, "It may be that some future visitor to Manhattan Island, viewing the remains of our present American civilization, will recall the names of those associated with the glories of New York, and that in some future museum will be found a reproduction in miniature of the Empire State Building, and beside it a picture of a famous Governor of the times who, like King Solomon, paid tribute to the workers in stone and metal."

Standing on this highest observation deck, reflecting on the symbolism of the monument he had helped bring into being, former Governor Smith spoke in lofty terms, while the men he intended to praise had returned to ordinary life on the streets below. No longer mythological heroes, the workers had fulfilled their function and might now become again representative types, indistinguishable elements of the great American upswing.

✳

The skyscraper, wrote architect Claude Bragdon in 1925, is "the symbol of the American spirit—restless, centrifugal, perilously poised." Its very form, Bragdon had contended earlier, provides a metaphor for American society. "Its steel framework, strong, yet economical of metal, held together at all points by thousands of little rivets, finds a parallel in our highly developed industrial and economic system, maintained by the labor of thousands of obscure and commonplace individuals, each one a rivet in the social structure."

The workers who built the Empire State Building were caught in an uneasy symbolic contradiction within the definition of "worker." Were they individuals or rivets? Craftsmen or appendages of the machine? In the first instance, the nature of their work itself was changing. "Certain tools used in skyscraper construction are more necessary to the work than any man," wrote the authors of a five-part series on skyscraper construction for *Fortune* magazine. "The great difficulty with the contemporary marriage of man and the machine is that it is not enough for the machine to be just about human. The human partner must also go halfway. Men must act, for the purposes of that relationship, just about like machines or the whole compact will fall to pieces." The idea was commonplace at the time. Journalist William Engle, admiring the hoisting derricks maneuvering their loads during construction, felt these machines performed a "portentous mazurka as though they were human; the agile ones who manned them seemed the automatons." The derricks seem human; the men tending them seem like machines. This awkward transposition surrounding how to understand the work of men in relation to the work of machines runs through almost every statement about the men who built the Empire State Building. The building's very design seemed to embody it.

"What gives this building its special character is this: that it was caught at the exact moment of a transition," wrote critic Douglas Haskell in his astute 1931 review of the Empire State Building for the journal *Creative Art*. In Haskell's view, the building teeters between two eras, "caught between metal and stone," and its architecture freezes halfway in the swing from human to machine labor, from "handicraft" to "industrial methods of fabrication." Haskell sees this transition everywhere in the design. The finished structure, he observes, buries its most advanced element, the steel frame, within an antiquated casing of brick and stone. Even the stainless-steel trim of the facade, its showiest, most modern feature, reveals the contradiction. "Here the metal is all that counts," Haskell asserts. "Exact repetition: window, spandrel, window, spandrel, window—set within parallel nickel guides, running up 725 feet without a break, and repeated across an area 185 feet wide; this is what is stunning and immense." The building's imposing size and design, Haskell maintains, are the result of industrial production. "Every one of those units was completely prefabricated; each carried its own complete pattern; the construction was simply an *assembly*."

Yet the architecture refuses to admit the truth of what it is. Instead, Haskell continues, it clumsily seeks to merge its innovative, repetitious, industrial form with a more traditional cladding of stone:

> The stone, on the contrary, follows the old handicraft tradition. It bulges here and is cut away there. The design cares nothing for the units. For the sake of the design as a whole, every unit has to be treated as a special job. You can see it especially in the broad six-story base of the building, which is entirely stone. Blot out the shaft of the tower, and you will find in this base an entirely different building—older in spirit by thousands of years. Judged by the tower, the base is dilettante; judged by the base, the main shaft in its swift and unfussy effectiveness is almost cruel. Past vs. future.

Like the building itself, its architects and builders were caught in this contradiction between an older rhetoric of craft and craftsmanship and the modern reality of industrial production. On the one hand, professionally, they are completely modern. In his article in *The Architectural Forum* discussing "The General Design," Empire State's chief architect, William Frederick Lamb, makes the designer's position explicit. "As far as possible hand work was done away with for in quantity production with thousands of pieces of each material identical in shape and size, the delay would have been disastrous. Windows, spandrels, steel mullions and stone, all fabricated in various parts of the country, were designed so that they could be duplicated in tremendous quantity with almost perfect accuracy and brought to the building and put together almost like an automobile assembly line."

Practically, for the men performing the labor, therefore, the innovations in construction methods produced a radically new kind of workplace. In a technical article describing the construction process, the author notes, "Special study was given to eliminate as far as possible material interdependence, to provide in every way for entire independence of manufacture and erection, and, where the elements were necessarily interrelated, to arrange so that the placing of any one group, once started, might proceed freely without being held up by another." In the example of the facade assemblage—the stone, mullions, spandrels, and windows, which form the face of the building—the work was conceived as discrete, disconnected operations, which meant that contact between the trades was eliminated as much as possible. The spaces between stone columns and window edges were spanned by the vertical rustless, stainless, chrome-nickel trim. As a result, as described in another article enthusiastically reporting this innovation, "no longer did the window have to be fitted to the stone, or the stone cut to an accurate arris at the window opening, since the metal strip covered the edge. See what that meant: if the stone gang was held up by delay, the window gang could nevertheless proceed. Again: the stones could come from the quarry ready-cut, since there was no further fitting to be done on the job. In short, there was almost such a thing as the Empire State as a factory assembly of standard units."

For stonemasons, then, rather than the complicated task of finishing stone around the frames of windows, the work required primarily setting stone in place. These technical innovations meant that the work of installing stone to a great extent ceased to require the skill of master stonemasons, even if master stonemasons still performed the work.

Nevertheless, conceptually and perhaps temperamentally, the architects and builders of the Empire State Building hewed to the beliefs and to the language of a bygone era. Lamb's partner, Richmond Shreve, had been president of the New York Building Congress from 1925 until 1929. It was under Shreve's leadership that the organization first conceived the idea of awarding Certificates of Superior Craftsmanship to construction workers. Lamb himself spoke at one of the Empire State Building's two award ceremonies. But in giving his speech, Lamb found himself in some difficulty. What did it mean to be a "craftsman" in the age of the assembly line? If the award did not honor the repetitious, standardized work itself—not strictly speaking craftsmanship at all—then what did it honor? "The finished product," Lamb said, "can never be the work of art and efficiency that it is without the cooperation of the workmen in the individual trades."

To the architect, artistry and efficiency are reserved for the structure, the product. As for the men who built it, their contribution is *cooperation*. Under the pressure of modern methods of construction, the ground has shifted beneath the concept of "craftsmanship." Cooperation is a skill, certainly, but a behavioral, not an artisanal one. It is a *virtue*, not a craft.

As Machine Age heroes, seen from afar, the men would be celebrated as the "spirit of the skyscraper." But closer to the ground, and more importantly, at the actual worksite, the men would be praised or criticized for their behavior, not their skill. And, unfortunately, when encountered up close as individuals, their behavior all too frequently would be found wanting.

Colonel William A. Starrett, one of the Empire State's builders, had intimate familiarity with the lives and habits of his labor force, as he describes in his 1928 book, *Skyscrapers and the Men Who Build Them*. What he sees up close is a class of men desperately in need of physical and moral uplift. "They are hearty eaters and gulp their food, frequently carried to the job cold, or if bought at the ubiquitous hot-dog stand, it is generally of the fried variety with little thought of the science of dietetics." The men are deficient not only in their diet but also in their personal habits. "The inordinate use of tobacco and small attention to dental hygiene, nowadays recognized as of such importance to middle-aged good health, leave them susceptible to the occupational ailments which their work sometimes engenders. Necessarily inconvenient are the sanitary facilities, and this, although the builder does his utmost to make proper provision, promotes constipation and stasis which usually are met by drug store quackery." "The admiring spectator sees young men," Starrett cautions, implicitly criticizing the "heroic" view of the workmen promulgated in the press. "The experienced builder, however, sees the prematurely aged building mechanic, sometimes a pathetic figure, standing on the sidewalk week after week, in the furtive hope that a job commensurate with his now narrowed abilities is available for him."

Surprisingly, Starrett sees the degradation of the worker to a narrow, pathetic figure as the result of the division of labor. Echoing Karl Marx, Starrett believes modern industrial relations diminish construction work from human craft to a mechanical knack and the worker from man to automaton. "To-day we have carpenters who do nothing but work on concrete forms, sawing and nailing year in and year out. Such a man can be taught to be skillful in this specialty in a few months." From the builder's perspective, the division of labor reduces the worker to a number, a line item in the contractor's ledger. "An employer must by the very nature of his relationship, snatch the men up, use him for a few weeks, and incontinently lay him off on the subdivision of an hour." For the worker, Starrett understands, the situation is both dehumanizing and alienating. He recognizes—at least in his own terms—the emotional consequences of the impersonal relationship, both to their employer and to their work, that industrial production creates for the workers. They are starved of genuine contact, Starrett observes, "savage and aloof toward any patronizing attitude." And yet, "they mellow instantly to the human touch. Discuss baseball, fishing, prize fights or local politics with them and they respond instantly. Even more alertly do they respond to serious comment on their own craft, in which they almost universally take pride." But while Starrett may agree with Marx about the problem and its consequences, he pegs its origin to a decisively different cause. The failure, Starrett concludes, does not lie with assembly-line work. It is not industrial capitalism that enforces these conditions. Instead, in Starrett's analysis, the men are hapless victims of labor unions. In stark contrast to Marx, Starrett lays the blame squarely on the collective organizations created to protect the men and their interests. "The guerilla origin of modern labor tactics bears the ancient traits inherited from barbarism, ruthless yet admittedly effective. Nurtured in combat and enforced through militancy, unionism has had little opportunity to learn the graces of civilization, to say nothing of civilization itself."

Adept only in the primitive social forms of barbarism, therefore, labor unions fail at their most essential task: elevating and caring for their members. In Starrett's view, unions provide no goal but combat, no education, and no path by which the men might evolve from their primitive state. Like a class of Huck Finns, the men are "savage" because their abusive and uncouth caretakers have failed to set a better example for them. Their unhappiness, the very roughness of their characters, can thus only be solved from above, by raising their sights. They need to be adopted and civilized. "Unionism," Starrett laments, "seems to have done little or nothing toward the solution of this, the most vital of labor problems." It remains for businessmen to take up the challenge.

"The question as to what business shall do in extending the hand of fellowship to these beloved malcontents in the solution of their most acute problems in which they continue to flounder is still almost wholly unsolved."

Let's return to former Governor Smith, mid-speech, addressing his guests on the Empire State's observation deck on opening day. "Too much praise cannot be given to the faithful workmen that put this monument in the air," Smith said. "We propose to put a tablet down in the main hall and inscribe upon it the names of the master craftsmen who received the awards for being the best in their particular line, so that their children and their children's children, when they come in the Empire State, can be able to point to the tablet with the pride that they will feel in the achievement of their forefathers."

Faithfulness, good work, family pride. The Craftsmanship Awards plaque, beyond noting the men's skill in the task of construction, becomes in Smith's speech something that allows the winners to participate in civilized society, in what the monumental building stands for. Perhaps Smith hoped the men's grandchildren would experience "down in the main hall" what he expected his own grandchildren to feel as they stood with him up on the observation deck. In this way, Smith encapsulated the fundamental philosophical motivation for the Craftsmanship Awards. To the men who created and conferred them, the awards aimed at something far higher than simply recognizing the workers' professional skill.

The archives of the New York Building Congress occupy sixty-four linear feet of space at the Tamiment Library and Robert F. Wagner Labor Archives at New York University's Bobst Library. The vast bulk of the collection covers the second half of the twentieth century. The holdings from the 1920s and 1930s are scant, a patchwork of governance documents, administrative records, minutes from committee meetings, trade union contracts, a few publications, and scattered photographs of Congress officers and events. The records covering the origin of the Craftsmanship Awards are even scantier, held in eight folders.

The New York Building Congress was founded in 1921 in the aftermath of World War I. A consortium of architects, contractors, materials suppliers, investors, and others involved in the construction industry, the organization aimed "to take over into peacetimes the cooperative ability developed in the building industry during the stress of the last war." In response to the sometimes violent confrontations between building trade employers and the building trade unions that had characterized the tumultuous first decades of the twentieth century, the Building Congress was conceived as a single entity through which to resolve conflicts and to regulate conditions within the industry. Among its activities, it provided apprenticeship training; undertook arbitration of commercial disputes, specifically, between general contractors and subcontractors; and it advocated for changes in industry practices, for example, promoting year-round construction as a means of securing steady work for laborers and avoiding winter layoffs. By 1930, when construction of the Empire State began, the New York Building Congress had more than 1,100 participating firms.

Recognition of craftsmanship counted as one of the Building Congress's primary goals. To this end, it formed the Committee on Recognition of Craftsmanship in 1925, composed almost entirely of architects and builders, including Arthur Loomis Harmon, the third member of the firm that designed the Empire State. Architect William Orr Ludlow, the Building Congress's vice president, served as committee chairman, and the surviving documents from this formative period reflect his distinctive vision.

William Orr Ludlow, son of Reverend James M. Ludlow, a pastor of the Collegiate Reformed Protestant Dutch Church, Forty-Eighth Street and Fifth Avenue, was born in 1870, four years before Lewis Hine. He had come of age as an architect in the legendary Beaux Arts firm of Carrère & Hastings, designers of the New York Public Library, the Standard Oil Building, and the House and Senate office buildings in Washington, DC. Ludlow formed his own firm in 1895 and continued in private practice with different partners through the 1940s. He is credited with designing the former offices of *The New York Times*, at 229 West Forty-Third Street, the former Chase Tower at 10 East Fortieth Street, and numerous college campuses, banks, and hotels from St. Augustine, Florida to Sitka, Alaska. Ludlow served as Chairman of the New York Building Congress's Committee on Recognition of Craftsmanship for fifteen years.

Under Ludlow's leadership, the committee aimed to stimulate interest in "true craftsmanship," recognizing workers on specific building projects and so convincing the wider public of the value of craftsmanship in modern construction. A document prepared in 1929 expressed the purpose of the Craftsmanship Awards in this way: "In an age of mass production good work and all that goes into it are too frequently overlooked. The first step in a revival of the spirit of artisanship is to single out and to honor the workmen who excel in the various trades." As its signature activity, therefore, the committee proposed that every architect or builder associated with the Building Congress award a Certificate of Superior Craftsmanship to one man in each of the building trades involved in construction of any project they completed. "The Committee also recommends that there be erected in the building a bronze tablet bearing the names of the workmen so recognized."

The New York Building Congress devoted considerable effort to establishing and publicizing the Certificates of Superior Craftsmanship, and the practice grew in popularity during the boom years of the 1920s. By the time the first workers on the Empire State were recognized in October 1930, the Building Congress had conferred more than 1,900 awards at more than one hundred buildings. When former Governor Smith announced the lobby plaque for work on the Empire State, therefore, the presentation of Craftsmanship Awards was already a routine feature of the inauguration of new skyscrapers in New York.

Winners of the award received a framed fifteen-by-twenty-one-inch certificate, signed by the officers of the New York Building Congress and presented at a public ceremony conducted on-site before the assembled workforce. The owner, the architect, and prominent public officials were enlisted to give these ceremonies an impressive and newsworthy character. Later, a gold button or lapel pin was added to the distinctions accorded the men. Finally, winners became honorary—that is, nonvoting—members of the New York Building Congress. It was imagined that the winners would constitute an informal council, "and the advice of these superior men is to be sought in further extension of the craftsmanship movement."

It was at this point, however, that the Committee on Recognition of Craftsmanship plunged headlong into the ambiguity within the idea of "superior men." According to William Orr Ludlow, the aims of the "craftsmanship movement" were more far-reaching than the simple recognition

The
NEW YORK BUILDING CONGRESS
awards this
CERTIFICATE
OF SUPERIOR CRAFTSMANSHIP
TO

....

IN CONNECTION WITH THE ERECTION OF

....

AND PLACES HIS NAME ON THE CONGRESS
HONOR ROLL OF CRAFTSMEN

Presented this .... *day of* ....

COMMITTEE OF AWARD

HONORARY CRAFTSMAN MEMBERSHIP CARD

This card certifies that the bearer is an Honorary Craftsman Member of the New York Building Congress.

CONSTITUTION OF THE NEW YORK BUILDING CONGRESS

EXTRACT

Article III—Membership

"Any workman who has received an award for superior craftsmanship under the Rules and Regulations of the New York Building Congress shall be eligible as an Honorary Craftsman Member, without dues, when such eligibility has been certified to by the Membership Committee, and such member shall not be entitled to vote."

Honorary Craftsmanship Membership Card, New York Building Congress.

of a workman's skill. The very existence of the award, he hoped, would assure workers of their valued place within the industry. In the committee's words, it "will prove a powerful stimulant in bringing to the worker an appreciation of his importance in the economic scheme." But beyond recognizing a worker's ability and his value to the industry, the award had a further symbolic goal. Ludlow was interested not solely in artisanship, but in the *spirit* of artisanship. "These selections are made not alone on the basis of quantity and quality of work performed, but for the spirit of cooperation and loyalty shown and pride of the mechanic in his work."

In an interview from April 1928, published in *The New York Times*, *The Washington Post*, and elsewhere, Ludlow stated, "the majority of the evils in the building industry are due to a lack of interest and pride of the workman in his work, and [we] look back longingly to the days when every mechanic was an artisan." Borrowing language and ideas from William Morris's Arts and Crafts movement, which emphasized the nobility of handicrafts and manual skill, Ludlow hoped his own "craftsmanship movement" would help to "restore" a utopian ideal of artisanship. Fueled by nostalgia for preindustrial labor relations and, above all, for preindustrial laborers, the underlying motive for the Craftsmanship Awards was thus not the recognition of physical craftsmanship, the workers' actual labor, but rather the desire to instill in the men a higher purpose, the proper attitude toward their work, the proper spirit.

"It is most desirable," Ludlow wrote in 1929, "to put the whole matter where it deserves to be placed,—on the high plane of great and splendid service not only to the building industry but to every individual concerned,—for the stirring of ambition to do nothing but a high grade of work ennobles a man's whole life, brings him a contentment that he has not known before, makes him a man of finer ideals, and in a word does something to create a better citizenship as well as a far worthier nation."

Because the ethos of Ludlow's "craftsmanship movement" was craft for craft's sake, any suggestion that the award should entail a monetary component was emphatically rejected. In an article the committee placed in the trade journal *Building Age* in June 1927, the author states, "Cash payments are recognition for services performed. Gold lapel buttons and framed certificates are evidence of something just a little bit above the plain duty owed to one's employer; a recognition of something that has been done by the worker for the good of his own soul and for the best interest of the trade in which he works." Giving explicit expression to this ethos, John D. Rockefeller Jr. spoke at the ceremony for award-winning workmen on the Riverside Church in June 1930, saying, "on this work I am positive that no one thought of his own appointed task merely as a 'job'—something done solely for economic reward. And there was no shirking. We are impressed with the loyalty, devotion and fine class of craftsmanship you have put in this structure."

Unlike Colonel William A. Starrett, who surveyed the labor conditions of workers subjected to the industrialization of their craft and concluded the problem lay with labor unions, William Orr Ludlow, chairman of the Committee on Craftsmanship, observing these same conditions, diagnosed the problem as spiritual. And this spiritual malaise, according to Ludlow, was pervasive, afflicting not only workers but owners as well.

For Ludlow, the Committee on Craftsmanship's mission was not restricted solely to elevating workers to a higher plane. Professionally situated between building owners on one side and trade laborers and unions on the other, the architects who led the committee found themselves fighting a two-front war against decadence. In a pamphlet entitled, *Recognition of Craftsmanship: How It Is Put into Effect*, Ludlow delineates the incentives for each party to participate in the program. The architect, he confesses, "is glad of a certain amount of acclaim which will come to him as the architect of the building." Above all, however, the architect "is the one, more than any other, who is interested in insisting on the good quality of the workmanship that goes into his building." The owner's motivation, by contrast, "is rather more sordid." At a total expenditure of approximately ten dollars apiece, the Craftsmanship Awards represented "a comparatively small item on a building enterprise involving hundreds of thousands of dollars." Nevertheless, in Ludlow's estimation, the compelling factor for the building owner to join in the craftsmanship movement was narrow self-interest. "The owners readily recognize the considerable advertising advantage which they get from awards being made on their buildings, even though they may not have a broader vision of the splendid ideals upon which the movement is founded."

"As to the men themselves," Ludlow concludes, "little need be said as to why they appreciate this recognition. One simply has to imagine oneself in the place of these men to know how he is likely to feel when in the presence of his fellow workmen, he is called to the platform to receive from the hands of the representative of an impartial body a handsomely framed certificate and gold button and told he has 'made good.'"

The social hierarchy is clear: Architects are the keepers of the craftsmanship ideal. Owners, lacking vision, care only for their own advantage. Of the men themselves, little need be said. The highest inducement to perform their jobs with pride, Ludlow believed, was the hope of receiving approval from above in the presence of their peers. Their motivations are so simple and childlike, anyone can easily imagine them.

In this way, the idea of craftsmanship has become a question of spiritual fitness, and any physical connection to the men's actual labor has been erased. What makes a "good" craftsman? In the 1929 pamphlet, *Recognition of Craftsmanship*, Ludlow gives this definition: "The craftsman is distinguished by his love of good work for its own sake and for the character molding values of integrity, thoroughness, intelligence, reliability, loyalty and cooperation." Like the word "craftsmanship" itself, the term "good," rather than signifying any quality of the work, has now come to have a moral or behavioral meaning, identifying desirable and aspirational qualities in the men themselves.

Far from an aberration in Ludlow's usage, these terms became definitive for the Craftsmanship Awards in general. Colonel William A. Starrett, speaking at the Craftsmanship Award ceremony held at 40 Wall Street in late 1929, saw the awards as the solution to the problem he had diagnosed a year earlier in his book. Referring to the barrier that modern labor practices had established between workers and employers, Starrett said, "We have given thought for twenty or thirty years as to how we could possibly break it down and find means of expression in the real soul of the building business which is the contact of the artisan and the employer. We have found it through this medium. These certificates go to you because of your excellence, not because any particular man is the fastest worker in the world, but because of his general workmanship, his ability as a worker, a true craftsman."

If Starrett's definition of "a true craftsman" is too vague, we can find clarification in the speeches held at the Empire State's two award ceremonies.

Honoring the men at the first award ceremony, October 8, 1930.

At the first, in October 1930, John J. Collins, secretary-treasurer of the Tunnel and Subway Constructors' International Union, who served as the Craftsmanship Committee's labor representative, assured the assembled workers: "Labor is proud of you men and to those who do not today receive certificates let me point out that you may merit one on some future building measuring up to the qualifications expressed on the certificate which are energy, loyalty, cooperation, service, thoroughness, industry, intelligence, and reliability." Speaking at the second award ceremony in February 1931, R. H. Hunter represented the builders, Starrett Bros. and Eken. "This building is an example of all the qualities expected of a master craftsman," Hunter said, "energy, industry, reliability, loyalty, cooperation, intelligence and service." And in case the honored workmen had not followed the list of expected virtues attentively, they were inscribed in the borders of the Honorary Craftsmanship Membership Card that each man received: "Energy, Service, Thoroughness, Cooperation, Loyalty, Industry, Intelligence, Reliability."

Some workers at the time uncontestably considered their work a craft. The New York Society of Craftsmen, the successor organization to the National Society of Craftsmen, was active in the 1920s, providing exhibition space and educational programming for all those "devoted to the applied arts and handicrafts." The crafts that the society represented included many fine arts such as painting and sculpture, but also applied arts and crafts, including bookbinding, ceramics, needlecraft, jewelry, stained glass, and furniture. In 1921, together with six other New York-based applied arts organizations, the Society of Craftsmen created the Art Center on East Fifty-Sixth Street, dedicated to decorative and ornamental design and "the practical application of American Art to trade and industry."

Workers in the construction industry, by contrast, were more typically referred to as "mechanics," as seen in the headlines announcing the Craftsmanship Awards: "Empire State Mechanics Rewarded for Good Work" in the *New York Herald Tribune*, or "Mechanics Hear Chrysler" in *The New York Times*. Contemporary usage of the word "craftsmanship" was reserved almost exclusively for the fine arts, musical instruments, or to enhance the appeal of luxury goods. On the same day the first Empire State Craftsmanship Awards were reported, for comparison, the only other appearance of the word across the largest New York City newspapers was an advertisement for a new Victor radio with "the most striking cabinet Victor ever designed . . . superb Victor craftsmanship . . . acoustically perfected." Similarly, with the exception of the Craftsmanship Awards, the word would be used in relation to workers only in advertising, to enhance the status of both the men and the products for sale. "The Work Shirt that Helped to Build the World's Highest Building—The grueling work with steel, stone, and mortar demanded the finest of craftsmen as this giant towered to its dizzy height of 110 stories—1260 feet— almost a quarter of a mile into the skies. What a testimony to Gladiator Work Shirts that most of the prize workmen in all branches of construction wore this sturdy work shirt, as did the superintendent of construction for Starrett Bros. and Eken, the builders."

In choosing to honor the work of building mechanics with the title of "craftsmanship," then, the members of the New York Building Congress had seized on a word with an elevated, yet also nostalgic and ill-fitting, ring. Beyond the word "labor," which described the men's activity but also referred to labor unions, and so was too grounded in the practical, contentious struggle over working conditions, there was no term that accurately captured the modern, industrial nature of the men's work. Just as the skyscraper escaped its mundane function as an office building in the transformation into a symbol of national aspiration, so the nature of work and the conditions of the building mechanics' workplace were "transcended" and rendered anodyne by the ideal of "craftsmanship."

Perhaps the fullest expression of William Orr Ludlow's craftsmanship ideal appeared in a richly illustrated pamphlet, *What Is a Good Craftsman?*, published by the Building Congress in 1928. The twenty-six-page document resides in its own folder in the Building Congress's archive. Replete with photos of Craftsmanship Award ceremonies, as well as an image of the bronze plaque mounted on the wall of the Central Savings Bank, now the Apple Bank for Savings, at Broadway and West Seventy-Third Street, the pamphlet closes with the text of a speech Ludlow gave at a luncheon for award winners in Carpenters' and Joiners' Hall on Madison Avenue on December 7, 1927.

"A good craftsman first of all is a man who does first class work in his trade; he is known by his workmanship; nothing he does is shoddy, ugly or of poor quality," Ludlow begins, addressing the question of physical skill in a sentence that defines good work by what it is not. The remainder of the speech focuses on virtues. "The good craftsman," Ludlow continues, "is loyal to his union. A good craftsman is loyal to the men of other trades." As if anticipating the spat between Belle Moskowitz and Edmund Wilson, Ludlow elaborates, "If he is a carpenter, he doesn't draw pictures on white plaster walls, and if he is a plasterer he doesn't drop mortar on a newly laid floor." When Ludlow does refer to the men's work, he reduces it to the level of a basic commodity. "A good craftsman is loyal, also, to his employer and the owner for he knows that he has sold to them his eight hours a day and has sold to them his skill, and he would no more expect to loaf on the job or do poor quality work than he would expect his grocer to take his money for a barrel of potatoes and then give him a barrel half full, or potatoes that were half rotten."

A craftsman, then, is a man who fills the barrel of his job. A *superior* craftsman, Ludlow emphasizes again and again, is more than this: He is a good person. "He is never a grouch, and when he is about, things seem to go better on the job." His good behavior becomes its own reward. "A good craftsman is a man with a happy look on his face. Why shouldn't he have a happy look, his day's work is no mere grinding out of so many hours for so many dollars, he has given to his work the most precious thing he has, his interest, his skill, his best effort." The virtues embodied in "goodness" thus represent the path upward, by which the not-quite-complete worker, subject to his machine, to his union, and to his own inadequate education, rises above the status of rivet or automaton to become a full human being. Having achieved this higher state, then, the beneficial effects of his "craftsmanship" radiate beyond the worksite. "Every day when he quits, he looks over his work with pride, for he knows he has done a good job, and he brings home to his wife and 'kiddies' contentment and happiness. Because he is a good craftsman, he is a good fellow, a good husband and a good father, a worthwhile man in his community—a good citizen."

As befits a splendid ideal, however, the ultimate goal of Ludlow's oration is not to be found on the earthly plane, at the worksite, or in the home. "Some day perhaps we shall stand before the Great Craftsman who made all things," he sums up, "and perhaps we shall be asked, 'What have you done?' I think the good craftsman will answer 'I did the best work I knew how.'"

SIX

"WHAT THE MEN THINK OF IT"

The Empire State Craftsmanship Awards were supposed to recognize men for their work. Perhaps as the men were handed their Certificates of Superior Craftsmanship at the award ceremonies, they felt pride in their labor, as the award givers hoped. What the men thought of the award, however, and more importantly, what the men thought of themselves, has not been preserved in the historical record. We might believe, like William Orr Ludlow, that their feelings would be easy to imagine. But the ease with which others assumed they could speak for the workers, and so define who these men were, is the most glaring of the many ways the culture worked to erase or disguise their actual lived experience.

The erasure of the workers' individuality extends beyond their photographs to their words as well. In the promotional pamphlet *Recognition of Craftsmanship*, the New York Building Congress helpfully included a page of quotations under the heading "What the Men Think of It." Like the statements attributed to workers in newspaper articles, however, the consistency with which the men express the exact sentiments desired by the Craftsmanship Committee leaves little in these statements that rings authentic. Sheet Metal Worker: "It is a pleasure to receive this award. I think occasions like this will cement the spirit of friendship and cooperation between employer and employee more than anything else." Hoisting Engineer: "I feel highly honored by receiving the certificate and the Missus feels that way also." Elevator Constructor: "The money in the pay envelope doesn't recognize craftsmanship—all journeymen get the scale. The award is different. It recognizes things that wages can't cover and it gives a man a lot of satisfaction to get one." Hoisting Engineer: "I feel honored in being selected to your membership, and I shall do everything possible to prove worthy of my connections with so encouraging an organization that sees fit to raise the Mechanic to so high a plane."

Among the journalistic profiles of workers who built the Empire State, a few mention the Craftsmanship Awards. But again, the oddly affected quality of the language renders it questionable whether these statements are, indeed, "what the men think."

Writing for the London *Sunday Express*, Ivor Griffiths relates his visit to the highest point of work on the Empire State:

> I came on a curious sidelight on America's handling of labour. I passed some casual remark about the pride and interest that the 5,000 workmen must feel at being concerned in putting up the world's tallest building. "Sure," said my guide. "And we help a man to take pride in his work here. A number of our men—engineers, metal-workers, stone-cutters, and labourers—have been given certificates and gold buttons by the New York Building Congress in recognition of their skill. The presentations were made publicly by Mr. Alfred E. Smith, president of the company that is putting up this building."

Margaret Norris, in her profile of ironworkers, also mentions a winner of a Craftsmanship Award, although not for work on the Empire State. Norris not only gives the man a voice, she identifies him, an ironworker called "Whitey," whose real name was Paul Rockhold. But little about Norris's depiction of "Whitey" survives closer scrutiny. She creates a character to fit her idea of who an ironworker should be. "Whitey is a young man around thirty, with a mop of tawny, wavy hair and shoulders at least half again as broad as his slim waist and hips. He comes from New England, of a family resident there for several generations and back of that English, and he is proud of it." In this instance, it is possible to document Norris's mythmaking in action. The record tells a different story. Paul Sommerville Rockhold was born on May 6, 1900, in Wirt County, West Virginia. Both his parents were also natives of West Virginia.

Almost every utterance about the men by the award givers and by the journalists who shared their orientation expresses an implicit or explicit wish to make the men into something else, something other than who they are, something "better." The men must be cleaned up, it seems, to be presentable in public. Whether with journalistic mythmaking or moral-spiritual uplift provided by the Craftsmanship Award's splendid ideals, the educated and upper-class figures betray their aversion to seeing the men as they are, in the actual conditions of their jobs. Beyond this lens of class privilege, only the smallest scraps of information remain, contained in documents, in the private recollections of their families, or in stray remarks captured almost by accident.

A letter to the editor of *The Brooklyn Daily Eagle* in August 1931 might provide one such fleeting insight. Noting the newspaper's contention that maintaining day wages for workers in the building trades would be difficult under prevailing economic conditions, the writer, a Joseph Brown from Brooklyn, explains, "Even if a skilled worker in the building trades were to work every day in the year he would earn no more than a policeman or fireman and little more than a milkman or a pie wagon driver. However, even in good years, he loses many days' work, pays $50 to $100 a year for dues and receives neither vacation nor retirement. He spends many days looking for work, furnishes his own tools and has practically no chance of advancement. His work is dangerous and disagreeable." Alongside this recitation of difficulties, however, Brown expresses something else worthy of attention. He concludes his letter with this simple statement: "The men who made the Empire State Building out of architects' drawings and raw material were building trades mechanics directed by foremen." The tone is subtle, and yet the demand for recognition of the mechanics' skill and significance is clear. We celebrate the Empire State Building, he implies, and yet we forget the men who actually built it.

As William Orr Ludlow insisted, pride in himself and his work was the most desirable attribute in a worker's character. But pride is a private thing. It cannot be imposed or assumed by another, and its subtleties of feeling are rarely trumpeted. Even the most self-confident worker might feel awkward when an organization or a nosy reporter insisted on the pride he ought to and must surely feel. He might be grateful for the recognition, and at the same time, privately, this gratitude could well be tinged with some skepticism or even resentment. Perhaps a hint of this ambivalence is captured in a notice entitled "Back-Pats" about the Craftsmanship Awards from November 1929, reporting that superior craftsmen "receive certificates and gold buttons, and they are not ashamed to take them." "Not ashamed" is a nice euphemism, but certainly it is not the same as unabashedly proud.

Like almost every other journalist of the era, Margaret Norris dutifully emphasizes the workers' pride in her quotations from Paul Rockhold. "Who wants to be a pencil pusher after he's worked with steel—or a common laborer either?" says "Whitey" in her account. "There's also the pride of achievement. It's nice to point to a suspension bridge or a towering building and say, 'I helped erect that.'"

In the context of this pride, Norris observes that "a framed Certificate of Superior Craftsmanship, awarded each year by the Building Congress to the outstanding man of his trade," hangs on the wall of Rockhold's Brooklyn home. Yet despite both Norris's and the New York Building Congress's efforts to enlist the Craftsmanship Award in the constitution of a worker's pride, Rockhold himself seems unmoved by the honor. Asked about his award, Rockhold's only comment is, 'Well, I got a good feed out of it.'"

What did the men think about it? Like the question of who they were, to answer this honestly without recourse to patronizing myths, we would need a record of an individual's thoughts.

Pietro di Donato was born in Hoboken in 1911 to Italian immigrant parents. His father, a bricklayer, died in a building collapse in 1923. His mother died shortly after, and di Donato, still a teenager, left school to support himself and his siblings. In March 1937, di Donato published a short story in *Esquire* magazine about his experiences as a bricklayer, "Christ in Concrete." In 1939, di Donato expanded the story into a novel, which was enthusiastically received. Charles Poore of *The New York Times*, who also covered the Empire State Building beat, admired the novel's experimental prose. "He can write, at will, like Sherwood Anderson, Dreiser, May Sinclair, Joyce," though the novel, Poore felt, "is Italian to the core." The book became a bestseller as well as a Book-of-the-Month Club selection, and di Donato was hailed at the time as an important literary voice, an authentic working-class writer exploring the immigrant experience. In the book, he paints an acerbically negative picture of the Craftsmanship Award.

The novel follows a bricklayer named Paul who, like di Donato himself, is forced to leave school as a young man to support his immigrant family after his father's death in an accident. In one extended scene,

Paul competes for a New York Building Congress Certificate of Superior Craftsmanship against his fellow workers.

"I must win the award! said Dave the only Jew bricklayer—said Frank the Scotchman—said Barney the Irishman—said Tommy the Englishman—said Hans the German—said Grogan the 'real' American—said they all. I must win! prayed Paul."

The effect of this competition, rather than enhancing the workers' pride in their work, instead proves divisive, causing them to turn against one another: "The men ran away with the job; to the delight of the foreman and the firm. Years of bricklaying sense were amplified to a point of acute accuracy and speed, and a man's spirit was mortified if he was a brick or cross-joint behind the next man. They never mentioned the award and became respectful strangers bearing each other a wholesome terrible hate."

When Paul is named the winner, he is invited to the ceremony to receive his award in the presence of his fellow workmen. "At noon the men were summoned to a large space on the second floor. Upon a wooden platform was the committee; the dapper bright-eyed mayor, officials, a stenographer, a few newspapermen, and three richly dressed women. When the workers saw the women they removed their caps and hats. Speeches were made while the men stared at the sheer-silked legs of the three rich women."

The honor of the award pales in Paul's mind next to his sudden, inexplicable proximity to the "glaze-skinned, soft, white-fingered men who owned the great building and the city." The class difference is simply too great for the workers and the owners to see each other as people. Just like workers as viewed by owners and journalists, in Paul's perspective, seen from below, *these* men appear hardly like human beings at all. "That afternoon while laying brick he marveled at the memory of the dainty pink-cheeked perfumed dolls of men who gave out the awards and spoke tired high-class talk."

When the details of a man's personal identity have dissipated with time, and his words have not been recorded or otherwise preserved, what remains of a craftsman is his labor and the open question of his private self-awareness, hinted at, perhaps, in a photograph. The names of four of

Thomas Walsh, derrickman.

the award winners can be recovered by attending to Lewis Hine's portraits of them performing their jobs.

Thomas F. Walsh, the hoisting engineer identified in Belle Moskowitz's *Empire Statements*, already demonstrated the difficulty of singling out a man with so common a name. There are thousands of Thomas Walshes in the 1930 US census—clerks, drivers, doctors, teachers, soldiers, dockworkers, farmers, bricklayers; there is a shipyard pipefitter, boilermaker, rope polisher, coal trimmer, nurse, and stenographer. Thomas Walsh, the award-winning derrickman, has nothing to identify him except his profession and his portrait.

In *Men at Work*, Hine identifies this as the "bell-man." The portrait of Thomas Walsh shows him sitting in the well of a column top, the traveling block and hook load of a much lighter derrick slung into a rivet hole. Hine often included some indication of a worker's profession in the setting or background of his formal portrait, as we see in the portraits of sheet metal worker Frank A. Moeglin and stone setter James P. Kerr, among others. In both images of Thomas Walsh, the derrick looms alongside him, as definitive as a signature. In the work portrait, Walsh gazes up at the derrick's boom and fall line, beyond the camera's frame, holding in his hands the two cords by which he relays signals to the hoisting engineer who tends the derrick's engine on a floor below, out of sight of the ironworkers. When we admire the pictures of daring ironworkers "riding the ball" of the derrick's hoist, it's instructive to recall that their lives depend on the concentration, coordination, and skill of the hoisting engineer and the bellman.

Gus Comedeca, steam shovel operator, is another of the award winners whose identity has been reduced over time to his profession. I could find no records at all for a Gus Comedeca.

In the 1930 US census, however, instead of Comedeca, there is an August *Camodeca*, a "stationary engineer" in the industry "steam plant." Could his name be misspelled on the lobby plaque? Newspaper announcements of the Craftsmanship Awards frequently misspelled or otherwise mangled the men's names. It would be a different matter, however, if the

Gus Comedeca, steam shovel operator.

name on the bronze plaque itself were incorrect. Yet this is not the only instance where a mistake of this kind may distort the worker's identity on the commemorative plaque meant to honor him.

Augustino Camodeca, known as "Gus," was born on December 29, 1893. A draft registration card from June 5, 1917, gives his birthplace as Hulberton, New York, near Lake Ontario. If this is the right man, he is thirty-seven years old in Lewis Hine's portrait, married with three children.

He shows up in the Newark, New Jersey, telephone directory in 1922, and in the Elizabeth telephone directory in 1928, both times with the profession "eng.," which must mean engineer. He's in the 1930 census, residing at 342 Florence Avenue, in Hillside Township, New Jersey, and again in the 1947 and 1951 telephone directories. His April 26, 1942, draft registration card shows him still living at the same address. According to that document, he's five feet eleven, two hundred pounds, with a "ruddy" complexion, working at the Naval Dry Dock in Bayonne, New Jersey. If

this is the correct man, then he died at sixty-eight years old on September 1, 1962. He is buried at Mount Olivet Cemetery in Newark, New Jersey.

The contingencies of historical memory and identification are starkly illustrated by Hine's work portrait of Gus Comedeca or Camodeca. In the photo, the name George J. Atwell is clearly visible on the steam shovel. While information about the steam shovel operator who helped to dig the foundations of the Empire State Building is not preserved, possibly including the correct rendering of his name, "Big George Atwell," a "gray-thatched, bulldog joweled man," appears in the newspapers with some frequency. In January 1931, in just one instance, he is mentioned for digging the foundation of 101 Wall Street, an excavation that inadvertently contributed to the archaeology of New York City, unearthing "pewter pitchers and plates, cannon balls, anchor chains, portions of the hulls of clipper ships," as well as the foundations for an old hotel on land that was once an island known as Hunter's Key.

Samuel Laginsky, glazier.

Samuel Laginsky won the Craftsmanship Award for his work as a glazier, installing windows on the Empire State. His identity is also confirmed by Lewis Hine's photograph of him at his job, and he can be found standing between Gus Camodeca/Comedeca and James P. Kerr in the newspaper photograph of the first award ceremony in October 1930.

According to a document related to his naturalization in 1922, Samuel Laginsky was born on May 15, 1894, in Teplik, Russia, now Teplyk, Ukraine, about 180 miles south of Kyiv. A manifest at Ellis Island, dated April 21, 1906, shows three members of the Laginsky family arriving in the United States, a mother with two sons. Their passage was paid for by the husband and father, Samuel Laginsky Sr., residing at 257 Monroe Street in Brooklyn, a three-story brownstone that still exists.

Laginsky's draft registration from 1917 makes him a year younger, with the birth date May 15, 1895. At that time, he is still listed as an "alien," not a citizen. But Samuel is already a glazier, employed by the Springfield Sash and Glass Company. He's married with one child. On the draft registration card, an address in Springfield, Massachusetts, has been crossed out and replaced by one in New Haven, Connecticut, where it seems the family had relatives. Samuel's brother would eventually settle there. According to related records, the brother, Morduchi in some documents, or Mordka in others, changed his name to Morris, and in still other documents went by M. Louis or Louis M. He and his wife ran a house fixtures store, which, according to the New Haven city directory from 1931, they called "The French Fixture Company." At the time Samuel received his Craftsmanship Award, he was thirty-three years old and lived with his family in the Bronx, on East 139th Street, a few blocks from fellow award winner Peter Madden. He and his wife, Sarah, age twenty-nine, had four children.

As is the case with other workers, while Samuel Laginsky remained anonymous, the products he installed were advertised in trade journals. In *Glass Digest* from June 1931, we can read, “The Empire State Building presents a phase of the modern building trend of interest to glass manufacturers, glass jobbers and distributors. The largest individual order for polished plate glass ever placed was filled by the Libbey-Owens-Ford Glass Company of Toledo, Ohio, supplying polished plate glass for over 5,000 windows in the Empire State Building.” According to the Starrett’s notebook, the window glass was installed by the Contractors Glass Company, and the window frames by the Campbell Metal Window Corporation of New York.

Samuel Laginsky suffered a gruesome death two years later. The *Poughkeepsie Eagle-News* ran a front-page notice on October 20, 1932, “Worker Killed in 10 Foot Fall. Glazier’s Skull Fractured as Window Frame Drops at Wingdale Hospital.” The accident, which had occurred the previous morning, October 19, is described in detail. Laginsky “pitched headlong from a window, 10 feet from the ground, under the impact of a heavy window frame that overturned on him as he went to work standing on the sill.” The district attorney ordered an investigation into the accident, citing the possibility of criminal negligence at the hospital, also known as the Harlem Valley Psychiatric Center, which had opened in 1924 and housed approximately five thousand patients. According to the article, Laginsky was thirty-five (in fact, he was thirty-seven or thirty-eight), and the father of five children, although the census lists only four. The oldest child would have been fifteen. In the aftermath of the accident, it seems the family moved in with their relatives in New Haven.

Adam Bigelow, winner of a Craftsmanship Award for dampproofing, is the final man I identified based on his profession. In the photo album created by the Starrett Corporation to document the Empire State’s construction, now in the collection of the Skyscraper Museum in lower Manhattan, there is an image very similar to this work portrait by Lewis Hine. There, the caption identifies the job the worker is performing, but not the worker. By naming the job, however, the album enabled me to identify Adam Bigelow. In Hine's portrait, Bigelow is applying a cement compound to a masonry wall to make it watertight. According to the in-house notebook, dampproofing for the Empire State was applied by the Hydro-Bar Corporation of New York City. Work began on July 14, 1930, and was completed five months later on December 10, 1930. As is visible in this photo, the process consisted of spreading a grout mixture, composed of lime, cement, and other ingredients, over the entire interior surface of all exterior walls. An asphalt emulsion was then applied to this first layer, forming an elastic sheet approximately a sixteenth of an inch thick.

The 1930 census record for Adam Bigelow is dated April 23, two months before the Empire State job would begin. He was twenty-eight years old and lived in Union City, New Jersey, at 314 Forty-First Street, with his wife and two stepchildren, ages twelve and ten. The census indicates that his wife, Madeline, was sixteen at the time of her first marriage. Adam was born in New York, the grandson of German immigrants.

Tracing Adam Bigelow backward, he appears in the 1905 New York State census, age two, living with his parents in Hell's Kitchen on West Fortieth Street in Manhattan. Adam's father, August, is a roofer, closely related to dampproofing, which remained the family profession for several generations. By 1915, they had moved out of the tenement neighborhood to West Nineteenth Street in Weehawken Township, New Jersey. By then, in addition to Adam, now age twelve, there are five other children. A seventh child is present in the 1920 census.

In 1940, ten years after Lewis Hine took this portrait, Adam Bigelow still lived in Union City with his family. The two children are no longer stepchildren. Bigelow must have adopted them. A family tree posted online shows that Adam and Madeline also had a son, William G. Bigelow, born in 1933. William became a roofer, like his father and grandfather. One of William's sons, Adam's grandson, went on to become a successful professional wrestler, "Bam Bam" Bigelow, who died in 2007 of a drug overdose.

The family tree was posted online by Adam Bigelow's great-niece. When I contacted her, she responded that only one member of the preceding generation was still alive, an elderly aunt, Adam's niece, who confirmed that her uncle's name is engraved on the plaque at the Empire State Building. According to this niece, several members of the family may have worked on the Empire State as roofers or dampproofers. Indeed, I found a Henry Bigelow, dampproofer, who may have worked alongside Adam

Adam Bigelow, dampproofer.

on the Empire State and who received his own Craftsmanship Award in October 1932 for work on the Union Inland Terminal.

Adam's great-niece regretted that she knew so little about him. Any papers or stories associated with his life had been passed down to other family members, now deceased.

"As far as Adam," she wrote to me, "he was born and raised I'm told in Hell's Kitchen in a large family. The family seemed to marry and slowly move one by one and buy houses in Bergen County in the Carlstadt/ Rutherford area. Some of them making a brief stop in the Union City,

North Bergen area of Hudson County as they moved from working poor to middle class."

A Craftsmanship Award conferred by the New York Building Congress may have been welcome recognition from above when these workmen received it. But two generations later, Adam's descendant remembered him for this other, very ordinary, American achievement, raising himself up into the middle class.

Lewis Wickes Hine, photographer, around 1930.

SEVEN

"LOOK HIM IN THE EYE"

The one workman present at the Empire State construction site for whom ample documentary evidence still exists is Lewis Hine himself. Hine published articles and essays; he wrote copious letters, which have been collected and published posthumously. During his lifetime, numerous journalists profiled him, and for three-quarters of a century, art historians and critics have been amassing a detailed literature, dissecting his images and assessing his importance as an artist. In the search to identify the workers, each scrap of information is significant as a clue to their lives. It ought to be much easier to approach Hine as a person and to understand what he brought to his work. Yet reading through his essays and letters and immersing myself in the critical debates surrounding his photographs, I find the reverse to be true. The mass of information and the various interpretations help situate Hine in a broader intellectual and historical landscape. But strangely, in establishing Hine's larger cultural importance, critics have muddled what seems to me the peculiar genius manifest in the individual photographs. Just as I have narrowed my focus from the conceptual to the specific in order to see the men in his portraits as people rather than symbols, so, to grasp what is most extraordinary about Hine as a photographer, I think we must separate the sources from the stories that have grown up around them—to separate, that is, what is said about Hine, even what he said about himself, from what happened in the instant he tripped the shutter.

No known photographs show Lewis Hine at his job on the Empire State. Yet that has not prevented writers from detailing vivid impressions of Hine at the site. Beaumont Newhall, like many other writers on Hine, provided a gripping, you-are-there depiction of the scene in his 1938 profile: "With the workmen he toasted sandwiches over the forges that heat the rivets; he walked the girders at dizzying heights." It makes for exciting reading. But how did Newhall know what Hine had done? Like every other description of the photographer at the Empire State, the stories come from Hine himself.

On November 25, 1930, just after completion of the steelwork on the building's mooring mast, Hine wrote an excited letter to Paul Kellogg, his friend and editor of *The Survey Graphic*. "My six months of skyscraping have culminated in a few extra thrills and finally achieving a record of the Highest Up when I was pushed and pulled up onto the *Peak* of the Empire State, the highest point yet reached on a man-made structure," Hine reports a little breathlessly. "Just before the high derrick was taken down, they swung me out in a box from the hundredth floor (a sheer drop of nearly a quarter mile) to get some shots of the tower. The Boss argued that it had never been done and could never be done again and that, anyway, it's safer than a ride on a Pullman or a walk in the city streets, so he prevailed." The experience was clearly exhilarating, and Hine felt his photographs taken in these moments had achieved something new. In his letter, he identified this new level of artistic achievement with the rise of the skyscraper itself. "Growing up with a building, this way, is like the account of the strong boy (was it Hercules?) who began lifting a calf each day and when they had both reached maturity he could shoulder the bull. I have always avoided dare-devil exploits and do not consider these experiences, with the cooperation the men have given me, as going quite that far, but they have given a new zest of high adventure and, perhaps, a different note in my interpretation of Industry."

Four years later, in 1934, Hine wrote another description of his exploits at the building site in a letter published in *Young Wings*, the magazine of the Junior Literary Guild, an organization devoted to young readers. "Dear Friends," he begins, "How would you like a year of 'High adventure', following the ins and outs, the ups and downs of a great Skyscraper as it grows gradually out of nothing into the greatest of human structures?" In the first part of the letter, while writing with compelling immediacy, Hine reproduces many of the clichés common to journalists of his era, enchanted with their own adventures in the rising structure.

> It was a new problem for me,—this Empire State Building,— full of surprises and thrills,—of hard, exhausting climbs up long vertical ladders with a heavy camera on my back,—of perching way up on the tops of columns and even the very tip

> of the 'mooring mast' for special shots,—of balancing across empty space on a narrow beam guided by the hand of a friendly worker,—and, finally, swinging out on the high-derrick a quarter-of-a-mile above the street. Always there was the danger of a mis-step or one of a thousand careless acts (of yours or others)—that means a fatal fall. Stepping on a loose plank, I saved myself by a miracle,—tripping on ropes and wires,—burned by showers of sparks from the welder up above,—dodging the derrick-loads of planks and columns,—everything that one could do and emerge I am sure I have done.

All subsequent descriptions of Hine at the Empire State, from Beaumont Newhall's on, derive from these letters, demonstrating how documentation is absorbed over time and amplified into legend.

Similarly, as we have seen, because Hine chose to suppress the identities of his subjects and instead to use their images to illustrate a more abstract ideal, critics have understood or construed the content of his photographs in equally general terms, as "work itself" or "American *virtue* manifested in the faces of American workers." Like the impression of the photographer at work, this interpretation of Hine's photographic practice, too, derives from Hine himself.

Hine had a very definite idea of himself as a photographer. "The ordinary way of viewing the newest and tallest building in the world is not the way of Lewis W. Hine, sociological photographer," wrote Hester Donaldson Jenkins in her August 1931 profile, "Man and the Skyscraper." Describing the Empire State project, she also reproduces many of the journalistic clichés of the era. "From these photographs, one can get a sense of the great adventure of this construction work, of the danger and thrill of a good deal of it, and of the virile quality of the workers." Noting Hine's history of work portraits, however, Jenkins understands that his goal extends beyond just showing individual workers. Hine is after something bigger, more abstract than any individual. On the job, she writes, "he immediately began to penetrate to the 'spirit of the skyscraper.'"

From his first work portraits until the end of his career, Hine would use the grand language of "spirit" and "the human" to define his intentions. In 1921, he spoke of showing "the Human Side of The System." In a February

17, 1933, letter to Florence Kellogg, wife of Arthur Kellogg and managing editor of *The Survey Graphic*, he writes, "It is for the sake of emphasis, not exaggeration, that I select the more pictorial personalities when I do the industrial portrait, for it is only in this way that I can illustrate my thesis that the human spirit is the big thing after all." A month before his death in 1940, Hine summarized his lifelong practice with these words: "Ever—the Human Document to keep the present and future in touch with the past."

Taking Hine at his word, writers and critics have understood his work as guided by a thesis, the illustration of a humanist ideal. Interpreting Hine, then, becomes a question of defining the ideal his photographs illustrate. Contesting Beaumont Newhall's more aesthetic reading of Hine, historian Kate Sampsell-Willmann construes the photographer as a social critic and concludes, "Hine was *not* making art for art's sake but for the sake of returning balance and harmony to social life being destroyed by the amoral demands of capitalism, which in turn resulted in immoral social relationships."

In his own writings, and in the profiles published during his lifetime, Hine provided abundant material for this line of interpretation. In a 1926 interview with the magazine *The Mentor*, Hine offers this brief autobiographical sketch:

> I came out of the Middle West a quarter of a century ago, after training to be a school teacher and after working also to express myself in various forms of art. My interest in the great movement of social uplift led me to throw myself into what was called 'social work.' For a number of years child labor and other lines of social welfare occupied my time, using the camera as a means of interpreting conditions and people to those who had but little contact with them. During the war the Red Cross activities in Europe were a fertile field for this kind of interpretation. My interest in the worker led me to spend a number of years interpreting his life and personality, and my collection of industrial situations stands as an apotheosis of labor. The philosophy that has guided me in my work is expressed in the words, "Whether it be an ornate stained-glass window, a gorgeous tapestry or a good piece of printing, a man's handiwork is never better than the mind that conceives it and the hands that fashion it."

Hine saw himself as a "sociological" photographer, an "interpretive" photographer, a photographer who conveyed ideas. If we follow his ideas to their intellectual roots, they emerge from some of the same sources as William Orr Ludlow's craftsmanship movement. In a 1906 article in *The Craftsman*, Gustav Stickley's magazine of the American Arts and Crafts movement, Hine already writes in the terms he would employ for the rest of his life. In that article, Hine expresses the mission of Felix Adler's Ethical Culture School, where he had been a teacher since 1901. The goal of education, Hine writes, is "to associate the work of the hands with the work of the head in a way to make every child understand how head work and hand work are bound together." In the pedagogical philosophy practiced at Ethical Culture, manual training was considered essential to a child's complete development. Yet as Hine explains it in 1906, the goal of associating mind and hand extends far beyond any practical skills children might develop. "Every child who has gained respect for manual labor by working hard with his own hands in competition with other children and by studying at the same time the history of industrial art has learned the significance of hand work in the advancement of history, and is prepared to respect labor and laborers for the rest of his life." In the ideals of the Ethical Culture School, respect for manual labor thus provided the foundation for a just and egalitarian society.

> To separate manual training from the usual mental training would, in Professor Adler's estimation, be creating class distinctions; it would be affording the embryo lawyer, the embryo musician, an opportunity to regard manual training as on a lower scale of business enterprise, and would also narrow the outlook of the artisan by shutting him away from the vital relation trade has to profession, industrial art to fine art, in the development of the world.

In theory, therefore, regardless of the child's background or future role in society, this education would instill an ethic of equality and respect for work, leading students "to become good citizens, whether boys or girls; to become good workers, whether lawyers or carpenters; to become earnest home-makers and State builders, whether rich or poor." This was Hine's ideal of "good craftsmanship." For the remainder of his life, he never strayed from this vision.

As Judith Mara Gutman observes, I believe rightly, "Hine always thought of himself as a teacher—teacher of children, teacher of adults, teacher of workers, teacher of corporations." Hine's mission of "interpreting conditions and people to those who had but little contact with them" may be understood as a fundamentally pedagogical goal. For him, to "interpret" meant to teach others how to see; to illuminate the life of an immigrant, a child laborer, or an industrial worker for an audience far removed from the realities of those lives; to make the "humanity" in that otherwise alien life evident and comprehensible. In his letter to Florence Kellogg from 1933, Hine wrote, "I think it is a very important offset to some misconceptions about industry. One is that many of our material assets, fabrics, photographs, motors, airplanes and whatnot 'just happen,' as the product of a bunch of impersonal machines under the direction, perhaps, of a few human robots. You and I may know that it isn't so, but many are just plain ignorant of the sweat and service that go into all these products of the machine." If Hine considered his audience "just plain ignorant," this was not the ignorance of the uneducated. Precisely the opposite. Hine criticized the ignorance of the educated, the snobbery and blindness of class and position, which prevented those "above" from recognizing and respecting a shared humanity with those "below," an ignorance that led the educated to feel falsely entitled to denigrate or characterize the lives and labor of others, whom they blithely considered automatons, "robots," less than fully human.

Twenty years after his article about Ethical Culture, Hine would describe the goal of his work portraits in similar terms. In his interview with *The Mentor* from 1926, he says, "As I see it, the great problem of industry is to go a step beyond merely having the employer and employee 'get along.'" Owners and laborers must be educated, Hine says, with each recognizing the role the other plays in the success of the enterprise. "Interpretive photography, properly used, will do that, I know, for it has been done. The great problem, of course, is to link the employer and employees in this method of education so that each sees the value in it." Regarding depictions of the laborer's craft, Hine writes, "The employer must think of it as genuine, not paternalistic; the employee must think of it as a sincere treatment of him and his work, not flattery."

When successful, Hine's sociological or interpretive photography would thus fulfill Felix Adler's pedagogical ideal. It would make manifest the relationship of mutual dependence between employer and employee—between the "head" and the "hand" of labor. The educated-ignorant viewer, led by the photo to recognize the worker as a person, not a robot, would cease to look down on him. And the worker, sincerely recognized for his labor and craft, would feel himself respected as an equal partner, rather than denigrated as the member of an underclass. This leveling, Hine believed, would lead to a more democratic society.

Yet in his role as pedagogue, Hine can easily sound pedantic—can sound, in fact, like a member of the New York Building Congress's Committee on Recognition of Craftsmanship, with the patronizing tone of a moralist instructing the worker how he ought to feel about himself. Unlike William Orr Ludlow, Hine did not see himself as a member of the "higher" strata of society. As a struggling, freelance photographer, he felt free to criticize the pretentions of those who assumed workers need only conform to their preferred ideal of behavior, and evil would be banished from the workplace. But Hine had his own ideal, and in expressing it, he can often display the same arrogance as Ludlow. In the 1926 interview, Hine sees his efforts tilted more toward educating the worker than the employer. "The employee must be induced to feel a pride in his work," he says, and Hine's means of "inducing" the worker to feel pride rings abrasively clinical. "I try to do with the camera what the writer does with words. People can be stirred to a realization of the values of life by writing. Unfortunately, many persons don't comprehend good writing. On the other hand, a picture makes its appeal to everyone. Put into a picture an idea and, if properly used, it may be transferred to the brain of the worker."

Hine—like Belle Moskowitz and William Orr Ludlow—was steeped in his generation's discourse of "social uplift." And as long as we only listen to what he says, then his commitment to "interpreting" workers lies open to the same criticisms as Ludlow's attempts to "recognize" them. He may be criticized as romantic, utopian, class based, and patronizing.

This is how George Dimock characterizes Hine's work. Hine's career, Dimock writes, "moved from a photographic practice rooted in activist reform to a later, rather unsuccessful and naive celebration of the dignity of labour within the corporate mainstream." Dimock does not comment specifically on the Empire State photos, since he considers them obvious evidence that Hine had sold out to corporate interests. His more pointed argument is that, even in his most socially engaged images, Hine is already an agent of oppressive social forces. Hine's child labor images, Dimock asserts, "should not be used to enlist his photographs unproblematically on the side of an alternative, working-class history of child labour." Instead, they "must be read carefully and cautiously 'against the grain' given their complicity in the construction of the working-class 'other.'" To Dimock, Hine's frontally posed subjects and their direct stares at the camera are not "evidence of Hine's sensitivity toward and respect for those whom he photographed." On the contrary, these poses are "a sign of the photographer's class dominance vis-à-vis his subjects. Hine is free to pose them as he pleases, positioning them frontally as objectifications of his political project, the fight against child labor."

Did Hine respect his subjects or use them? Were they subjects at all, or merely objects for him to shape according to his own ideals? Were they individuals or symbols? As I look through the portraits of the men who worked on the Empire State Building once again, I think the answer depends on whether you approach the images armed with concepts or look at them specifically as snapshots of discrete moments. In other words, what the photographs *show*, what they *are*, depends on whether you listen to what Hine said or look carefully at what he did.

To notice that many of his photos are posed does not delve very deeply into them. Hine's Graflex camera was physically demanding. It took time to set up, and from the Ellis Island portraits in 1906, through *Man with Wrench* in 1921, to the Empire State's workers in 1930, many of his finest photos show individuals frontally, looking at the camera, or posed at their work. The fact that Hine was composing the scene from behind the camera, while his subjects stood exposed in front of it, might in theoretical terms define a relationship of "dominance." But this argument hardly distinguishes Hine from any other photographer of his class or era or any other. This is how photographs are made. These criticisms are conceptual. The critic abstracts the photographic situation from each individual photo and assumes a generic knowledge of what any subject or any photographer wants or feels. As such, these objections fail to address what makes Hine distinctive, what differentiates his images from those of any other photographer. Hine was not the only one to take images of child laborers, nor, for that matter, of construction workers on the Empire State Building. But his are the photos we continue to ponder, ninety or one hundred years later. As with the conceptual interpretations of the Empire State portraits, these criticisms treat the images as generalities. And by seeing generalities, the critic ignores the specific lives of the individuals pictured, even as he claims to defend them. This misses what makes Hine's work important.

Reading Hine's writings, I think he was struggling to express something subtle, but using crude terms to do it. "I do not verbalize nearly as effectively as I visualize," he wrote in 1940 to Roy Stryker, head of the photography program at the Farm Security Administration, requesting assistance in composing a grant application for the Guggenheim Foundation. Hine understood he was not nearly as clear or precise a thinker in words as he was in images. Despite or because of his sociological training, I believe he never succeeded in giving conceptual articulation to what he wanted to convey with his sociological photography. Like most of his contemporaries, Hine was instead caught in the contradiction between a language of social uplift, of craftsmanship or human values, and the unprecedented challenge to individual autonomy represented by twentieth-century industrial production. In this language, as we have seen in the journalism of the day and in the speeches of men like William Orr Ludlow, a worker is a general type, not a full person but a cliché. In the most egregious examples, his identity is not his own but is imposed by circumstances, from outside, from "above." We see this in Ludlow's conception of the worker. His imaginary picture fully eclipsed any actual men in front of him, about whom "little need be said." The same might seem true of Hine, if you view his images through his statements about them. Hine spent his career documenting the relationship between man and machine, exploring in his photographs the tension between the human spirit and the particularity of individual lives lived under the often crushing conditions of industrial capitalism. In his mind, he photographed *types* of people—"immigrants," "newsboys," "child laborers," "workers"—representatives of an abstract ideal of the human, whether struggling, oppressed, or thriving. In this way, Hine seems to deprive his subjects of autonomy. In 1922, writing to Paul Kellogg to request changes in the captions associated with his portraits of truck drivers, he asks, "Cant [*sic*] you bring out, somewhere, the idea that the motor has helped them to hitch their wagon to the star,—Pegasus out of a dump-cart,—or words to that effect. If I could tell the story in words, I wouldnt [*sic*] need to lug a camera." In his writing, Hine relies on his erudition. "Hitch their wagon to a star," in this case, is a reference to Ralph Waldo Emerson's 1862 essay, "American Civilization," in which the philosopher describes the power of natural and metaphysical conceptions to raise human work above the mundane. "Now that is the wisdom of a man, in every instance of his labor, to hitch his wagon to a star, and see his chore done by the gods themselves." Even if, philosophically, Hine's suppression of individual identity was in the service of demonstrating a common humanity, still, like Ludlow, in his language he has replaced the specific individual with his own "elevated" ideal.

I think the photographs tell a different story.

When Hine sought to express his most important thoughts, the ideas that felt "biggest" to him, he turned to a literary or mythological vocabulary ("Pegasus," "Hercules," "Icarus"). He drew this language from his education, from the sociological terms of the National Child Labor Committee or *The Survey Graphic*; from the lyrical transcendentalism of Emerson or the ecstatic pragmatism of William James; from the pedagogical philosophy of John Dewey; and, above all, from the practical idealism of Felix Adler and Frank Manny, his mentors at the Ethical Culture School. To this extent, Hine's commentators are correct: These were the sources of his thought and the conceptual motivation for his practice. Relying on their vocabulary, Hine is implicated in the class-based, paternalistic attitudes of his era so grating to later readers.

But while the sources of his thought and writing may seem parochial to us, Hine's photographs contain more than the ideas he brought with him to his work. In the photographs themselves, the concepts that surrounded his practice became something else, something more direct and nonconceptual. Something very difficult, perhaps even impossible, to put into words.

Here is another version of Hine's portrait of Peter Madden, Empire State Craftsmanship Award winner for asbestos pipe insulation. What do we see? What does the image show or communicate? What is this portrait?

Peter Madden.

Perhaps, like Hine's critics, we see something *taken*, the photographer, from his position of power, stealing the man's soul. Perhaps we see a face that embodies *strength* and *character*, the general virtues that Hine wished to emphasize. Or perhaps we see a ravaged man, the victim of an oppressive and reckless corporate power, which has subjected him to dangerous, life-threatening work without regard for his safety. In this case, we see a victim photographed by a lackey hired to satisfy his capitalist client's wish to celebrate "the dignity of labor" without having to pay for its real-life costs.

The portrait may be any or all of these things, and many others. But one thing it most decisively shows, in addition to all we may think about it, is a precise moment of interpersonal exchange between Lewis Hine and Peter Madden. Hine positions Madden; Madden responds to Hine, who then takes his photo. In this exchange, something is also *given*—perhaps guardedly, cautiously, unconsciously, or nakedly. The very quality of this interpersonal exchange, so difficult to describe, is what appears in the photograph, and this is what distinguishes Hine's genius as a photographer from so many mediocre contemporaries. In his best photos, Hine documents a deep, meaningful, revealing, yet enigmatic response in his subject. This is what *makes* these his best photos. Yet we lack the vocabulary to describe this quality, this depth, as did Hine. If the photograph succeeds, we say the image captures the man's "humanity." We say he comes "alive," appears "real" or "present" in the image, using the most general, abstract terms to denote what is, in fact, most specific and individual about it. The portrait opens a space for us to witness this man's private interiority, without telling us what it is. As viewers, we then engage with the result of this revealing exchange, we experience or respond to it, creating our own relationship with what is visible, yet unknown about the man we see.

An awareness of these two dimensions captured within the photograph, the conceptual and the interpersonal, is mixed in with almost everything Hine wrote or said. We can glimpse it in a letter Hine sent in 1933, when applying for a job to document the Tennessee Valley Authority. He begins formally: "In this era of wide-spread visualization by movies and newspapers, it becomes quite essential that an enterprise like the Tennessee Valley Authority should have pictorial records of the many lines of activity from the very beginning through every step in the progress of the work." Hine then enumerates the different "lines," including the natural setting, the "cast of characters," and finally, from a sociological perspective, the transformational impact of the project, "the building of the new framework for the new community life and the new facilities for safeguarding the health, recreation and social activities of the people." He concludes in the language of his philosophy. "All these lines should be treated with patience, understanding, and tact,—to emphasize not the superficial oddities of the participants in this drama but their essential human qualities that have been their heritage from all the preceding generations."

This letter fits neatly with Hine's many statements of intention, recalling his comment to Florence Kellogg regarding the selection of "pictorial personalities" for "emphasis, not exaggeration," and especially prefiguring his final career summary, "Ever—the Human Document to keep the present and future in touch with the past."

But rather than his language of "essential human qualities," I am struck by his unnecessary insistence on the proper attitude of the observer, the need for "patience, understanding, and tact." These qualities, too, are things Hine learned from his training as a teacher and from his advocacy on behalf of working class and underclass laborers. He brought these qualities, too, to each portrait he made, along with his ideas about what he was doing. But these qualities cannot be conceptualized. They exist only in moments of interpersonal exchange, and then they dissolve into the photograph itself.

What he meant by human essence or human spirit was something I believe Hine did not himself know how to express in words. The portraits themselves are now the only evidence.

These two dimensions of Hine's sensibility—the grand language and the quiet, attentive sympathy—are evident in most of his statements about the men of the Empire State Building, though the conceptual imagery, as always, has attracted the most commentary. In Hine's letter to the readers of *Young Wings* from 1934 we can hear him conforming to the era's clichés of the heroic worker when he describes the men in general. After noting his personal adventures on the job, Hine writes: "All the time I was getting to know the men better,—trained in the school of experience, with muscles hardened by constant use, eyes and nerves trained to the highest pitch,—combining the team-work of the football field with the control of the acrobat,—it is a new race of men the Skyscraper has developed. They see life from a different angle from that of ordinary humans."

But at the same time, almost as an undertone, Hine evokes the manner of individual men toward him. "They taught me to 'walk-a-beam', laughed down my fear of falling off, helped me through the tight places. Patiently they argued with me about the dangers up there,—'Why, it's safer up here than it is down on the street,—down there you might get something dropped onto you.'"

Finally, to summarize, Hine again reaches for the language of his philosophy: "After all, I came to realize more fully that even a Skyscraper is what it is because behind all of it is the human spirit that made it."

Hine's text for *Men at Work* displays a similar pattern, a mix of contemporary journalistic cliché, interpersonal sympathy, and a grand, "philosophical" goal. He begins with a quotation attributed to William James's 1906 essay, "The Moral Equivalent of War": "Not in clanging fights and desperate marches only is heroism to be looked for, but on every bridge and building that is going up today." Defining his project by this quotation, Hine writes, "This is a book of Men at Work; men of courage, skill, caring and imagination. Cities do not build themselves, machines cannot make machines, unless back of them all are the brains and toil of men. We call this the Machine Age. But the more machines we use the more do we need real men to make and direct them." Then, as in the letter to the Junior Literary Guild's *Young Wings*, Hine speaks more personally: "I have toiled in many industries and associated with thousands of workers. I have brought some of them here to meet you. Some of them are heroes; all of them persons it is a privilege to know."

I find this mix of registers—the high, conceptual language of the human spirit and the specific, interpersonal language of relationships with individuals—everywhere in Hine's writing. It is present even in some of the profiles. In Hester Donaldson Jenkins's 1931 article, after she notes Hine's sociological goal of penetrating the "spirit of the skyscraper," she describes another dimension of Hine's presence at the site. In contrast to Newhall and many later critics, she is attentive to more than just courageous exploits and virile workers. She hears Hine describe relationships:

> And yet Mr. Hine tells of the consideration of these brawny fellows toward the slim photographer with the sensitive, whimsical mouth and understanding eyes. For this new job took him into strange places. He climbed endless stairs laden with his camera, he had to cross on great girders many

> floors from the ground, and here the men led him by the hand, to keep him from slipping. When they swung him out in a derrick, ninety stories above the street, these men who dared such things naturally themselves, were full of admiration for the pluck of the slight fellow. "I didn't think you'd do it," said one of them admiringly.

Looking at the Empire State portraits that Hine published in *Men at Work*, or at the many that are not included in that selection, we can let our eye be led by the phrases Hine chose for his captions, as his critics generally are. If we view the portraits as the documentation of an individual encounter, however, and not as the illustration of an ideal, we come face-to-face with the paradox that animates Hine's work.

In the moment he photographed an individual, Hine encountered a person and sought to document what they brought to the exchange, an unknowable interiority or otherness. He believed this very privacy to be something all humans share. Yet we *share* it solely in the abstract, as a word, something empty and vague. Only in an individual life does it become specific, precisely, inexpressibly individual. The paradox is that what we all share abstractly is what makes each of us distinct, separate, and unknowable. Hine's language was not precise enough to differentiate this paradox. When Hine spoke of it, he used a conceptual language of generality, the human, the spirit. But his images always show the particular. They become "symbolic" *because* they show the particular.

The most revealing caption Hine wrote, I think, is not found in his published work but is scrawled on the back of his portrait of Peter Madden, now located at the George Eastman Museum. Hine identifies Madden there only as "one of the workers on Empire State," noting that he won a Craftsmanship Award. Then, perhaps to himself, or perhaps as a challenge to the viewer, Hine writes, "Look him in the eye."

Who can say what this means? Maybe Hine felt he had captured some essential quality in Madden's expression, and so understood his own note conceptually. In his telling letter to Florence Kellogg from 1933, Hine distinguishes his own form of documentation from more "artistic" approaches to portrait photography. "I have a conviction that the design,

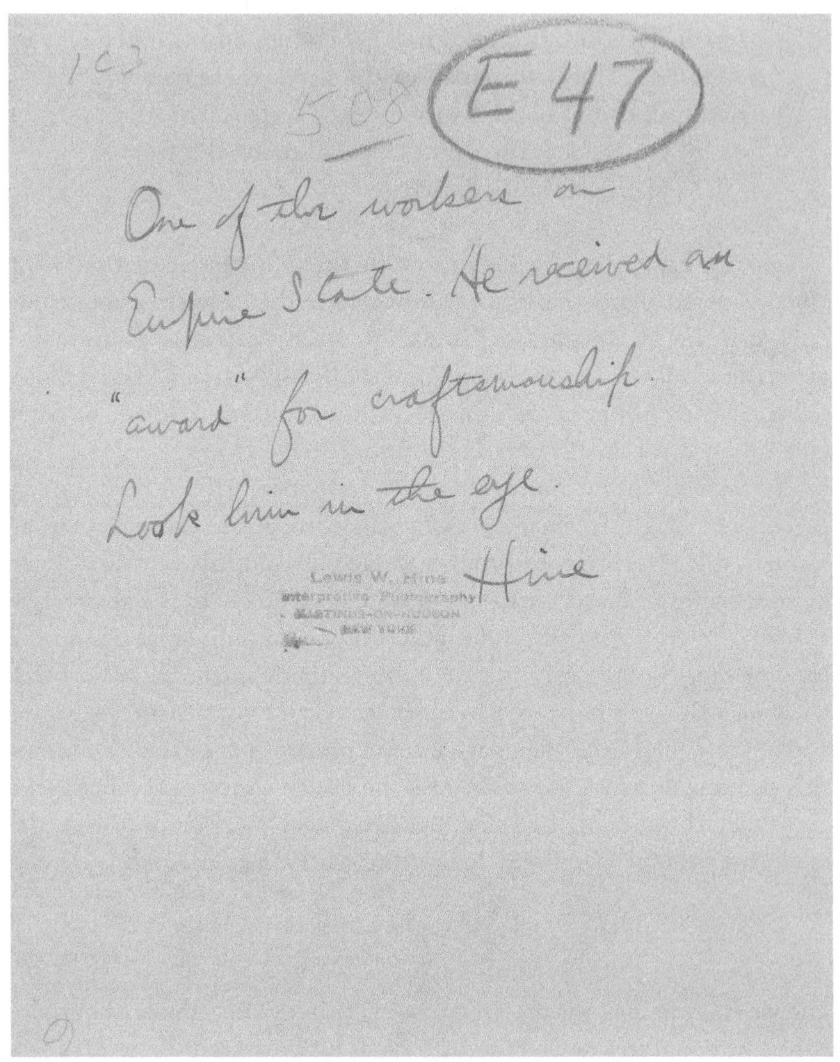

Hine's handwritten note, "Look him in the eye."

registered in the human face thro [*sic*] years of life and work, is more vital for purposes of permanent record, tho [*sic*] it is more subtle perhaps, than the geometric pattern of lights and shadows that passes in the taking, and serves (so often) as mere photographic jazz." Hine may have understood Madden as a type, and may have drawn attention to the face, not for its individuality, but for its "essential" design, suitable as an example of the human in the permanent record.

It's up to us, the viewer, to decide how we see and hear what Hine has captured, the sociological, symbolic, or the interpersonal, how an individual face registers "years of life and work," how the person *presents* in the photo. Both dimensions are manifest. But while Hine writes as if the symbolic were his aim—and critics follow him in this—I believe Hine photographs from the opposite perspective, from the perspective of witnessing the face, the years, the work.

Strangely, in this way, Hine captures exactly what he said he meant to, the "human document." But what does this vague phrase mean? Reading his photographs, critics have seen them through various theoretical lenses, taking his subjects as illustrations of a concept. They look away from the photograph itself to the world of ideas, and then attribute the idea to the photograph or identify it as Hine's intention, his meaning. Yet none of this explains the quality that emerges so powerfully in Hine's images. I believe Hine did something different than he said. Behind the camera, with a person on the other side, he did not think in conceptual terms. Kate Sampsell-Willmann notes, "Hine's work at Ellis Island, and indeed for the rest of his career, was not candid. It was purposeful, intentional, self-conscious, and direct." But by thinking only of *Hine's* activity, critics miss the most salient quality of his practice. His work was *personal*, in the sense that it captured the moment of a relationship created by the fact that Hine and his subject were *together* producing a photograph. In these moments, the human document meant the challenge of documenting this particular human, depicting how he or she shared their distinctive interiority, how their general humanity has been made specific, shaped by the unique conditions under which this individual lived and labored.

With his caption on the back of Peter Madden's portrait, I think Hine meant to draw attention to the man in the photo, to what we cannot know about him, the elusive quality that makes him who he is. Instead of seeing a representative of something else, seeing a generic human or worker—that is, a cliché, an other already conceptualized—I believe Hine meant for the viewer to encounter this specific, unknowable instance of what we all share. Hine meant we should *respect* Peter Madden in his otherness and his unknowability. Because that is what makes him human.

Respect for the individuality of others does not mean we see them or their lives as they see themselves. On the contrary, it means we accept that we cannot know them fully. We accept this fundamental, painful gap in our knowledge, without attempting to fill it with our own ideas. This respect is what William Orr Ludlow and his colleagues at the New York Building Congress failed to show, and its lack is what makes their pronouncements regarding "good" craftsmen condescending. Hine, in profound contrast, captured this gap, the unknown that makes the individual *individual*. His photographs create a space within which this individuality might appear. The subjects of his photos are therefore unknowable, indeed other. That is, the content of their interiority may be unknowable—who are we to say what constitutes another's "authentic" self? But in recognizing, witnessing, and respecting this interiority, this gap between us, we meet the other with empathy, as a fellow human, an equal, an ordinary person, without resorting to preconceived concepts or clichés to fill in what we cannot know about them.

Whatever Hine may have said or thought subsequently about his photos, in that moment of interpersonal exchange, he was not there to photograph class divisions, an oppressed figure, or a worker. Instead, what each of his portraits shows—from the immigrants at Ellis Island to the workers at the Empire State Building—is an individual meeting the camera's gaze, responding in their own way to Lewis Hine, a man who looked this person in the eye.

EIGHT

"THE NEW WHO'S WHO"

The commemorative plaque mounted in the Empire State Building's lobby was always intended to be an artifact. As Al Smith emphasized each time he spoke of it, future generations were the plaque's true audience, the winners' "children and their children's children and on down through the ages." With this bronze tablet, the New York *World* assured its readers, the workmen "will be immortalized." Yet, as with most artifacts, although the object has survived, only a fraction of its meaning has come down to us. While the plaque remains in place, its history fell away. Now it hangs on the wall, unremarked and devoid of context. The names are preserved, and perhaps descendants retain personal recollections of their relatives. In every other sense, however, the men it honors have been forgotten.

Even in 1930, the significance of the Craftsmanship Awards was ambiguous. *The New York Sun* praised the award, extolling the New York Building Congress for its "graceful and appropriate" recognition of the workmen. "Not in the heyday of fine craftsmanship, when gothic cathedrals were springing up in medieval Europe, were workmen so signally honored." Simultaneously, however, by the time Al Smith made his proclamations addressed to future generations, Craftsmanship Award ceremonies were common enough that journalists could deride them as formulaic. *Fortune* magazine included this laconic description of a Craftsmanship Award ceremony in its series on skyscrapers, published in March 1930: "When a great skyscraper is near completion the New York Building Congress gives out its awards for the best work done in each of the various trades. The laborers nominated by their foremen gather in the lobby of the building with its unfinished bronze and marble and its painters' scaffolds and its dangling lights. The owner comes in. Some dignitary from the builder's office makes a suitable speech. There is a round of suitable applause. And the buttons are handed out."

Construction of the world's tallest skyscraper was a historic project, and the presence of the honorable Alfred E. Smith as president of Empire State Inc. lent everything connected with it a degree of public notoriety. But Smith's stature only highlights the ambiguity inherent in the Craftsmanship Awards themselves. Were they important because of the important men who *gave* them? Or were they important as recognition of the ordinary men who *received* them? Looking back in the archives, this fault line runs through the newspaper coverage. "Smith to Honor Workers," announced *The New York Times* on October 8, 1930, marking the first Craftsmanship Award ceremony, honoring men from the "structural" trades. Four months later, announcing the second ceremony, held on February 11, 1931, and recognizing the "finishing" trades, the paper again emphasized the prominent man presenting the honor, rather than men who were to receive it, "Smith to Make Awards."

By contrast, the New York *World* and the *New York Herald Tribune* framed the events around the men. "Building Craftsmen Rewarded for Skill," said one; "Empire State Mechanics Rewarded for Good Work," said the other. The difference in perspective, perhaps reflecting the expected readership of these different papers, affected the content of the articles. When the news was about former Governor Smith, the articles were several paragraphs long and included relevant quotations from his speech and those of his fellow dignitaries. The men were not mentioned at all, although one article noted that, in addition to the award winners, "about 500 workmen, clad in their overalls and munching their lunches, were present." When the focus was on the award winners, on the other hand, the only thing newsworthy was the fact of the award itself. These articles consisted simply of one or two sentences explaining the purpose of the award and a list of the men's names, often misspelled or garbled.

As William Orr Ludlow understood, *giving* the awards was symbolic. *Receiving* the award, by contrast, was specific and individual and carried no further public significance. I think this is reflected in Al Smith's comments about the meaning of the plaque. Its presence in the building's lobby commemorates the ceremonial granting of the award. This aspect of its meaning belongs to the story of the monumental structure and its symbolic significance as an American achievement. The men's identities, the names themselves, however, were of no symbolic importance. They were the private concern of the men and their families, and Smith expected only they would remember them down through the ages.

Once the plaque becomes an artifact, however, persisting beyond the circumstances of its original placement, its meaning undergoes a peculiar reversal.

As a symbolic event, Craftsmanship Award ceremonies provided owners, builders, and architects an occasion for publicity. They made speeches of self-congratulation, often quite unsuitable, while the men sat silently listening. Walter Chrysler provided an extreme example of this in the address he gave to the winners of Certificates of Superior Craftsmanship for his building on January 20, 1930. "If it weren't for craftsmanship, the construction of great buildings like this one would be an impossible feat. It is an honor paid to me when I see that you have enthusiasm for what you have done." Even when the speeches did not entirely overlook the men they were intended to honor, frequently enough, they schooled the men in the abstract virtues expected of them, "integrity, thoroughness, intelligence, reliability, loyalty and cooperation."

Often, more programmatically, the remarks asserted a larger, national virtue. Addressing award winners for the building at 40 Wall Street in December 1929, Colonel William A. Starrett insisted, "The awarding of craftsmanship shows the democracy of the life in which we live." Walter Chrysler, too, gestured toward democracy in his speech to the workmen receiving awards for his building. "You built it as a monument to yourselves and to me. We are all made from the same putty, from the same mould," he declared. And in a speech on May 27, 1930, announcing his intention to install the bronze plaque in the lobby of the Empire State Building, Al Smith similarly claimed that the Craftsmanship Awards were a sign that, in America, workers and owners were united in democracy. The award, he said, "builds up a better standing, a better feeling and a much better society so to speak, as between the men that are supposed to be at the top and the man that is supposed to be at the bottom, whereas, as a matter of fact, they are all equal and they are all even. We have no class distinction in this country."

Nevertheless, class distinctions define the history of the award. Seen as an honor received by ordinary working men, the Craftsmanship Awards exposed the emptiness of the symbol and the patronizing language used in granting it. In the week after the first award ceremony, cartoonist Will B.

"The New Who's Who," by Will B. Johnstone (Oct. 18, 1930).

Johnstone poked fun at the award and, implicitly, at the men, in a drawing syndicated in papers around the country. Johnstone may be best known today for inventing the character of the victimized taxpayer, stripped of both his earnings and his clothing until he is left destitute, wearing only a barrel and suspenders. In subsequent years, he collaborated with S. J. Perelman on scripts for the Marx Brothers, including two of their most famous films, *Monkey Business*, released in 1931, four months after the Empire State Building's grand opening, and *Horse Feathers*, which premiered the following year. But in October 1930, Johnstone penned a wry commentary on the idea of honoring "ordinary" workmen. Entitled "The New Who's Who," in a nod to lists of high society members, his cartoon features caricatures of four men from the first group of Craftsmanship Award winners: Vladimir Kozloff (called "Valmir Kozleff"); Gus Comedeca or Camodeca (called "Gus Comedech"); Michael (called "Mike") Tierney; and Giuseppe Rusciani. "That's Valmir Kozleff, the champion wrecker!" exclaims an onlooker. "Nice form!" responds his companion. Comparing the workers' activity to a sports competition—rock driller Michael Tierney is depicted as a golfer—Johnstone implies that naming a "superior" wrecker or excavator is ridiculous. The mark of distinction between riveters, in this view, would be who's loudest.

A handwritten annotation on the copy held in the archives of Empire State Inc. affirms, "the names correct," which is not entirely true. On the scale of the ordinary individual, details like this tend to grow fuzzy. As we have seen, the commemorative plaque itself may have misspelled some award winners' names.

A second cartoon, published around the same time, mocked the idea of granting awards to building trades in the first place, expressing a view similar to that of Maurice Heaton in his article denying bricklayer Charles E. Sexton the title of "craftsman." Drawn by artist Harry Haenigsen, the cartoon implies that once awards are given to construction workers they might as well go to bootblacks, telephone operators, and the milk wagon horse.

Perhaps I am misinterpreting Haenigsen's cartoon as ironic. Perhaps in his opinion the bootblack and milk wagon horse, like construction workers, were truly unacknowledged heroes who did their job well every day and so deserved to be recognized, though they never would be, unless in a cartoon. The ambiguity only underscores the paradox of recognizing ordinary people as extraordinary, a paradox inherent in the

"After All These Years," by Harry Haenigsen, honoring the bootblack, telephone operator, and milk wagon horse (Nov. 6, 1930).

Craftsmanship Awards themselves. Why create a lasting commemoration to someone simply doing their job, and a job so common and fleeting?

Al Smith himself unwittingly confronted this division at the heart of the Craftsmanship Awards during the second ceremony at the Empire State Building. As an important man and the corporate president, Smith was fluent in the symbolic language of grand events, as his many encomiums to the building and the awards demonstrate. But Smith was also a master politician, more sensitive to the concerns of individual workers than many of his peers. Born in New York's Lower East Side tenements,

Smith had famously gone to "school" at the Fulton Fish Market and had worked himself "up from the city streets" to high office. (A joke circulating at the time noted that, despite his failed run for US president, as the head of Empire State Inc. Al Smith still occupied the highest office in the land.) At the first award ceremony, on Wednesday, October 8, 1930, Smith spoke quite movingly, holding to a middle register between worker and employer, without the patronizing tone that invariably characterized Colonel William A. Starrett's or William Orr Ludlow's speeches. On that occasion, Smith expressed what sounds like genuine awe and appreciation for the work the men had accomplished.

"In less than seven months there has arisen upon this lot the greatest monument in the world due to the ingenuity, ability and craftsmanship of every man taking a part in the construction of the Empire State Building," he began, including all the workers, not just the award winners. "It may occur to those who look upon it that there is some great debt of gratitude coming to the large army of men who during the long hot days of June put everything they had into it. And the New York Building Congress, mindful of that fact, desired to make some award, some recognition to the master craftsmen in the different trades as a testimonial to them and as something to be cherished because they have made a substantial contribution to their city, their state and their country."

Here, Smith speaks to the men, presenting the award as a testimonial to their significant, individual contributions. It is a respectful tribute to the workers assembled to hear him.

But Smith was just as susceptible to the grand, symbolic gesture, in which the workmen all but disappeared. At the second ceremony, on February 11, 1931, rather than speaking *to* the men, he demonstrated the characteristic ease with which journalists, architects, builders, and owners felt they could speak *for* the men. On this occasion, one of the habitual orators, John J. Collins, the secretary-treasurer of the Tunnel and Subway Constructors' International Union, arrived late and missed his appointed time slot. Former Governor Smith, who held honorary membership in several unions, dating to his time as governor, rose in Collins's place. "As a bona fide member of the Bricklayers' Union, the Teamsters' Union, and the Shovel Hoisters' Union, or whatever the name is, I'll speak for labor," the former governor volunteered, displaying how quickly precise names cease to matter when symbolism is the goal. Responding on behalf of the workers, *as* a worker, Smith ventriloquized. "We are glad we have displayed our energy and ingenuity and are proud of our work here." Smith seemed to enjoy his role, which received enthusiastic reviews from the newsmen. "Smith as a Laborer Helps Honor Workers; Adopts Role to Speak in Place of Union Leader at Building Exercises," reported *The New York Times*. But Smith's playacting—as a young man, he had aspired to be an actor—went a little farther than he meant. Perhaps intending to continue his speech with a recitation of the lofty ideals the award represented, he then said, "These certificates should mean more to us than just a frame and a paper." But what *should* the Certificate of Superior Craftsmanship mean, from the workers' perspective? In this moment, Smith's role had reversed, and instead of granting the award, he stood for a moment trying to imagine what it meant to receive it. This new role broke the symbolic sheen that surrounded the awards for the men of the New York Building Congress, and so Smith confronted the central ambiguity of the Craftsmanship Awards from the workers' perspective. In the symbolic view, the award represented the splendid ideals of energy, ingenuity, and pride. But from the individual worker's point of view, what significance did they hold? Almost as if his brief impersonation had awoken in him for the first time an awareness of the men beyond the scope of the Building Congress, Smith departed from the formulaic talking points. In this moment, unique in all the award ceremonies of the era, Smith improvised a new, sadly unrealistic note in his speech. Remaining in character, Smith expressed a wish rather than an ideal, one that honestly acknowledged the practical challenges workers faced in February 1931. "Builders and architects should give some consideration to those who are out of work who have received this recognition, and give them jobs whether they need more men or not."

From the recommendation letter Al Smith wrote on behalf of Peter Madden in 1932, we know that his expression of sympathy for workers was not feigned. Yet expressions of sympathy and earnest wishes could not resolve the conflict within the Craftsmanship Awards. Rarely in good times, and so much less so in February 1931, would employers contemplate hiring a worker because he had won an award, regardless of "whether they need more men or not." As an exercise in publicity, or even as a sincere exhortation to aspirational ideals, the award ceremonies exhausted their significance in the act of presenting the award. Beyond that, the award became the private concern of the winners, no longer of interest to Empire State Inc. or the New York Building Congress. The plaque proudly placed in the lobby by the owners would commemorate the award and the symbolic act of publicly awarding it. The men themselves, as private individuals, would have to determine what *receiving* the award meant and whether it held any practical value for their prospects of future employment. Ultimately, their descendants would be responsible for preserving this private meaning, pondering for themselves what lasting significance the award carried by connecting the individual lives of their ancestors to the names inscribed on the list.

It is ironic, therefore, that the commemorative plaque has survived. The symbolic bubble of the Craftsmanship Awards burst almost as soon as the award ceremony was over. The event was reported in the newspapers, and the articles were clipped and collected in Empire State Inc.'s scrapbooks, destined to yellow in the archives. But the plaque, which records the men as individuals, has survived in public view. As an artifact, isolated on the wall, what it communicates is fragmented, nearly illegible. Nevertheless, by virtue of having survived, the plaque, rather than the speeches or grand ideals, now carries the significance of the event into the present. To us, today, its meaning has been inverted from what those who placed it understood. No one remembers the public presentation of the Craftsmanship Awards or the speeches held to ennoble it. But now, almost by accident, the list of individual names has attained symbolic importance. Against the backdrop of so many anonymous workers, what had been the private concern of a few men and their families now constitutes the plaque's public significance. Regardless of why the Building Congress granted the award, the names on the list have become the sole portal through which to recover pieces of this otherwise forgotten history.

Steelwork on the Empire State's peak, its celebrated mooring mast, "the highest point yet reached on a man-made structure," required only seventeen days and was completed on November 21, 1930, six weeks after the first Craftsmanship Award ceremony. Lewis Hine was on hand to document the momentous achievement, as ironworkers hoisted the final beams and drove the last rivets. Despite the legend, repeated in many corporate histories, that Al Smith "shot" a golden rivet to complete the structure, there's no evidence to support it. Smith was afraid of heights.

Meanwhile, economic conditions for the men whose jobs on the Empire State Building were now done continued to worsen. Just two days after completion of the mooring mast, on November 23, 1930, Al Smith announced that six truckloads of leftover wood from the building's construction would be donated daily to a free woodpile on West Thirtieth Street to help heat the homes of the city's unemployed. That same day, an abandoned pier at the foot of East Twenty-Fifth Street, near where steel for the Empire State had arrived by ferry, was transformed into a cafeteria and barracks for the jobless. Two thousand men waited in line for mutton stew, four slices of bread, and coffee.

When steelwork on the building came to an end, and the ironworkers were out of a job, the men of the finishing trades were still working far below—the tile setters, electricians, plasterers, and painters. The last of these workers did not complete their contributions to the building until months later, in April 1931. Yet the four months that separated the first and second award ceremonies for the Empire State's superior craftsmen saw a marked change in the public mood, dramatically reflected in how the two groups were treated.

In October and November 1930, business leaders like John Jakob Raskob and Charles M. Schwab, president of Bethlehem Steel, were still predicting that the economic situation had stabilized. "The indications of the past six or eight weeks are that the bottom has been reached," announced Raskob, quoted in an article entitled, "Schwab Sees Record Prosperity." In their view, things were looking up. Articles aimed at boosting the public mood claimed that "the cloud of depression is not without its silver lining." Those with "small salaries but steady jobs," one journalist trilled hopefully, might enjoy the "increased buying power of money." "A pair of real silk hose can be bought for less than a dollar." By February and March 1931, however, such pronouncements had mostly ceased.

While the stock market surged on Wednesday, February 11, 1931, the day the second group of Craftsmanship Awards were presented, closing at its highest level for the year, the headlines on the business page of *The Brooklyn Daily Eagle* expressed the uncertain situation: "Hardware Demand Is Only Moderate," "Commodity Prices Are Still Wobbling," "Steel Demand Spotty," "Refined Copper Stocks Decrease." The following day, *The New York Times* reported that the seventy-nine breadlines in New

York City, serving seventy thousand meals a day, would coordinate their mealtimes, in order to "curtail the necessity for men spending nearly all day going from one bread-line to another to obtain enough food to sustain them." The same article noted that salaries for white collar workers in January 1931 had declined 30 to 50 percent compared to January 1930.

Lewis Hine produced portraits of all sixteen (or seventeen) Craftsmanship Award winners in the first group, representing the structural trades. He photographed fewer than ten of the sixteen winners from the finishing trades. Perhaps these portraits are simply missing. Or perhaps, caught up in the thrill of following the ironworkers to the pinnacle, Hine spent less time with the men whose more prosaic work took place indoors. Or perhaps, like the newsmen and even Belle Moskowitz's publicity office, Hine's interest waned once the drama of structural ironwork concluded. Yet clearly, the publicity office had commissioned him to photograph the winning craftsmen. When Hine left this part of his assignment unfinished, Belle Moskowitz hired another photographer to supply the missing portraits. Hiram Myers, a colleague of Hine's, whose darkroom he had occasionally used since at least 1919, photographed five of the men absent from Hine's documentation of this second group of award winners. At least initially, Publicity Associates intended to create a complete set of portraits. Had Belle Moskowitz planned a second photo spread of winners for a later edition of *Empire Statements*, recognizing men from the finishing trades? Or did she imagine some other publication or commemoration, devoted to all the award winners? If so, it did not come to fruition. With the building's grand opening looming, the publicity office may have been absorbed in more pressing matters. Whatever the reason, this second group of award winners fell by the wayside. Two men—William Deneen, an elevator constructor's helper, and George R. Adams, a painter—were not photographed at all.

In every respect, the men of the second group of award winners were treated differently. While many of these men appear among Lewis Hine's photos, none of the prints that ended up in the archives bears a name or other clue to the man's identity. Indeed, none of Hine's prints of the second group that I viewed had handwritten notes of any kind, in significant contrast to the first group. Additionally, there seem to be fewer images of these men, and frequently no images of them at their jobs. These sixteen award winners were equally honored by Al Smith, the contractors, and the New York Building Congress at a public ceremony. But they appear to have suffered from coming second and, perhaps, from belonging to less picturesque and "heroic" trades. While the ironworkers benefitted from being symbols of American achievement, and were featured in photo-essays and news outlets, no reporter published a profile of a plasterer. Journalistic attention made men of the structural trades exceptional, raising them from obscurity to momentary visibility, occasionally even preserving their full names. The men of the finishing trades had no such symbolic role to play. They remained ordinary workers, cloaked in unexceptional invisibility.

This invisibility has practical consequences for my search to reconnect the names on the Craftsmanship Awards plaque with the men in Lewis Hine's photos. The lack of notes, the absence of work portraits, the lack of follow-through by the publicity office—these break the already fragile thread that connects the images to the individuals they document. Coincidentally, some of the men in the second group had particularly common names—John Connolly, John E. O'Connor. They were not just ordinary people in the usual sense, but additionally in this respect, fading more swiftly and thoroughly into the dark background of anonymity. As a result, they are more like their fellow workers who were not recognized with awards and whose association with the building has disappeared entirely. The only thing that distinguished the award winners was the award itself, and this was no more than a snapshot, in which they appeared for an instant and as quickly disappeared again.

In addition to the archives of Empire State Inc., the Avery Architectural and Fine Arts Library at Columbia University holds fifteen archival boxes of uncatalogued materials donated by the architectural firm that designed the Empire State Building, Shreve, Lamb, and Harmon. Most of these files concern famous visitors to the building—Queen Elizabeth, Winston Churchill, the king of Siam, movie stars, beauty queens, sports teams. One box, marked "1955, 1956," includes a folder labeled "Birds Killed at ESB," but contains no photos or articles about dead birds. Instead, it holds images of crowds waiting to enter the observatory. Another folder, enigmatically labeled "Empire State Bldg., hold for decision by Carl Willes," harbors additional photos of the building under construction, including unidentified portraits of three workers. The folders in the final, unnumbered box contain a seemingly random mixture of photographs—a dozen of those dead birds; a series showing the building's opening ceremony; celebrity visits; a handful of construction photos, most likely by Lewis Hine but hitherto unidentified; and five portraits of craftsmen from the second group of award winners, with their names, professions, addresses, and the names of their employers handwritten on the back. All these portraits were taken by Hiram Myers.

Hiram Myers was born in 1888 in New York and died in 1967 in Florida. He came of age amid the same progressive social reform movements that had nurtured Lewis Hine and Belle Moskowitz. Like Hine, Myers became a social worker and "social photographer," documenting the lives of immigrants and the working classes. Like Hine, he had photographed the appalling conditions of child laborers in the United States for the National Child Labor Committee. Indeed, a 1910 photograph attributed to Hine, showing a family in a ramshackle tenement, and now in the collection of the Art Institute of Chicago, may be misattributed. It features the same stamp on its back as the photos by Myers of the Empire State Building workers in the Avery collection: "Publication Subject To Written Permission Or Invoice Hiram Myers." Elsewhere, Myers is identified as the head of the "Association for Improving the Condition of the Poor, New York City," and a notice in a 1929 edition of *The Survey Graphic* describes him as "a commercial photographer in New York who does a great deal of work for social agencies." Myers's selection to complete the job Hine left unfinished once again betrays the influence of Belle Moskowitz, who evidently used her position at Empire State Inc. to undertake her own, small-scale jobs program, employing photographers whose social commitments she respected and who were hit especially hard by the difficult economic times. But perhaps because Hiram Myers did not become famous, no one has previously recognized that both he and Hine were commissioned specifically to document the Empire State Craftsmanship Award winners. These five portraits have never been linked to Hine's work. While Hine's images were collected, celebrated, and decontextualized, Myers's images remained unknown in these folders.

There are many differences in technique and nuance between Hine's portraits and those taken by Myers. But even considered solely as contract work, the portraits were handled differently. While Hine was hired with a more expansive brief, Myers's contribution appears to have been limited exclusively to these five portraits. And unlike Hine's prints, which frequently bear his handwritten notes, the only inscriptions on the portraits taken by Myers, likely by a member of Belle Moskowitz's staff, identify the men by profession and by employer. The publicity office was more interested in their affiliation with subcontractors than in the men as individuals. Nevertheless, like the plaque itself, the intentions of the publicity office have been reversed by time. The notes allowed me to confirm the identities of these five men, the only confirmations from Empire State Inc. for all the award winners in the second, neglected group.

The portrait of steamfitter Louis Hummell illustrates the difference between photographs by Hiram Myers and those by Lewis Hine. Although similar in composition and approach, they differ in the very quality that distinguished Hine's genius. Myers's portraits, like Hine's, pose the men frontally or show them at their jobs. To my eye, however, Myers's work lacks the personal depth, the dimension of interpersonal exchange, that characterizes those by Hine. The expressions reveal less, communicate less. The men seem more self-conscious and so somehow less themselves. The photographs are both less specific and less symbolic.

The caption on the back of Louis Hummell's portrait names him and his employer. The firm, Baker, Smith & Co., was responsible for the installation of the heating and ventilation on the Empire State. In the notebook documenting the date on which the most workers were present at the construction site, the company had 189 men working, seventy-five on heating, and 114 doing ventilation work. Additional men from the company may have been involved in pipe covering. At that time, Baker, Smith & Co. was already an old firm. An advertisement in *The New York Times* from May 5, 1865, features a "low pressure steam heating apparatus," patented by Baker, Smith & Co., located at 37 Nassau Street. Other documents show the company in existence prior to the Civil War.

Details of the job Hummell and his coworkers performed at the Empire State Building can be found in several articles from the time. One, published in *The Architectural Forum* in October 1930, was written by Henry C. Meyer Jr., of the firm Meyer, Strong & Jones, the mechanical

Louis Hummell, steamfitter, photographed by Hiram Myers.

engineers for the Empire State Building and a company that still exists today. Here we learn that the building would contain seven thousand radiators with a total of 227,000 square feet of heating surface. The heating plant was divided among several different zones, with equipment in the subbasement, the twenty-ninth and fifty-fourth floors. To accommodate these heating mains without reducing the ceiling height in offices, the structural design for those two upper tower floors extended to seventeen feet, instead of the more typical eleven feet six inches. Further technical information about the plumbing and drainage systems, "interesting to all readers," appeared in *The Plumbers and Heating Contractors Trade Journal* in November 1930. To handle its massive plumbing, the Empire State Building, which the author refers to as "this noble pile," was outfitted with "two 8-inch soil stacks and their two 8-inch vents, four 6-inch soils and their 6-inch vents, one 5-inch sink stack, and six 4-inch waste stacks with separate 5-inch vent stacks all reach to the very top of the structure," where some twenty-five pipes stick out "into the ozone so to speak."

While documentation of the job he performed is plentiful, records for Louis Hummell, with two L's, are hard to come by. There was a steamfitter named Louis Hummel with one L, however, and the US census intimates a concise family history. Is this another instance in which the award winner's name is misspelled on the commemorative plaque?

In 1920, Louis Hummel, eighteen, lived with his widowed mother and two brothers, on Second Avenue between Fifty-First and Fifty-Second Streets. By this time, Louis was already a steamfitter. An earlier record included an older child, Irene, but by 1920, she no longer lives with the family. The children were all born in New York, while their mother, Agnes, and their deceased father were both born in Ireland. Agnes is a laundress for a private family. A 1921 photo of Fifty-Second Street between Second and Third Avenues, held at the New York Public Library, shows a rundown neighborhood with loose cobblestones sticking up from a giant pothole in the middle of the street. A 1927 photo of Fifty-Second Street reveals a mixture of two-, three-, and four-story buildings, some dilapidated, while several lots are undergoing excavation for new construction.

In 1918, Louis George Hummel registered for the draft. This document provides a birth date, September 6, 1900. He registered on September 12, 1918, which would put him just a week past his eighteenth birthday. However, the New York City Births Index shows Louis G. Hummel was born on October 6, 1901. It seems likely that he lied about his age to join the army.

On July 14, 1925, Louis G. Hummel married Edith Margaret Melia, born in 1903. She may have been a girl next door, because she shows up in the 1920 census living with her mother just around the corner from the Hummel family, in her grandmother's apartment on East Fifty-Second Street. There is a birth record for a daughter, born to Louis and Edith, on December 20, 1925, five months after the marriage license.

For the next twenty years of their lives, however, I could find few documents for Louis George Hummel or for his family. It appears that Louis and Edith separated or divorced. The 1940 census shows Edith living with a man named Nelson, though it misspells her name as "Thummel." And in 1942, when Louis again registers for the draft, he lists his mother Agnes as his closest contact. Louis is still working as a steamfitter, now for the Whitney-Dierks Heating Corporation, located in Long Island City. Agnes M. Hummel died on June 9, 1943, and is buried in Mount Saint Mary Cemetery in Flushing, Queens. Louis G. Hummel died of heart disease on May 15, 1954, and he is also buried at Mount Saint Mary Cemetery.

On August 14, 1930, the date documented in the sole surviving Daily Job Report, the Otis Elevator Company had four foremen, ninety-eight mechanics, and 113 helpers at work installing elevator rails, piping, and wiring. Signal work, then a novelty which allowed elevators to function with both greater autonomy and more centralized control, occupied an additional twenty-eight men, bringing the total at work that day to 243. Because of the unprecedented size of the building, new kinds of hoisting motors, along with other safety innovations, were necessary to make elevator service practical. Indeed, as in the case of the dancing derricks which so appealed to William Engle, these autonomous elevators were sometimes seen as figures for the ideal worker. "Here we have a mechanism which is about as human as mechanical ingenuity can make it," wrote a *New York Times* correspondent, identified only as "W.K." "It has a sort of mind, because it takes and obeys orders. It responds to signals, remembers all the stops that it must make, never missing one, speeds itself up and slows itself down at a rate which is not distressing to the pit of the stomach, flings doors open and shuts them, watches intently whether so much as a hand is stretched between the car floor and the landing and refuses to move until the hand is withdrawn to safety."

But while the surviving Job Report recorded the highest number of laborers at the building in total, it does not appear to reflect the peak of elevator installation. According to a celebratory pamphlet issued by the Otis Elevator Company describing their work on the Empire State Building, twenty-seven elevator constructors began work at the site on May 5, 1930, when steel had reached the sixth floor. By July 11, 280 men were employed constructing the fifty-eight passenger elevators, six freight, two tower, and a final mooring mast elevator for the finished building, as well as maintaining and extending the material lifts for construction supplies and the independent, temporary elevators necessary to bring workers to their jobs throughout the rising structure.

One of these men was thirty-year-old Thomas McWeeney. Thomas Francis McWeeney was born on February 5, 1900, the son of Irish immigrants. In the 1905 New York State census, the family, including three children, lives on Second Avenue in Manhattan between 103rd and 104th Streets. The father, John, is a driver.

Thomas McWeeney enlisted in the US Army in April 1917. He served overseas as the bugler in the Fifty-Eighth Artillery company for a year and was discharged on May 7, 1919. By 1930, when he received the Craftsmanship Award, he was married and living in a rented two-story, two-family home on Eighty-Ninth Street in Queens with his wife, also the daughter of Irish immigrants, and two young children.

By 1940, McWeeney was an elevator inspector for the Argonaut Insurance Company in New York. His family had grown with the birth of a son in 1932. They lived in a rented home on Forty-Fifth Street in Queens. Thomas was making a good living, with an annual income of $2,440, at a time when the median income was $956.

Like his father, McWeeney's older son, also named Thomas, joined the armed forces, and he served in the Marines during World War II. He was wounded twice, and items about him appear in *The Brooklyn Daily Eagle* on August 29, 1944, and again on June 20, 1945. The articles note that his parents live on Eighty-Second Street in Jackson Heights, Queens. Sometime after the war, like so many families, the McWeeneys moved out of the city to the suburbs, settling in Garden City, Long Island. Thomas McWeeney Sr. died on August 31, 1978, and is buried in Long Island National Cemetery, East Farmingdale, in Suffolk County.

"He was a great guy," his grandson George McWeeney recalled. "You wanted to know him. He always came out as being smarter than most people in the room, always had stories to tell, and when he started to tell a story, people listened. One of these guys you like to have around."

George McWeeney was seventeen when his grandfather Thomas died. But he visited his grandparents often, and for years Thomas and his wife Mary would come from New York to spend a month with George's family

Thomas McWeeney, elevator constructor, photographed by Hiram Myers.

in Chicago. These visits created problems for Thomas's daughter-in-law, George's mother. Mary, it seems, was a difficult house guest.

"I remember those days—and I remember them because they made my mother so miserable," George said. "Tom's wife, Mary, she was not well educated. But she would always expect to be treated like a princess. A certain kaiser roll in the morning, a certain marmalade. I would stay up late and hear my mother sobbing about how Mary made her feel. She'd complain to my grandfather."

I asked George whether his grandfather ever talked about his work on the Empire State Building.

"He never even spoke of it," he responded, somewhat disappointedly. "Different generation, different times. Maybe sometimes, when we would see from time to time pictures of the construction, then maybe he'd talk about it."

Was it something that people talk about in the family today? I wanted to know.

"It's been so long now," George said, "he's been gone forty-five years."

But George felt a lingering sense of achievement.

"I'm always amazed myself. I understood the importance of it. He didn't finish school or go to college, and there he was working on the Empire State Building with his name on a plaque in the lobby, which is exactly one more than I have!"

George had never seen the photograph that Hiram Myers took of his grandfather in 1931.

"He looks very serious," he said when I sent it to him, "like he's worried about where next month's rent is going to come from. Looking at it reinforces what I felt before. He wasn't a particularly happy guy, and he seems a little dour in that picture."

According to George's father, the atmosphere growing up in the household was still characterized by the challenges of the Great Depression.

"Times were really tough for him," George said. "He didn't have a college degree. They lived through some hard times." And this experience left a lasting impression on the mood at home. As George put it, "Like all the time, they were sort of asking, 'Why was I dealt this hand of cards?'"

George recalled his grandfather sharing one embarrassing moment from that time. "One story he told, this was during the Depression, he was going to get a meal, and he got to the counter to pay for it, and he had stolen some sugar packets—sugar was being rationed or something in those days—and the guy says, 'it's $2.40 for the meal. And 40¢ for the sugar.'"

Nevertheless, as a grandfather, Thomas seems to have escaped the pall of those times.

"I have nothing but fond memories of him," George said.

I wondered whether George had ever seen his grandfather's Craftsmanship Award.

"I had pictures of it!" he exclaimed.

He was referring to the bronze plaque in the lobby, partly confirming Al Smith's belief that the plaque would remain a touchstone for the award winners' families down through the generations. But George was unaware that his grandfather had received an award certificate and a gold button at a formal ceremony in the building.

"I never saw that," he said of the framed Craftsmanship Award and the gold lapel pin, of which the New York Building Congress was so proud. "And I'm sure I'd remember if I had."

It wasn't something he had hanging on his wall at home? I asked.

"Definitely not. I remember going to his home often, and I never saw anything like it. It wouldn't have surprised me if, when they were moving some time, say from house A to house B, he said, 'Aw, screw it. I don't need that thing.'"

Frank W. Pierson Jr. came from a family of metalworkers, two of whom were named Frank Pierson. This created some confusion in identifying the man in Hiram Myers's photo. In the 1910 census, Frank W. Pierson, then thirty-four years old, lived on West 125th Street with his wife, two sons, and his father. Frank was born in May 1875 in Chicago. His younger son, also named Frank, was born in New York in January 1908. By 1930, both Franks were metal lathers. Which one appears in Hiram Myers's photo? The younger Frank Pierson was twenty-two years old in 1930. Judging from the portrait itself, it seems more probable that the father, by then age fifty-four, received the award. But perhaps both men were on the job at the Empire State Building.

An employment record shows the elder Frank W. Pierson working in the Panama Canal Zone in 1914 but does not specify his profession. According to his 1918 draft registration, however, he was a metal lather for Henry Steers & Co., located on the Brooklyn-Queens waterfront.

At the Empire State Building, as indicated on his portrait, the award winner Frank W. Pierson worked for Martin Conroy & Sons Inc., a subcontractor for metal lathing and plastering. On August 14, 1930, the company had forty-nine men at work on the Empire State: forty-five lathers, three laborers, and a foreman, performing work on the tenth through seventeenth floors.

In 1940, the father, by now a widower, lived with his son and daughter-in-law on Woodycrest Avenue, the Bronx. Both men were still working

Frank W. Pierson Jr., metal lather, photographed by Hiram Myers.

as "wire lathers." The father, Frank W. Pierson, died in 1953 and is buried in Sparkill, Rockland County, New York. An entry in the official Florida Death Index shows that the son, Frank Woodruff Pierson Jr., died at age seventy-eight, on March 13, 1986, in Pinellas County, Florida.

⁂

Owen Scanlon, the marble setter's helper photographed by Hiram Myers, worked for William Bradley & Son Inc., a legendary marble yard located in Long Island City. *Transportation*, the giant sculpture adorning the entrance to Grand Central Terminal in New York City, was carved from Indiana limestone at the yard. The firm also cut the marble for the Chrysler Building, the Frick mansion (now the Frick Collection), and many other famous buildings in New York. The fact that Scanlon worked for William Bradley & Son Inc. helps to place him more specifically at the worksite. This company subcontracted for the marble work in the Empire State Building's lobby. Interior marble work above the lobby was performed by a different subcontractor, the Traitel Marble Company.

Setting the marble in the Empire State's lobby proved to be a serious challenge for the builders, beginning with the selection of the stone, since few quarries could supply sufficient quantities in the time necessary to complete construction. "The final selection," as H. R. Dowswell, a member of Shreve, Lamb, and Harmon's staff, reported in *The Architectural Forum*, "was Belgian Black base surmounted by a colorful combination of Estrellante and Rose Famosa." Yet this decision presented practical problems.

> Colorful marbles are invariably unsound and consequently difficult to cut, transport and set. On the Empire State Building, it was felt that the unusual height of the marble wall facing, some of which extends through three stories, demanded that every precaution be taken to insure permanency. It was accordingly decided to line completely the back of all Estrellante and Rose Famosa marble facing with an absolutely sound material. Ozark Missouri Gray marble 7/8" thick was accordingly secured, with German cement, to the back of each piece of wall facing, and the double thick material set and anchored in the usual manner.

Further detail is revealed in an advertisement placed in the Delaware *Milford Chronicle*:

> It may be interesting to know that the L.D. Cault Company supplied the material that was used in the interior construction of the Empire State Building, New York. After the famosa

Owen Scanlon, marble setter's helper, photographed by Hiram Myers.

> stone was cemented on the limestone and placed in position in the building, the famosa stone separated from the limestone and fell in the corridors. This was due to the difference in the expansion of the two stones when subjected to a marked change in temperature. When this condition took place The Caulk Company was called into consultation and in their research department developed a material that met their every requirement and enabled the contractors to finish their contract on time. So when you visit the Empire State Building and you look upon the beautiful interior finish of the corridors, it will be interesting to know that the cement which holds the beautiful stones in place was manufactured by The L.D. Caulk Company, Milford, Del.

It's possible to trace Owen Scanlon with comparable precision to his birthplace in County Leitrim, Ireland. He appears in the Irish census of

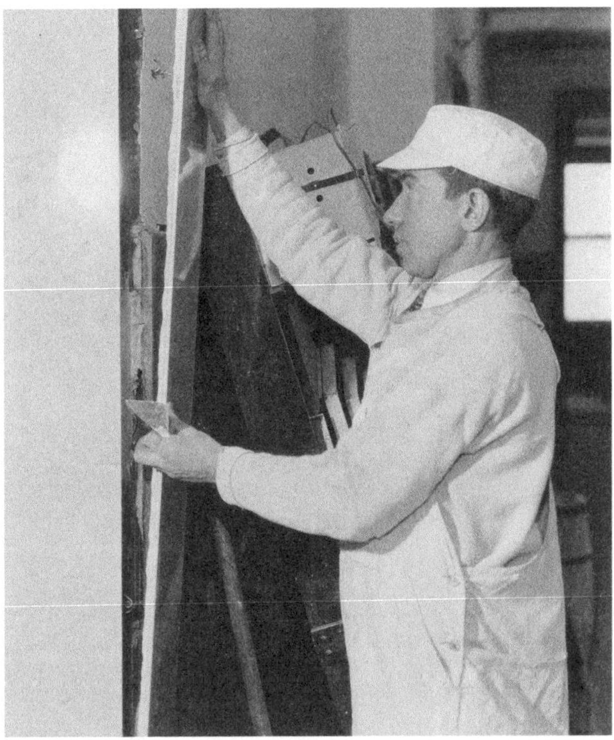

1911, age five, living on a farm with his parents and five older siblings. His 1927 Declaration of Intention indicates Scanlon immigrated to the US aboard the ship SS *Samaria*, arriving in New York on October 26, 1926. In the Ellis Island database, an Owen Scanlon does arrive with his father on this ship and date, headed for the home of his brother, Thomas, at 407 West Fifty-First Street between Ninth and Tenth Avenues. Thomas, nine years older than Owen, had arrived in the US six years earlier. On the Declaration of Intention, Owen gives his birthday as May 15, 1906, meaning he was twenty-one when he arrived. According to that document, he had a "ruddy" complexion. He's five feet nine, 150 pounds, with brown hair and gray eyes.

While Owen's profession is initially "laborer," his brother's declaration lists "Marble Setter's Helper" as his occupation. Owen's professional path thus appears to have been preordained. One year later, in 1927, when Owen petitions for US citizenship, he has also become a "Marble Setter's Helper." That document is witnessed by his two brothers, Thomas and James. James, too, is a marble setter's helper. In 1930, when Owen Scanlon won the Craftsmanship Award, he lived with Thomas, by

Ferruccio Mariutto, terrazzo worker, photographed by Hiram Myers.

then thirty-two, and his sister Rose, age thirty, on Amsterdam Avenue in Manhattan between Eighty-Eighth and Eighty-Ninth Streets. All three brothers may have worked on the Empire State Building.

Six years later, Owen Scanlon died in a car accident. The *Poughkeepsie Eagle-News* for August 6, 1936, reported that Scanlon had "lost control of the car on a steep grade" while driving on Tongue Mountain, near Lake George, New York. Scanlon initially survived the accident with two broken legs. But he died in the hospital the following day. He was twenty-nine years old.

Ferruccio Mariutto, the award-winning terrazzo worker, is the last craftsman identified in the photos taken by Hiram Myers. Mariutto was employed by the De Paoli Del Turco Foscato Corporation, which had its office on West

Forty-Fifth Street in Manhattan. On the note scribbled on the back of his portrait, Mariutto's home address is given as 931 Quincy Avenue, the Bronx.

Both Mariutto and another award winner, Pietro Vescovi, are mentioned in an article by Javier Grossutti of the University of Trieste, discussing the contributions to American construction by craftsmen from the northern Italian region of Friuli. According to Grossutti, the company, L. Del Turco & Bros., was established in 1910 by Louis Del Turco, an immigrant from Sequals, about sixty-five miles north of Venice and a famous center of terrazzo work for centuries. Del Turco soon after joined with a company founded in 1899 by Vincent Foscato and continued by his two sons. The combined firm did terrazzo and tile work for many New York buildings, including the Steinway Building, Rockefeller Center, Lincoln Center, the United Nations Building, the Holland and Lincoln Tunnels, and the Guggenheim Museum. Despite virulent racial prejudice against Italians, Grossutti writes, mosaic and terrazzo workers from the Friuli region were recognized as "highly specialized labourers." They were well paid and belonged to "the upper class of the labour force."

Ferruccio Ettore Mariutto was born on January 14, 1912, in Koblenz, Germany. This is documented by both a 1931 and a 1933 Declaration of Intention to become a United States citizen. The latter document bears a photograph that confirms this is the same man who appears in the portrait by Hiram Myers. According to the 1933 document, Mariutto had immigrated on December 7, 1928, on the vessel *Roma* from Genoa. His previous residence was Cavasso Nuove, Italy. His occupation, "Terrazzo mechanic." He's five feet five, 160 pounds, and seventeen years old.

At the time of his work on the Empire State Building, Mariutto was nineteen. He lived as a boarder at the home of Arthur Miani in the Bronx. A 1928 photo shows the neighborhood populated by single-story, wood-frame homes, though it was not far from the former Henry C. Overing mansion, a grand residence which had by that time become the headquarters of the Eastern Mission Association, run by the Apostolic Lutheran Church. Mariutto's living arrangements were auspicious because a few years later, on May 5, 1935, he married Anna Miani, the niece of his landlord. Their connection does not appear to have been coincidental, however. The Mariutto and Miani families had been intermarrying for generations. Ferruccio's sister Luigia married Gino Miani, himself the son of a Miani-Mariutto match. And a generation earlier, Ferruccio's uncle, Angelo Pietro Mariutto, had married Luigia Miani.

In 1940, Ferruccio and Anna were living with their two-year-old son and Anna's extended family at the same address on Quincy Avenue, on the eastern edge of the Bronx, near the current on-ramp to the Throgs Neck Bridge. The household included her parents and her three siblings, ages fifteen to twenty-two, as well as her father's brother and his family, thirteen people altogether. All the adult men were terrazzo workers.

The documents do not show how the family weathered the Depression. However, they seem to have prospered. In 1938, now age twenty-six, Mariutto traveled to England aboard the *Queen Mary*. He described his profession as "manufacturer," though he still lived at the same address in the Bronx. In 1950, Mariutto appeared twice in *The New York Times* as the purchaser of property in the Bronx. Ferruccio Mariutto died on January 1, 1976, and is buried in Mount Hope Cemetery, Hastings-on-Hudson, New York.

"I'm brokenhearted as I hear you talk about this," said Robin Mariutto, Ferruccio's granddaughter, when I shared with her what I had learned from the documents. "My dad and my uncle Fred would have loved to talk to you. And my grandmother, Anna, she would have been a font of information. She could have given you the names of everyone on the crew."

Robin was only eight years old when Ferruccio Mariutto, her grandfather, died of lung cancer, possibly mesothelioma related to asbestos exposure. According to Robin, Anna's father, Ugolino Miani, had been the foreman at the Empire State Building on the terrazzo crew that included Ferruccio.

"I do remember my grandmother telling me—here's how she put it: when the Empire State Building was going up, they were giving out the Craftsmanship Award, and she called it 'a project to make the men feel better about building the skyline of New York.' And what she said was—Ugolino had won the award on the Chrysler building. When they wanted to give it to him for the Empire State Building, too, he said, 'I've already won it. Give it to my son-in-law.'"

This may be an instance where family memory and documentation collide. Ugolino Miani is not listed as one of the award winners for the Chrysler Building. Indeed, I could find no record of Ugolino Miani's Craftsmanship Award, either in the *Building Congress News* or in contemporary newspaper accounts of the many award ceremonies. However, not all awards were reported, and the *Building Congress News* mentioned only some ceremonies and listed the award winners' names for only some of these. Perhaps his award was for an unremarked, lesser-known building, or perhaps the story serves more as a description of Ugolino's character than as a verifiable fact beyond family history.

"Tile, terrazzo, and marble have been in our family a long, long time," Robin recalled, adding that whenever the family went out to a store or a restaurant, the men would look at the floor and critique the job.

"My uncle Fred talked about 'the dance,'" she continued. "When they're putting down terrazzo floors, there are chips that are shiny, that sparkle. The only one who's allowed to lay those is the foreman. They carry a bag—what do they call it? A crossbody, with the marble chips."

For the Empire State Building, the marble chips were of three types, Botticino, imported from Italy, Belgian black, from Belgium, and Cardiff green, from Maryland.

"To get a good distribution," explained Robin, "you have to spread them evenly. You do this wild-ass throw that distributes the marble chips across the floor. That's the mark of the artist. That's the sign of the master, that spread of the marble." Robin sighed. "I wish I had a video of him doing this."

As the documents had shown, the family lived together in the Bronx, eventually building their own house.

"The three brothers, each had a floor in the house they built. There was land all around them," Robin said. "Though it's hard to believe now, they literally would go out on Thanksgiving morning and shoot a pheasant for Thanksgiving dinner." She added that Ferruccio was an avid hunter and fisherman. The family still has a video, taken on a family vacation in Florida, that shows Ferruccio fishing. "And the look on his face," Robin marveled, "it was the happiest my father had ever seen him."

Perhaps because Robin's stories came down primarily through her grandmother, Ferruccio's wife, Anna, the figure of her great-grandfather, Ugolino, was especially important in her recollections. According to her, Ugolino had sponsored Ferruccio when he emigrated to the US. The family had retained close contact with their relatives in Italy, and as Robin recounted it, Ferruccio's father had written to Ugolino, worrying, "If he doesn't get out of this town, he's going to end up a criminal." Ugolino had taken the young man under his wing.

"He came to this country as a skilled schoolboy," Robin said. "He apprenticed while he was here." Robin also had the suspicion that Ferruccio and Anna's marriage may have been arranged, "part of the agreement for bringing him over to the US."

While Ferruccio died relatively young, at age sixty-four, Anna had a much longer life. "Grandma Anna, she was my personal hero," Robin said. A widow for more than thirty-eight years, Anna lived to one hundred and remained devoted to Ferruccio's memory.

"She wanted to make sure the grandkids knew him and knew how proud he and she were to be Americans," Robin said. "I asked her once in the 1990s if she missed him—he'd been gone for a long time by then. And she said, 'Yes. It's such a shame he's missing out seeing his grandchildren growing up.'"

I wondered what Robin remembered of Ferruccio directly.

"He spoke with a very heavy accent," she replied. "If you'd told me he was talking Italian, I would have been, 'Okay.'" She laughed at the recollection. "This was a man who taught himself English by reading Dear Abby in the newspaper! And you know how they have the questions and answers? He would always say 'An-*swear*.'"

But Ferruccio's memory was important to her, and the Craftsmanship Award had, in its own way, become the medium though which Robin and her family remembered him.

"My relatives, they did take me to see grandpa's name in the Empire State Building," she said. "And anytime a friend tells me they're going to New York, I tell them to go see the plaque in the lobby." She laughed again, "And every time they go, they bring me a picture of it, as if I'd never seen it before."

Yet the work on the Empire State Building and the Craftsmanship Award were not something that had occupied the family while Ferruccio was alive.

"I can tell you honestly, no. It didn't become a thing until after he died. That plaque, that award, it gave the grandchildren a connection to their grandfather, who they might not otherwise have had a chance to remember," Robin said. "I wish you had called eight months ago," she continued after a pause. "In June my father passed away. I know he would have enjoyed this call." She choked up at the missed opportunity.

It wasn't the Craftsmanship Award or even the Empire State Building in any general, public sense that moved her, but rather this personal, intimate feeling, the connections and losses that suddenly became present to her when she thought about the role the award played in her family.

Second Craftsmanship Award ceremony, February 11, 1931.

The notes on the back of Hiram Myers's photographs are the last documentation from Empire State Inc. concerning the men who won Empire State Craftsmanship Awards. For the remaining eleven men, connecting their names and faces, and determining details of their lives, depended on the contingencies of public documentation, which create their own random selection process, allowing some men to step forward against the dark background, while others remain vanishingly faint.

All of the sixteen Craftsmanship Award winners in the second group appear in a photo published in the *Building Congress News* in March 1931, documenting the ceremony that took place a month earlier, on February 11. The men are arranged in two rows, each holding his award certificate. Based on the information scribbled on the back of Hiram Myers's portraits, it is possible to identify five of the men. Two more men, whose portraits do not appear to have been taken by either Lewis Hine or Hiram Myers, can nevertheless be identified as well.

Painting and decorating on the Empire State Building required only two months and did not begin until March 1931. Perhaps by this time, both Hine and Myers had moved on to other projects. But George R. Adams, the award-winning painter, can be seen standing in the center of the group photo in white overalls, displaying his Certificate of Superior Craftsmanship with a hint of a smile on his face. I was able to identify him by locating another photo, taken years later and published online on a genealogy website. In the later photo, Adams looks at the camera with a down-turned mouth. But in both photos, he has the same oval, bald head and slightly bulging forehead, unmistakably the same person.

When he worked on the Empire State Building, the painter George Adams was thirty years old and lived with his wife and their daughter, in Hempstead, Long Island. He was born on August 5, 1899. His father was a housepainter as well. The family can trace its roots at least as far back as Buckley Adams, born 1788 in Lincoln, Massachusetts. He appears to be distantly related to the second US president, John Adams.

George R. Adams,
painter and decorator.

According to his obituary in *The Brooklyn Daily Eagle*, George Robert Adams died on March 21, 1949. The article describes a man deeply connected to his community. He was "active in church and fraternal circles"; was a member of the Advance Hook and Ladder Company in Wantagh; and was a member of the advisory board of Bellmore Assembly, Order of Rainbow for Girls. George Adams's granddaughter confirmed these details. But she had no personal or family recollections of her grandfather, who had died long before she was born.

William Deneen, elevator constructor's helper, is another man who seems to have escaped the notice of both Lewis Hine and Hiram Myers, but who can nevertheless be identified in the group photo of the Craftsmanship Award winners.

Originally, I had identified someone else as William Deneen. Lewis Hine took both a portrait and a work photo of another elevator constructor, with a caption that clearly identifies the man's job.

But a fragile thread of genealogical research was sufficient to find William Deneen's son, also named William Deneen, known as Bill, who quickly corrected my mistake.

Unknown elevator constructor, photographed by Lewis Hine.

"The photo of the worker which you sent does not appear to me to have any resemblance to my father," he wrote when I shared Hine's portrait with him. Instead, he identified a different man in the photo published in the *Building Congress News*.

"My father died when I was ten," Bill Deneen said. "He was working for Sealtest Dairies. He actually died on the job, a heart attack. I think he was a delivery man."

The Social Security Administration lists Deneen's date of death as June 25, 1958. He was fifty years old.

"I remember him as a big, strong man, though that's probably from a ten-year-old's perspective. Hard worker, very religious. Catholic."

William Deneen, elevator constructor's helper.

After William Deneen's death, Bill and his family moved from Ardsley, New York, to North Carolina, where his mother had relatives.

"They were reserved people to begin with," he said. "And in North Carolina, they were pretty isolated."

I asked whether William's work on the Empire State and his Craftsmanship Award were something the family talked about.

"No. They didn't make as much of a to-do about it as we do these days," he replied. He could not recall anyone speaking of it during his childhood, even when his father was alive.

"I don't know that we ever went to the Empire State Building when we lived in New York."

I wondered then how he knew about his father's contribution to the building.

"It was probably finding this commemorative plaque," Bill responded, referring to the award certificate William Deneen holds in the photo. "It was packed away. My mother had it, but you didn't exactly see it. And when my mother died, I was the executor. The first time I saw it was when I went through her stuff. My wife had it framed for me."

The certificate now hangs in Bill's office.

"There's a certain amount of pride that your father was such a well-respected person," he admitted.

Bill's son, Andrew, had taken an interest in the award when he saw it as a young man.

"I have a recollection of the certificate showing up framed in our house, and then asking about that," he remembered.

He had tried to find more information about his grandfather's work on the Empire State.

"I've spent a lot of time looking through the Hine photographs that are available in the online collection," he said. "It's been a dream to get into the archive and find the definitive photo of my grandfather."

One man among Hine's portraits of Craftsmanship Award winners may be tentatively identified by his clothing. Perhaps this man is Frank J. Klein, plasterer. It would be typical for plasterers and painters to wear white overalls, as can be seen in the photo of the second group of award winners, where George Adams, painter, is also in white. In this photo, the distinctive hat would also tend to identify the man as belonging to the indoor trades. Spots of plaster or paint can be seen on the brim of his hat and on his neck. In the background, we see unfinished masonry surrounding a structural column and what may be the edge of a ladder, just above the man's shoulder.

The name Frank J. was common among German or Austrian immigrants, who bore the Americanized version of the Hapsburg kaiser's name, Franz Josef. Three men in the 1930 census seem like possibilities. One was a mason, one a paint mixer at a paint factory. The third is a plasterer, although the census gives the industry as "house building," not construction. This Frank J. Klein is twenty-two years old, living on East Seventy-Fourth Street, Brooklyn, with his parents. But visually, that seems too young to be the man in this photo.

Whether or not this is the right man, the Frank J. Klein who won a Craftsmanship Award on the Empire State Building probably worked for Martin Conroy & Sons Inc., 110 West Fortieth Street in Manhattan. The plastering contract for the building was large enough to warrant its own paragraph in *The New York Sun*. The plaster supplier, Structural Gypsum Corporation, also placed advertisements in several trade journals, boasting that its products were being used on the highest building in the world. But none of the men who performed the work is mentioned in the newspapers.

⁂

Frank J. Klein, plasterer (tentative).

Pietro Vescovi, who won a Craftsmanship Award as a terrazzo worker's helper, is the final member of the second group of award winners who may be tentatively identified, in this case, by his mustache. In a strange coincidence, a professional contact of mine happened to mention that his college roommate was the grandson of an Empire State construction worker named Vescovi. Indeed, Jim Vescovi's grandfather, Antonio Vescovi, was a terrazzo worker, who himself won a Craftsmanship Award in April 1930

Pietro Vescovi, terrazzo worker's helper (tentative).

for his work on 40 Wall Street. Pietro Vescovi, who won the award for the Empire State, was a cousin or an uncle. As a child, Jim heard stories about him, passed down from his grandfather to his father to him.

"He was short, pretty stocky, and very strong," Jim related when I spoke with him on the phone. "Pietro and Antonio would argue about who was stronger."

One story involved each man lifting the other over his head to prove his strength. Beyond that, Jim said, "he loved to drink white wine. He would come over to my grandfather's on Saturdays and drink. Most of them made their own wine and kept it in the cellar."

Jim never met Pietro Vescovi. But looking at Lewis Hine's photos, he identified this man. "That looks a lot like my grandfather," he said. "Same mustache."

Genealogical information, however, makes this identification highly tentative.

Like Ferruccio Mariutto, the other terrazzo worker to receive a Craftsmanship Award, Pietro Vescovi is mentioned in Javier Grossutti's paper, "Emigration from Friuli Venezia Giulia Towards the United States." This source identifies Vescovi's birthplace as Berceto di Parma, about halfway between Genoa and Bologna, in northern Italy. But this turns out to be incorrect.

Pietro Vescovi does indeed arrive in the United States from Castellonchio, Parma, about five miles from Berceto, aboard the SS *Giulio Cesare* on September 19, 1923. He's sixteen years old, which would make him twenty-four in 1931 when he won a Craftsmanship Award, too young to be the man in this photo. When this Pietro Vescovi arrived in the US, he joined his father, Giuseppe, who had emigrated much earlier, in May 1875, at age twenty-four. The father had immigrated with another Pietro Vescovi, perhaps the grandfather. But in 1923, the younger Pietro, who would go on to help build the Empire State, was returning to the US, not arriving. He was born in New York, not Italy. A handwritten note on the 1923 manifest indicates that he presented his birth certificate on arrival. His birthdate was June 2, 1907. A New York City record shows a "Peter" Vescovi born on this date to a family residing at 42-15 Twenty-Third Avenue, in Astoria, Queens. The only other record I could find for Peter Vescovi was the Social Security Death Index in January 1986. His last residence was Long Island City, just a few blocks from where he was born.

⁂

For the final winners of Craftsmanship Awards—seven from the second group, and one from the first group, cement mason Gino Santoni—my search was inconclusive. At the first award ceremony, in October 1930, Al Smith had said the names on the bronze plaque in the building's lobby would be preserved as a statement, a testimonial to the men's contribution to their city, their state, and their country. But as the publicity surrounding the award ceremonies died away, and attention turned to the grand story of the building as a monument, these names were left in its shadow. At the scale of the individual, where precise names become significant, not enough information survived for me to connect the names and the faces. Only in a few cases did biographical research yield some material. I could find no Gino Santoni, for example, but several Eugene *Santinis*. Perhaps this name, too, is misrepresented on the award plaque. Here is where the image becomes blurriest and the bronze tablet in the building's lobby turns opaque. We know the men's names, more or less. It seems probable we have at least some of their photos. But for now, at least, the connections between the names and the faces cannot be restored. Like Hine's dissociated portraits, they confront us not as statements, but as questions. The new who's who.

These are the remaining names:

John Connolly, Roofer;
Joseph Leffert, Tile Setter's Helper;
R. Maddalena, Tile Setter;
William L. Moran, Steamfitter's Helper;
John E. O'Connor, Plumber;
Gino Santoni, Cement Mason;
Louis Shane Jr., Marble Setter;
Clifford Smith, Electrician.

And these are the faces of unidentified workers on the Empire State Building, at least some of whom, based on their resemblance to men who appear in the group portrait published in the *Building Congress News*, were winners of Empire State Craftsmanship Awards.

Unidentified workers.

Unidentified workers.

NINE
THE SKY BOY

On June 16, 1931, columnist Henry W. Clune noted one very conspicuous way that Belle Moskowitz made use of Lewis Hine's magnificent photographs of the men who built the Empire State. "Turning the corner of this fantastic modern Babel recently, I noticed a whole main-floor window devoted to photographs of the workmen who actually had lifted up and secured in place the tiered beams that reached ultimately to the lower stratum of cloud mists." Shortly after the building's grand opening, the corner windows at Fifth Avenue and Thirty-Third Street became a showcase for Hine's portraits. Clune, one of the first to review Hine's Empire State photos, provides a characteristic gloss on the men. "Below the serrated lines of forehead, clear eyes that held the half twinkle of D'Artagnan adventures looked straight out at their beholders."

Nor was Empire State the only office building to highlight Hine's extraordinary images. An undated memo from Publicity Associates indicates that "the New York Times has agreed to place a number of Mr. Hine's photographs in their Times Square windows." As the Great Depression entered its second year, Moskowitz must have recognized the public relations value of celebrating the building's May 1 opening with a heroic display of workmen, rather than as a triumph of American business. Noting this about-face in the building's publicity strategy in *The Skyscraper in American Art, 1890–1931*, Merrill Schleier writes, "Raskob's and Smith's working-class roots, Hine's sympathetic views of the skyscraper builder, and the realities of the Depression shifted the emphasis from the businessman to the common man. In the face of rampant unemployment, the omnipotent workman was a source of hope and a role model for the struggling masses." A contemporary note in *The Daily Worker* offered a less detached perspective on this display of Hine's photos. "I wish to call your attention to the irony of the recent picture exhibition shown in the windows of the Empire State Building. They are 'art-photos' of the proletariat who constructed the skyscraper. Now they are out of work. And all the benefit and value of their labor goes to Al. Smith [*sic*] and company." Another contributor to the *Daily Worker* was harsher. "The gall of Al Smith and other owners of the building, to show a photo exhibition of workers who built it, workers who gave their lives to put it up—who own not one brick in it, and are not allowed to enter it except to scrub the floors and are now jobless and hungry."

In pictures of the display, found in the archives of the architects, we can see rock driller Michael Tierney featured prominently, along with many other Hine photos that would eventually become among the best-recognized images in American photography. The exhibit itself attracted public attention and over the coming months it would appear in other venues as well. Hine titled it *The Human Element in Skyscrapers*.

These prominent displays, along with the excitement and ubiquitous publicity in the run-up to the building's grand opening, gave a lift to Lewis Hine's career. *The Survey Graphic* published a well-received, multipage spread of Hine's images in January 1931, titled "Up from the City Streets," in a nod to the 1928 biography of Al Smith, written by Belle Moskowitz's husband, Dr. Henry Moskowitz. A few weeks later, Hine delightedly informed Paul Kellogg, "World's Week has just waked up to my existence and is using special stuff and wants more. A raft of lesser lights are using the skyboys and altogether a little stream of shekels trickles in and the applecart job seems more remote." Hine began to garner national attention for his work, and he shared his gratitude with Paul Kellogg in another letter ringing in equal measure with vindication and humility. "It was only a year ago, come St. Patricks' (the birthday of Al's Big Shanty), that I decided to move out into the open spaces where there is less overhead and more under foot, for I thought I had shot my best bolts and was ready for the armchair by the fire. Some subsequentials would indicate that there is a lot of wallop in the old Model T, if only the supply of gas and oil holds out. There is nothing to brag about but a deal to be thankful for." In a touching addendum to one letter, Hine thanks his friends for their years of support. "I want to tell you I shall always remember what a factor you two and Survey have been in putting my stuff on the map, to

Hine's photos on display in the Empire State Building, May 1931.

say nothing of what your appreciation and encouragement have meant all through the first quarter century of Hineography. The other three quarters ought to be that much easier."

Hine expected the success of his Empire State images to lead to more opportunities, and he requested advance copies of *The Survey Graphic*'s photo story to present to Josef Israels, Belle Moskowitz's son and partner at Publicity Associates. Israels responded enthusiastically, promising "to circulate it among the directors of Empire State."

But despite the powerful men who had employed him, no further work came from Empire State Inc. Belle Moskowitz, who might have continued to promote Hine's work, died suddenly on January 2, 1933, from complications following a fall. Her death marked the end of Hine's support from Publicity Associates, and it marked the end of an era for Al Smith, as well, whose outlook turned increasingly embittered and politically conservative.

Economic conditions continued to worsen, and the success Hine hoped for failed to materialize. Some magazine work came his way, and the Red Cross hired him to document the plight of flood victims in Mississippi. But soon the commissions died down. *The Survey Graphic* was unable to provide sufficient work to sustain him. And while he was briefly successful in obtaining a position documenting the Tennessee Valley Authority in 1933, differences with management led to Hine's early departure. He never again had a major photographic project.

By 1936, he was writing to Paul Kellogg, "I certainly appreciate your many efforts to keep the Work Portraits idea alive,—I often feel the results do not justify all the bloodshed." In 1938, Hine applied for a grant from the Carnegie Corporation, and then in 1939 from the Guggenheim Foundation. The project he proposed was entitled, "Photographic Interpretation of Some Phases of American Craftsmanship." Writing to Henry W. Kent, secretary of the Metropolitan Museum of Art, to ask whether Kent would serve on the new project's advisory committee, Hine described it as "an interpretive photographic survey of our American craftspeople and the adaptation of their crafts to present-day needs." Using terms familiar from his previous statements of intention, he added, "This is not a personal matter but is one that could have a deep, social significance as a means of education for the present and future generations." He was turned down for both grants.

In a June 21, 1938, letter to Roy Stryker, Hine complained of his impoverishment. "The Hine fortunes are at an all-time low and if they do not change in the near future, or at least show some evidence of real prospects, the Home Owners Loan Corp. will have to foreclose on the place and we will wander forth to cheaper pastures." The letter of foreclosure arrived at Hine's home in Hastings on September 1, 1939. Hine concluded an arrangement with the bank to rent the house on a month-by-month basis. But the Federal Home Loan Bank Board repossessed the formal deed on December 19, 1939. Just a few days later, on Christmas morning, Sara Rich Hine, Hine's wife of thirty-four years, died.

In October 1940, Hine conceived a new project, for which he again sought foundation funding. "I propose making a series of photo-studies dealing with the life of representative individuals of foreign extraction to show their reactions to and influence upon our American democracy." His "Plan for Work" shows Hine remaining faithful to his pedagogical language and to the ideals of Ethical Culture. "If 'Our strength is our people,' this project should give us light on the kinds of strength we have to build upon as a nation. Much emphasis is being put upon the dangers inherent in our alien groups, our unassimilated or even partly Americanized citizens—criticism based upon insufficient knowledge. A corrective for this would be better facilities for seeing, and so understanding, what the facts are, both in possible dangers and real assets."

Hine did not live to fulfill the project. He died a month later on November 4, 1940.

"Hine was a pure 'primitive.'" He was "a naïve, untaught, determined little man . . . quiet, incorruptible." "Kindly, trustful, wistful, amazingly innocent. He looks like an unworldly schoolteacher, needing protection from the rigors of the everyday world."

It was left to journalists and art historians to define Hine as a man and as an artist. Elizabeth McCausland, a prominent art critic, who, along with her partner, photographer Berenice Abbott, met Hine in his last years and helped to mount a retrospective of his work in 1938, commended his "genuinely simple and sturdy soul." As a subject of critical attention, Hine thus suffered a fate similar to the Empire State Building workers he had photographed. Like the workmen, he was defined by others' ideas about him, fashioned into a one-dimensional symbol of American virtue. In an essay from 1938, "Portrait of a Photographer," written to accompany the retrospective, McCausland wrote: "To understand the character, both of the man and of the period, we cannot turn to literature. The nineteenth-century American writers furnish no prototype for men like Hine. Yet Hine is as American as the 'Oshkosh B'Gosh' from which he hails." In McCausland's rendering, Hine was an example of "Yankee genius," a man of ingenuity, cunning, and a tough moral clarity. "Certainly, if ever a man spoke the American vernacular it is Lew Hine. He looks like a wheat farmer. Despite his Pd.M. from New York University in 1905, he talks like one." The image stuck and seventy-five years later, it still defined him. Instead of a man of grand vision, instead of an artist of deep insight or empathy, he was portrayed as a kind of folk hero, with "a naivete both lovable and sad." Daile Kaplan, who discovered a large cache of photographs Hine made for the Red Cross during World War I, writes, "Hine remained the perennial innocent whose personal values were rooted in a traditional Midwestern upbringing—independent, moral, and at times perhaps a bit corny."

Almost as soon as they became public, Hine's Empire State photographs drifted away from the circumstances of their creation and became instead free-floating symbols, subsumed in the grander narrative of American progress. The interpersonal qualities that made Hine's portraits so affecting did not translate well into the conceptual language of art history. Unable to discern in Hine himself the bearing suited to the importance of his achievement, critics reached for larger concepts by which to lend the images the desired stature. Daile Kaplan argues that "the Empire State Building series . . . mirrored the socialist-realist 'heroic worker' portraits produced by the Soviet photographer Alexandr Rodchenko." Art historian Freddy Langer believed the photographs express "faith in technology and the ideal of a new, progressive urbanism." Kate Sampsell-Willmann, who recognizes the sympathy Hine felt for the men he photographed, interprets this as evidence that Hine identified with them. In her reading, Hine saw himself, too, as a craftsman, and his portraits of workers are really self-portraits. "From the sky boy to the watchmaker, Hine's workers were competent, confident, and happy. Hine obviously found joy in his own craft and saw the same emotion in others."

The Certificates of Superior Craftsmanship, which had honored the Empire State workmen by name, also dissociated from their historical context. Over time, the history of the awards and the identities of the men themselves—everything *but* their names—were forgotten. The bronze plaque that Al Smith proudly placed in the lobby became a bypassed curiosity, lost in the building's physical grandeur and the lobby's commercial busyness. Many of the men's faces, by contrast, became world famous, preserving their concentration as they worked and perhaps something of what we might call their humanity. But because Empire State Inc. emphasized their abstract value as publicity photos, and because critics seized on them as decontextualized symbols, the images ceased to honor individual men. This process was endorsed and accelerated by Hine's own quest to turn the men into representatives of the human spirit. Ironically, therefore, like the Craftsmanship Awards themselves, Hine's supremely personal photos of the men who built the Empire State Building finally obscured the individuals they documented in the same moment they preserved them. Hine deprived the men of their names. As a result, as individuals, they were rendered mute by the expressiveness of the photographs as art.

But the loss of context and connection was inherent in how Empire State Inc. had understood the project and made use of Hine's photographs. It was not a gradual effect of art history, nor the result of Hine's sociological ideals. "We all feel sure that your contribution to Empire State has been a most important one and that your pictures will be a reminder for many years to come of the fine human elements which went into the construction of Empire State," wrote Al Smith in a note of acknowledgment to Lewis Hine on June 19, 1931, six weeks after the grand opening and while Hine's images were on display in the building's windows. Smith thanked the photographer for his thoughtful work. "These interesting studies of the spectacular steel workers and more especially the fine portraits of ordinary working men do a great deal to humanize and popularize this monumental structure." Despite more than a year relentlessly touting the significance of the Craftsmanship Awards, former Governor Smith failed to recognize that the "ordinary workers" in the photographs were the same "superior" men whose hands he had shaken just months earlier, when he lauded them as "leaders in their particular line of trade" at two public ceremonies.

So quickly was the connection between names and faces severed.

Instead of the award winners, whose contributions to the building the commemorative plaque was supposed to immortalize, other men, other faces, became briefly famous in images that more neatly served the story of the

...aring Bird Perches 'Mid Forests of Steel

WAVING TO YOU—A "top-o'-the-morning" greeting is being waved to you by Carl Russell, one of the steel-nerved workers on the 102-story Empire State Building, at 5th Ave. and 34th St. He's at 1,048-foot altitude, with steel fastnesses all around him.

(International Newsreel)

Carl Percy Russell, "daring bird."

"omnipotent workman" as "a source of hope and a role model." These, too, were often disconnected from names and always from the actual lives the men led. But like the Craftsmanship Awards plaque, the significance of these images has been inverted by time, and rather than perpetuating an idealized cultural narrative, they may now become a form of individual memorial.

During the week of September 30, 1930, as steelwork on the eighty-sixth floor came to an end, a syndicated photo ran in papers around the country showing an ironworker sitting on top of a lone, jutting column. In one paper, the image ran with the title "Daring Bird Perches 'Mid Forest of Steel."

"A 'top-o'-the-morning' greeting is being waved to you by Carl Russell, one of the steel-nerved workers on the 102-story Empire State Building, at 5th Ave. and 34th St. He's at 1,048 altitude, with steel fastnesses all around him." Here again, a particular man is used as an example of a worker, and as a result he is both identified and generalized. The caption plays on the common misconception that all ironworkers were Irish, which Russell was not. It is a small instance, but still instructive for how in almost every case involving a worker, the needs of cultural mythology overwhelm accuracy and respect for the individual.

Carl Percy Russell was born on April 2, 1903, in Rainy River, Ontario, Canada, and died at age eighty-eight on November 29, 1991, at his home in Charlotte, Florida. His parents were Canadian of Scotch ancestry. The Canadian census of 1911 shows Russell, age eight, here called "Percy," living with his parents and five siblings in Algoma West, Ontario. In 1930, when this photo appeared in papers around the country, Russell was twenty-seven years old. He'd been in the United States since 1923 and had been married for five years to a woman named Lucille. The couple had a 2½-year-old daughter and lived in Leonia, New Jersey, just across the Hudson River from Manhattan. It's possible to find a few other snapshots of Carl Percy Russell. The record of his border crossing at Niagara Falls on June 23, 1923, exists. Then twenty years old, he is identified as an "elec. Helper." He was "seeking employment," headed to Globe, Arizona, where an uncle lived. Three years later, in his naturalization document from February 26, 1926, Russell had become an ironworker and lived at 96 Park Place, Brooklyn. He was 5 feet, 7½ inches tall, weighed 160 pounds, with blonde hair and blue eyes. Four years after that, he appeared in the newspapers, sitting on a steel column high over Manhattan and waving at the camera.

Other publicly accessible genealogical databases make it possible to follow Russell's daughter through her subsequent marriage up to the present time with the names of Russell's grandchildren and great-grandchildren, another way in which this immigrant helped to build America.

"My grandfather Carl Russell was an adventurer who was born on a farm in Saskatchewan, Canada," wrote Gail Lincoln, Carl Russell's granddaughter, in an email. "He left home at age 15 or 16 & worked his way across the country doing everything from logging to singing to make a living. He wound up in NY around 1910 & joined the iron workers union. He became part of a small group daring enough to work atop the skyscrapers with barely a net. He was completely fearless."

As is often the case, family memory and official documents tell different stories. According to Russell's naturalization papers, he did not arrive in the US until 1923, not 1910, as Gail believed; and according to his death certificate, Russell's birthplace was not Saskatchewan but Ontario. In contrast to cultural myths, the history of an individual, even recalled by a member of his own family, leads to questions and discrepancies. There is no way to determine whether the documents or the family lore are accurate. But when Gail searched for other mementoes of her grandfather's life, she rediscovered a brief biography, written as a family keepsake by Carl's brother, known as Jack. From this, a few personal details about Carl Russell came to light. He had worked on Rockefeller Center and the Golden Gate Bridge. During World War II, he helped to build the Alaska Highway. Following the war, he took jobs in South America. Professionally, he chose to go by his unused first name, Carl, although his family knew him as Percy. On the job, according to his brother, he grew "tired of being called a 'Limey'—the name Percy is very British."

Ninety years after he worked on the Empire State Building, Carl Percy Russell's identity is preserved in an anecdote. Reflecting on these details in her great-uncle's memoir, Gail Lincoln felt closer to her grandfather, whom she had known only as a child.

"It was nice to have the opportunity to see the book again. I first saw it as a teen & didn't appreciate at the time what a remarkable life he led."

In November and early December 1930, another isolated ironworker on the Empire State Building became momentarily famous in a syndicated

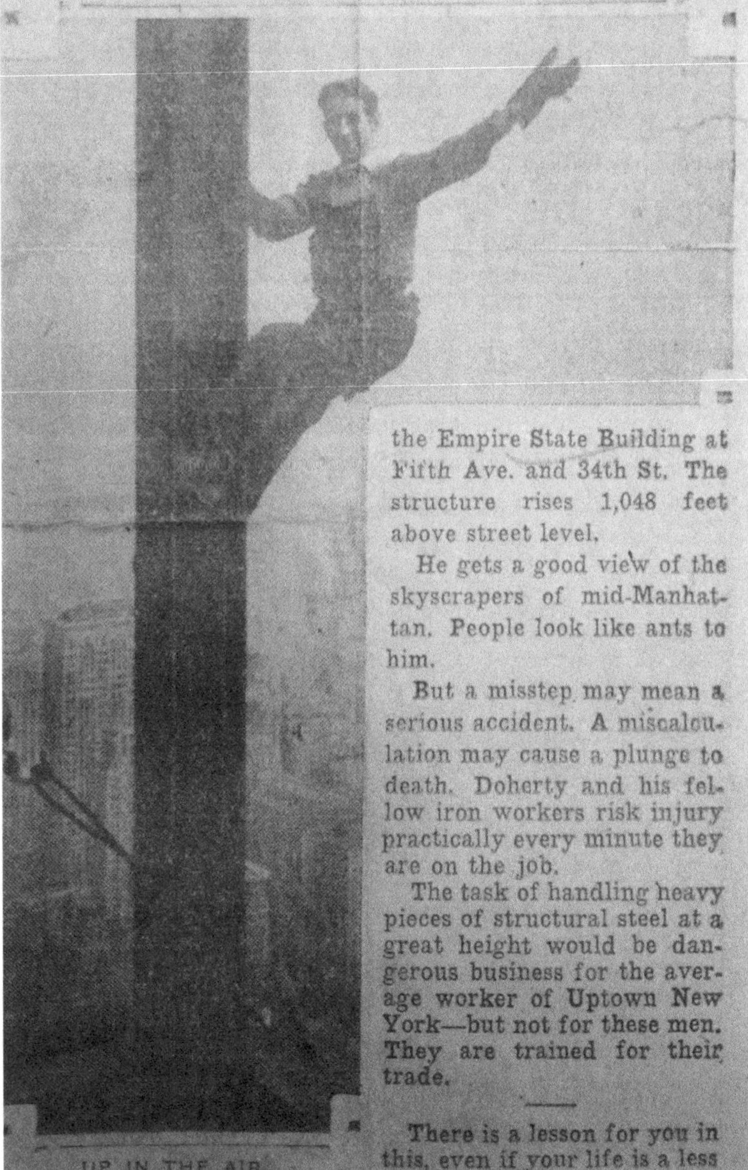

He Knows How

He Is Not Afraid.

Here is Neil Doherty, one of the unsung heroes of the air. Doherty, an iron worker, who lives at 1755 Jarvis Ave., The Bronx, is shown atop of the highest building in the world—the Empire State Building at Fifth Ave. and 34th St. The structure rises 1,048 feet above street level.

He gets a good view of the skyscrapers of mid-Manhattan. People look like ants to him.

But a misstep may mean a serious accident. A miscalculation may cause a plunge to death. Doherty and his fellow iron workers risk injury practically every minute they are on the job.

The task of handling heavy pieces of structural steel at a great height would be dangerous business for the average worker of Uptown New York—but not for these men. They are trained for their trade.

There is a lesson for you in this, even if your life is a less

UP IN THE AIR

Neil Doherty, "unsung hero of the air."

photograph, which shows him clambering halfway up a steel column. Papers captioned the image with a variety of blurbs: "Daring iron worker Niel [*sic*] Doherty, perched on the summit of the new Empire State Building, 1048 feet above the street. Pedestrians seem like bees and autos like toys to him." "It isn't everybody who can look down upon the Chrysler Building, which may be seen in the background, rearing aloft its silvered spire." In one instance, a paper provided not only Doherty's name, but also his home address, 1755 Jarvis Avenue, in the Bronx. Beneath the heading, "He Knows How. He Is Not Afraid," the caption reads: "Here is Neil Doherty, one of the unsung heroes of the air."

Neil Doherty was comparatively well documented at the time. He was among the small group of Empire State ironworkers who followed the construction all the way up, from its foundations through the topping out of the main structure on the eighty-sixth floor, and then went on to build the building's mooring mast. He appears in numerous photographs by Lewis Hine. One of these illustrates Margaret Norris and Brenda Ueland's article "Riding the Girders," published in *The Saturday Evening Post* on April 11, 1931, and was subsequently included in Norris's book, *Heroes and Hazards*. In this image, Doherty stands on a beam holding a heavy rope. He is not identified.

But Hine knew his name. On the back of a print of this photograph located at the George Eastman Museum, Hine had jotted it down, along with an address, and the note, "release," indicating his intention to publish the photo.

Doherty was also among the very few ordinary workers allowed to have his own voice. "It's just like anything else," he is quoted as saying about his job in an interview published in the New York *Home News* on November 9, 1930. "A person on solid ground never has any fear of falling. That's just the way you become up on the girders after a while, and you have to watch yourself as soon as you find yourself taking that attitude. Usually the two days off at the end of the week are enough to take away this carelessness. Going up to the top on Monday mornings, you are always inclined to be more careful for some reason or other."

Alone among all the surviving profiles of ironworkers, Doherty is granted a moment to reflect on his job, beyond its dangers and the thrills that excited journalists. "It's beautiful up there," he says, "and often I get a couple of minutes to watch the clouds down below us. They stretch out about 50 feet below us at times, and hide the whole city from view, but

Neil Doherty, ironworker.

they're nice to look at. We can look over into Jersey or up into Westchester, and on a clear day we can see as far as the Pocantico mountains, way up in North Westchester. The beam when the sun shines through the clouds is a pretty sight, too, and looks just like a long gold shaft of metal."

According to the article, Doherty was one of two Irishmen in his gang. In fact, Neil Doherty was born in Boston on September 28, 1898, the son of Irish immigrants. He died in Marlborough, Massachusetts, about thirty miles west of Boston, in September 1969.

*

Of all the workmen who helped to build the Empire State Building, however, two figures photographed by Lewis Hine have come to overshadow all the rest. Often referred to interchangeably as "the Sky Boy," the men in these two images became the enduring symbols of the skyscraper, the era, and the nation. One of them was profiled in 1931 and his identity has been known since then. The other remains a mystery.

Because so little information has survived, popular accounts of the construction of the Empire State Building usually converge on Victor "Frenchy" Gosselin. The very rare combination of personal details and exhilarating photos has made Gosselin the single best-known worker on the building. He was photogenic and charismatic, and in every portrayal of him, he epitomizes the cultural ideal that has so powerfully shaped our image of the workmen who built the Empire State.

Over the course of one or two days in September 1930, as steel construction was nearing its completion, Hine followed the work of a derrick gang, which raised and set the columns and girders in place. One man in particular caught his eye, and Hine took more pictures of him in these days than of any other worker at the Empire State. In these photos, the man is shirtless, wearing cutoff work pants. Sometimes he has the stub of a cigar in his mouth. One photograph especially appealed to Hine. In it, the worker hangs precariously on the load block of his derrick, an insouciant smirk on his face.

Prints of this photo, which are housed in numerous museum collections and research archives, frequently bear Hine's captions or notes on the back. One copy, at the Avery Architectural and Fine Arts Library, identifies the man by name, though the handwriting is not Hine's, leaving uncertain who provided the information.

Another extraordinary copy of the same image shows Hine at work, turning his original print into the iconic portrait that became world famous. Ruler-drawn lines show Hine preparing to crop the image, emphasizing Frenchy's pose and minimizing the context. Precise, pen-drawn outlines enhance the border between Frenchy's form and the sky beyond. Black shading on his features accentuates his expression. With these enhancements, the image became one of the two most reproduced photographs of the construction of the Empire State Building, published widely at the time and since, and eventually appearing along with eleven other Hine photos as a USPS Forever stamp in 2013, titled

"Man on Hoisting Ball, Empire State Building," from the series *Made in America: Building a Nation.*

Victor Gosselin was also profiled in John Cushman Fistere's article, "No Timid Man Could Hold This Job," published in June 1931 in *The American Magazine*. In an installment of the column Interesting People, Fistere reports on his "luncheon conference" with Frenchy on the unfinished eighty-fourth floor of the Empire State Building. Typical of this genre of reporting, Fistere first comments on the spectacular and dangerous location, "an open platform about two feet this side of some little white clouds," and confesses his own trepidation at visiting it, "I suppose the people on Fifth Avenue below look like little microbes from that height, but to tell the truth, I didn't get close enough to the edge to be able to say what they looked like." Equally as typical, Fistere portrays Frenchy as a romantic hero. Tearing a page from a *Boy's Adventure* magazine, Fistere writes, "The earth never did seem big enough to Frenchy. Before most kids know their way around the block, he knew all the bends and byways along the Montreal water front. The stuffy basement where he lived with his three brothers, father, and mother was a prison to his restless spirit." According to Fistere, as a "tousled-headed youngster" whose "blue eyes sparkled in eagerness," Frenchy stowed away on a ship and "began a life of wandering and adventure that has carried him all over the world, cast him into every sort of rough-and-tumble job, and finally poised him at the peak of an astounding profession."

When I first read this article, early in my search for the identities of the men in Lewis Hine's photos, I was delighted to have found a man so expansively documented. But rereading it often as my search progressed, I began to wonder how Fistere knew these details. How would the journalist know anything at all about this man's life, except by repeating the stories Frenchy told him or by indulging his own imagination for the sake of "effect"? Having spent so long trying to separate the men as individuals from the uses made of them, I now see Fistere's article as the epitome of the mythmaking that has rendered the men so difficult to discern in retrospect. Perfecting the journalistic and cultural clichés of his era, Fistere creates Frenchy as the apotheosis of an American type, the devil-may-care cowboy of the skies, a stock figure since the dawn of the skyscraper age and still prevalent today. The beams of the new skyscraper, the journalist writes, were "set in place by the powerful arms of Frenchy

Victor "Frenchy" Gosselin, ironworker.

(*Right*) Hine at work, creating the iconic image.

and his hard-boiled swearing, dare-devil gang of steel erectors. Every one of them is a 'tough guy' in the real sense,—and Frenchy is the toughest of the lot. Frenchy is the King of Steelmen! Victor! A name for a king!"

As a character, Frenchy is irresistible. Between bites of "a huge steak sandwich," he relates his history. He has been a ship's mate and a deep-sea diver. "I always wanted a job out in the fresh air. The best one I ever had was lumberjack," Frenchy says. "That's the life I like—out there in the woods. If you wanna real thrill, you wanna ride them logs; that's something big, believe me! And those babies are tough. I almost got killed up there one day. We was on a job in Vancouver, riding them in. I slips off into the water and gets pretty nearly ground up." As for ironworking, Frenchy came to the profession by accident. "First job was down in North Carolina on a bridge. I needed a job, and the fellow in charge says, 'Well, you can go to work on the steel if you got any nerve.' I didn't know if I had any nerve or not. Nobody ever asked me—so I goes to work. The job was going along fine, and then one day a fellow falls off; the river was bout one hundred and fifty feet below. I didn't feel so good the rest of the day, and the foreman sees me. 'You wanna quit?' he says. I just give him a look. 'Who? Me?' I says. 'What for?'"

Here is a man who fits the era's American ideal perfectly. He is brash, funny, capable, considerate, clever, practical. He is even emotional, though not so much that it interferes with doing his job. The personality that shines through in these quips may accurately reflect the man Victor Gosselin. And yet each quotation also ticks a box in the roster of desirable American virtues. "Everybody seems to think you have to be a superman or something to work on steel," Frenchy says. "Of course, it ain't no picnic, but then there's lots of jobs I'd pass up for this. I wouldn't wanna be no taxi-driver, for instance. Lokka them guys down there, dodging in and outa that traffic all day long. A guy's apt to get killed doing that."

Reading this profile now, it's impossible to say how close this comes to the man himself. Nevertheless, I admire the journalist's skill. With a few details, possibly made up or embellished, and with a winning portrayal of "working-class" speech patterns, most likely freely interpreted from hasty notes, Fistere creates Frenchy as an enduring character. His story even has a happy ending. After years of wandering, Frenchy has now settled down with a good woman. "She knew I was a steel worker when she married me four years ago, and never kicked about it," he answers when Fistere asks about his wife, whom he'd met while building a theater in Atlanta, Georgia. "If women ha jobs like these, she'd want one, sure," Frenchy says. But doesn't she worry when you leave in the morning? the journalist wants to know. "I dunno, she never says nothing but, 'Good-by, baby; don't get hurt.'"

Victor Joseph Gosselin was born on January 27, 1896, in Saint-Étienne-de-Lauzon, Lévis, directly across the St. Lawrence River from Québec City. As Fistere noted in his profile, Victor had three brothers, two older, one younger. Fistere or Frenchy neglected to mention he also had four older sisters. Genealogical records go back three generations, to his great-grandfather, Joseph, also a native of Lauzon, Lévis, Quebec. Although nicknamed "Frenchy" by his fellow ironworkers, and celebrated as a symbol of the United States, his family almost certainly belonged to the Kahnawake Mohawks, the First Nation or Native Americans whose territory straddled the US-Canadian border before these countries existed.

A 1915 US Department of Labor record shows Gosselin arriving at the port of Montreal. He's a "laborer." Two years later, on his US draft registration card, his profession is "lumberman," and he's employed by Township D, Franklin County, Maine. This document contains a peculiar detail, especially considering Frenchy's later career. In answer to the question, "Has person lost arm, leg, hand, foot, or both eyes, or is he otherwise disabled (specify)," Gosselin writes, "Has lost big toe on left foot."

Frenchy's tales of world travel can be documented in small part. In 1919, he appears on a ship's manifest, returning to New York from Boulogne-sur-Mer, France, aboard the SS *Nieuw Amsterdam*. He is twenty-three years old, five feet nine, with brown hair and gray eyes. His profession is "bridgeman," which means he was already working with steel. His destination is Pittsburgh. He has no home address. In 1922, like many ironworkers of the era, he ships out from Brooklyn to Cristóbal, Panama Canal Zone. In 1929, Gosselin surfaces on yet another ship's manifest, this time returning to the US from Port Said, Egypt. His profession is now ironworker, and his residence is New York, New York.

Just four months later, on April 14, 1930, about six months before Lewis Hine photographed him at the Empire State Building, Gosselin is listed in the 1930 US census. He is thirty-four years old and lives on West 149th Street, in the Sugar Hill neighborhood of Upper Manhattan, with his wife of four years. They shared a relatively expensive apartment, compared with other Empire State workers, with a monthly rent of sixty dollars. As a union ironworker on the Empire State Building, Frenchy would have earned seventy-seven dollars a week. But since Post & McCord, the subcontractor, as well as Harris Structural Steel, which provided men for the job, were both open-shop companies, it's impossible to say what he actually earned. As Frenchy mentions in Fistere's article, his wife, Helen Amy Duncan, came from Cherokee County, Georgia. She was born in 1908. The five-story building where they lived still exists today, with its seven-step stoop, handsome white-brick facade, and arched windows.

Ten years later, in 1940, the couple has moved to West 180th Street, just north of the on-ramp to the George Washington Bridge, which was constructed contemporaneously with the Empire State and opened five months after it in 1931. Frenchy had worked on its steel towers. The couple now has two young sons, ages eight and four. Victor's birthplace, however, has transposed from Quebec to Maine, and in subsequent documents his birthplace is given as "Bumes," almost certainly a misspelling of Bemis, Maine, near where Gosselin had worked as a lumberman in the late 1910s. The monthly rent was fifty-eight dollars, indicating that Frenchy was still employed. But ironworkers frequently traveled for their jobs, and a second 1940 census also lists Gosselin as a crew member on the USS *Sailfish* at the Portsmouth Naval Shipyard in Kittery, Maine. The *Sailfish* was a submarine that had led a previous life as the USS *Squalus*. Commissioned in 1938, the *Squalus* sank during a test dive in 1939, but was salvaged and recommissioned as the *Sailfish* in May 1940. The census taker in Maine spoke to Frenchy just a few weeks before this, on April 4, 1940, indicating he was probably employed repairing the ship.

In 1942, at age forty-six, Gosselin again registered for the draft. He was now living with his family in Joppa, Maryland, and once again working on naval vessels, this time at the Bethlehem Steel Sparrows Point Shipyard, north of Baltimore. Despite how imposing Frenchy appears in the photographs we have of him, and the record of his height in 1919, he is described on the draft registry as quite slight: five feet five, weighing 121 pounds.

Less than a year later, Victor Gosselin died. The US Social Security Death Index has an entry for Victor Joseph Gosselin dated August 21, 1943. On August 29, *The Baltimore Sun* ran this brief account of his death: "Victor J. Gosselin, 46, of Magnolia, was killed when his automobile left

Buddy Turner, left, and Victor Gosselin.

the Philadelphia road near the Ebenezer road and overturned six times." The accident occurred about eight miles from his home. His widow was thirty-five years old. His sons were eleven and seven.

Pictured in Lewis Hine's masterful photograph, and profiled so engagingly by John Cushman Fistere, Victor Gosselin has become the archetypal ironworker, a representative for all Empire State workers. He seems to unite in himself all the most admirable qualities of the American worker of the 1930s, as conceived by newsmen, and to embody the essential human spirit that Hine sought to illustrate. This combined portrait lives on, a symbol of the nation's strength during hard times, the human face of the grand story of the Empire State Building, itself the representative of twentieth-century America in all its glory and power. But if we attend only to these images, these myths of the American character without context or connection, we erase the actual lives of the ordinary individuals who built, and who continue to build, the nation. So little remains by which to grasp the life of Victor Gosselin. Still, enough can be found to perceive the man as an individual distinct from the symbolic use that was made of him. Distinguishing Victor Gosselin, the man, from the figure in Hine's iconic photograph does not make him any less heroic. Instead, it allows us to see the photograph more fully, and it roots Gosselin's genuine heroism in a real life, tragically short and mostly unknown, rather than in a fantasy.

If we view the Empire State Building from the perspective of the men who worked on it, rather than from the more common, generalized perspective, a richer, more personal, and nuanced story of its construction emerges. "My experience on the Empire State Building was a real love affair—I liked the work—I liked the people I worked with and above all it was the most important project in the world at that time." In the 1984 documentary film, *America and Lewis Hine*, director Nina Rosenblum interviewed Harold McClain, identified then as the last surviving ironworker to have built the Empire State. In these interviews, and in a handful of personal letters he sent to Rosenblum during the film's production, McClain reflected on his experience. Despite the many books and articles written about the Empire State's construction, and the widespread historical and critical attention devoted to Lewis Hine's dramatic photographs, for fifty years, McClain had been unaware of the photographer's work or the cultural influence exerted by his images. At the job site, McClain recalled, Hine's presence was not noteworthy. "I don't remember Lewis Hine as a person," he said. "We as an organized gang erecting steel with a derrick were pretty busy." Encountering the photographs in Hine's *Men at Work* for the first time as an older man, McClain was amazed and gratified to recognize himself and his brother, Jerome McClain, known as Romie. "For years and years I wondered why we didn't get more attention," he remarked at the opening of Rosenblum's documentary film. "Now I'm finding out we did. I was just not paying attention."

Like ironworker Neil Doherty, Harold and Romie McClain had worked the central or "tower" derrick during construction, one of the last derricks remaining when the steel frame topped out at the eighty-sixth floor and the only one used for erection of the decorative mooring mast. Annotating a copy of *Men at Work* for Nina Rosenblum, McClain was happy to explain what the images depicted. "Each derrick used ten men. There were forty eight [*sic*] riveting gangs at 4 men each. Bolting and fitting up required two man crews. Plumbing up and planking over the open floors many more." What most animated his recollections, however, was the network of relationships he had with fellow workers, relationships that nurtured and depended on mutual respect and cooperation. So many men were employed on the project, he recalled, most of them remained strangers. But his derrick gang was composed of men he had known for years.

"Many of us were friends from preceding jobs. Romie McClain, Myself, Nig Fuller, Frenchy Goslin [*sic*], Buddy Turner, Oscar Johnson from the Geo. Washington Bridge and many others."

Invisible to any outsider, these relationships constitute another, crucial dimension of the building, seen on the scale of individual men, that falls away entirely when its history is told as a tale of romantic heroes or in a few photographs selected to emphasize a lone, anonymous worker. Looking at the images, McClain recalled the men, intimating the context that has been lost.

"Shorty McDermott was the burner," he wrote in a remarkable letter, providing a running commentary as he flipped through the pages of Hine's book. "Frenchy Goslin and Buddy Turner posing on the load block," he exclaims, recognizing the men in the famous image Hine had captioned, "Like spiders spinning a fabric of steel against the sky."

For McClain, the experience of building the Empire State was not captured in photographs or immortalized in the Craftsmanship Awards. On the contrary, the photos and the award, by purveying the myth of the lone ironworker or the "superior" craftsman, only severed the connections that constituted the work. The images and the award isolated men and moments from the flow of the job and from the relationships, both personal and professional, that gave it meaning.

"The hoisting engineer. A very important man with our lives in his hands," McClain explained, describing one photo. For another, he writes, "Frenchy Goslin (the Big Frog) is unhooking from a beam." It had not been recorded that "Frenchy" was also known as "the Big Frog."

What remained memorable for McClain was not any of the abstract, individual virtues enshrined in the Craftsmanship Awards, but the mutual respect of the workers. "The biggest part of our safety was the quality and the type of men we worked with. They were our buddies. We looked out for each other in the gang. It was a team."

Perhaps a faint hint of this lost dimension may be seen in Hine's photograph of the ironworkers who comprised the topping-out gang for the mooring mast.

In this group portrait, Harold McClain, slouching in the back row, center, wearing a dark coat, stands with his brother, Romie, beside him. Another man McClain identified, "Blackie" Bavona—probably Anthony Bivona—is partly hidden behind Romie's shoulder. These three men were the connectors, which means they were responsible for placing and ultimately removing the final fifteen-ton guy derrick, which rose above the height of the building itself and was used in constructing the 205-foot mooring mast. This made them "highest in the world on a man made structure," as McClain proudly recalled, employing a phrase frequently repeated by those associated with the building. McClain also identified the man standing in front, wearing an open peacoat and holding his hat. Oscar Johnson was his foreman, the boss of the derrick gang, with whom he had worked on the George Washington Bridge.

Lewis Hine photographed some of these men individually, and they appear in *Men at Work* in isolated portraits. The older man with the shaggy mustache in the front row, center, can be seen in Hine's book above the caption, "Young and old, they all say it isn't really as dangerous as it looks." On the back of a working print of that image, Hine writes, "old steelworker . . . who keeps up with the boys." McClain does not mention this man's name, and I have not been able to identify him. But this photo locates him in the context of a few specific "boys."

Indeed, these were the men Hine accompanied in their work, who taught him to "walk-a-beam" and laughed down his fear of falling. They are the men who helped him through tight places, and who swung him out on a derrick to capture the final rivets on the mooring mast.

The man Harold McClain identified as the foreman, Oscar Johnson, appears in another photo, likely taken the same day as the group shot, along with another man McClain identified, "Slook," the bolting-up boss. In this photo, the two men dangle over the city in a box suspended high above the street. This is undoubtedly the same contraption in which Lewis Hine swung out with his camera, and one of these men was the "boss" who said it was safer than a ride in a Pullman or a walk on the street. Oscar Johnson sits on the right, while "Slook" stands holding one of the cables.

In the commemorative album created by Starrett Bros. and Eken, now held at the Skyscraper Museum in lower Manhattan, there are other photos of both Johnson and "Slook," identified there as "Sluke" Ryerson. Based on the 1930 census, I believe his real name was Burt Ryersen. He was forty-one years old, an immigrant from Norway, who had arrived in the US in 1925.

Other men that Hine photographed separately may also appear in this group photo. Though McClain does not mention the name, Hine made a series of striking portraits of Dick McCarthy on or around September 16, 1930, the day steelwork was completed on the eighty-sixth floor.

Hine scribbled various captions on his prints of these portraits. One copy in the Avery Library archive has the inscription, "One of the 'Sky-boys' on Empire State, with a long record of big buildings he has worked." Copies in the George Eastman Museum identify him as "The Bolt Boss" and "Boss of a structural gang." On another print, also found in the Eastman collection, Hine writes: "Dick McCarthy Bros."

Although Richard McCarthy is a common name, I found a 1930 record for him, age thirty-one, living in Brooklyn. Further searching revealed that Richard was the youngest of three, and his brother, Andrew, was also an ironworker.

The topping-out gang: Harold and Romie McClain, center, third and fourth from the left. "Blackie" Bavona (probably Anthony Bivona), far back center. Oscar Johnson in the dark coat, front right. Behind him, possibly Andrew McCarthy and Dick McCarthy.

“Safer than a ride in a Pullman.” “Slook” or “Sluke” Ryerson, left, and Oscar Johnson.

"The Bolt Boss." Dick McCarthy, ironworker.

Richard Aloysius McCarthy was born in New York on November 9, 1898, a second-generation American, grandson of Irish immigrants. In September 1930, when he helped complete structural steelwork on the Empire State Building and was photographed by Lewis Hine, Richard "Dick" McCarthy was just a few weeks shy of his thirty-second birthday. He lived with his wife, Mary Agnes Finley, born in 1905 to Irish immigrant parents, and their three children in a house they owned, worth $6,450, on East Thirty-Seventh Street, Brooklyn. The family eventually included six children. Dick McCarthy remained in Brooklyn until his death on July 1, 1983.

Andrew Francis McCarthy, seven years older than his brother Richard, had married Gertrude Cronin in August 1916. In 1930, he was thirty-seven years old and lived with his family on Twentieth Street in St. Albans, Queens. The census gives his profession as "riveter." Andrew lived the rest of his life in Queens and died there on January 5, 1948.

Rejoining names, faces, and snippets of personal details is perhaps all that can be done now, so many years later, to see these men as individuals and to erect a fragile bulwark against the pressure of mythology. The more difficult, now far more tenuous step is to restore the context and connections that single photos and heroic narratives sever. It has been possible to do this for some of the men who won Empire State Craftsmanship Awards. Is this possible now for Dick and Andrew McCarthy?

Two men who look remarkably like brothers, one of whom closely resembles Dick McCarthy, appear in the group portrait that includes Harold McClain, his brother, Romie McClain, along with "Blackie" Bavona or Bivona and Oscar Johnson. Could the man standing just behind Oscar Johnson be Andrew McCarthy? And the man at his side, on the right of the group, could he be Dick McCarthy? He stands with his head tilted in what was clearly a characteristic slant to the left, seen in all the photos in which he is positively identified.

Icarus or *The Sky Boy*. The photo as it became famous.

Icarus or *The Sky Boy*, an alternate view.

The question is significant, because Dick McCarthy may also be the figure in the second of Hine's most iconic images of the construction of the Empire State Building, the photo he frequently captioned *Icarus*, though it appears in *Men at Work* with the title *The Sky Boy*. This one inspiring and masterful photograph has seemed to embody everything the skyscraper stood for as a symbol. Today, a life-size transparency of it forms the centerpiece of the tourist gallery on the Empire State Building's observation deck. But the worker has never been identified. The photograph has so fused with the heroic image of the building that, for all these years, it has seemed beside the point to ask the man's name.

In the most famous version, Hine once again cropped the image to isolate the figure. In *Men at Work*, he provided this caption: "One of the first men to swing out a quarter of a mile above New York City, helping to build a skyscraper." But in his notes, Hine left no clue to the man's identity. Instead, he seems to float alone above an abyss, although other prints and alternate shots provide a wider field of view and reveal additional workers looking on.

The Sky Boy has become so famous and has been reproduced so many times it is difficult to look at it afresh to see the man whose work is pictured. In the absence of a name or other information, the worker takes on mythological dimensions, which billow out over time to become a cloud, obscuring what is specific in the image. This obscurity envelops not only the man himself, but the nature and human cost of his labor, the facts of Lewis Hine's employment by Empire State Inc. and every other element that makes the photograph *documentary* in any meaningful sense of the word. In the end, this mystification becomes so extreme we may have a description of the Sky Boy entirely untethered to anything but a writer's fantasy, like the one offered by Alexander Nemerov in his book about Lewis Hine, *Soulmaker*. "An adventurous lad, the sky boy sets out alone, on a journey like no one else's. Free of constraints, of 'real-world' requirements and obligations, he floats in some aerie of private exploration, the biographical ideal of the sovereign self in full flight, lifted like Lindbergh in ecstatic solitude."

We may never know the truth about the man in this photo. But everything in Nemerov's description is false.

After almost one hundred years, the Sky Boy confronts us as a question. Who is he? What can we learn about this man who helped to build

Dick McCarthy, left, and the Sky Boy, right.

the Empire State Building? As a tantalizing start, the man in the photo bears a strong resemblance to Dick McCarthy.

Can we restore the Sky Boy's identity, recognizing his features as evidence of a specific individual? Can we reconnect him now with the professional and personal context that gave his life and his work their meaning, and that constitute the real greatness of America, seen from the workers' perspective, the only worthy symbols of the nation's strength?

Do we know his name? Or, like the thousands of other workers who built the Empire State, must we honor him now as an individual only by asking why he has remained isolated and anonymous?

Because *The Sky Boy* is not only an abstract embodiment of the American character, the apotheosis of labor and the human element in skyscrapers, a symbol of the rising American and human spirit. The photograph is also the *specific* embodiment of these grand, empty concepts, a snapshot of a particular man doing his job, one moment of one day, tightening the guy wire of a derrick while the other men in his gang look on and wait. An unremarkable moment, in this perspective, extraordinary only because Lewis Hine was there to capture it, enabling us to witness this man at work. The image is symbolic, therefore, of all the other moments, all the other men, and of all their labor, which we do not see, and of all we do not and cannot know about this one man, how he climbed down from the wire after tightening the bolt, continued working the rest of the day. How he went home to his family, perhaps in Brooklyn, what he thought and felt about himself and his circumstances, how he got up the next morning and, if there was work, if he was hired, did his job again. One moment of one day in a long career of similar jobs, the hard, unsteady work of building an ordinary, American life.

ILLUSTRATIONS AND PHOTO CREDITS

Chapter 1: The Named and the Unnamed

1.1: *The Sky Boy*. Courtesy of the George Eastman Museum.

1.2: The grand entrance. Photo by the author.

1.3: The Craftsmanship Awards plaque. Courtesy of the George Eastman Museum.

1.4: One of Al Smith's cats and her kittens. Courtesy of the Skyscraper Museum.

1.5: Lewis Hine's handwritten note, "See also photos of men." Courtesy of the George Eastman Museum.

Chapter 2: Men Who Make Our Modern World Safe

2.1: "Character—An Empire State Craftsman." Hine's portrait of Arthur Jones. Courtesy of the George Eastman Museum.

2.2: Arthur Jones at work, award-winner for ornamental iron and bronze. Courtesy of the George Eastman Museum.

Chapter 3: "Who Is the Craftsman?"

3.1: Matthew M. McKeen, carpenter. Empire State Building archive, 1930–1969, Avery Architectural & Fine Arts Library, Columbia University.

3.2: Michael Tierney, rock driller. Empire State Building archive, 1930–1969, Avery Architectural & Fine Arts Library, Columbia University.

3.3: Michael Tierney, rock driller. Empire State Building archive, 1930–1969, Avery Architectural & Fine Arts Library, Columbia University.

3.4: James P. Kerr, stone setter. Empire State Building archive, 1930–1969, Avery Architectural & Fine Arts Library, Columbia University.

3.5: James P. Kerr, stone setter. Empire State Building archive, 1930–1969, Avery Architectural & Fine Arts Library, Columbia University.
3.6: Charles E. Sexton, bricklayer. Empire State Building archive, 1930–1969, Avery Architectural & Fine Arts Library, Columbia University.
3.7: Charles E. Sexton, bricklayer. Courtesy of the George Eastman Museum.
3.8: Peter Madden, asbestos worker. Empire State Building archive, 1930–1969, Avery Architectural & Fine Arts Library, Columbia University.
3.9: Peter Madden, asbestos worker. Empire State Building archive, 1930–1969, Avery Architectural & Fine Arts Library, Columbia University.

Chapter 4: "The Man on the Job"

4.1: *Empire Statements*, volume 1, no. 2. Empire State Building archive, 1930–1969, Avery Architectural & Fine Arts Library, Columbia University.
4.2: Steven or Stephen Coons, structural ironworker. Empire State Building archive, 1930–1969, Avery Architectural & Fine Arts Library, Columbia University.
4.3: "One of the Boys" (Oct. 26, 1930). *Daily News* (Oct. 9, 1930) photo by the author.
4.4: Frank A. Moeglin, sheet metal worker. Empire State Building archive, 1930–1969, Avery Architectural & Fine Arts Library, Columbia University.
4.5: Vladimir Kozloff, wrecker. Empire State Building archive, 1930–1969, Avery Architectural & Fine Arts Library, Columbia University.
4.6: Vladimir Kozloff, wrecker. Empire State Building archive, 1930–1969, Avery Architectural & Fine Arts Library, Columbia University.
4.7: "Craftsmen Rewarded." The first award ceremony, October 8, 1930. *The American Magazine* (Oct. 9, 1930) photo by the author.
4.8: Thomas F. Walsh, hoisting engineer. Empire State Building archive, 1930–1969, Avery Architectural & Fine Arts Library, Columbia University.
4.9: Thomas F. Walsh, hoisting engineer. Empire State Building archive, 1930–1969, Avery Architectural & Fine Arts Library, Columbia University.
4.10: Thomas F. Walsh, hoisting engineer. Empire State Building archive, 1930–1969, Avery Architectural & Fine Arts Library, Columbia University.
4.11: Giuseppe Rusciani, laborer. Empire State Building archive, 1930–1969, Avery Architectural & Fine Arts Library, Columbia University.
4.12: James Irons, stonecutter. Empire State Building archive, 1930–1969, Avery Architectural & Fine Arts Library, Columbia University.

4.13: James Irons, stonecutter. Empire State Building archive, 1930–1969, Avery Architectural & Fine Arts Library, Columbia University.

Chapter 5: "Splendid Ideals"

5.1: Honorary Craftsmanship Membership Card, New York Building Congress. Honorary Craftsmanship Membership Card, n.d., New York Building Congress Records, WAG.167, box 5, folder 16. Tamiment Library & Robert F. Wagner Labor Archives, New York University.

5.2: Honorary Craftsmanship Membership Card, New York Building Congress. Honorary Craftsmanship Membership Card (verso), n.d., New York Building Congress Records, WAG.167, box 5, folder 16. Tamiment Library & Robert F. Wagner Labor Archives, New York University.

5.3: Honoring the men at the first award ceremony, October 8, 1930. Empire State Building archive, 1930–1969, Avery Architectural & Fine Arts Library, Columbia University.

Chapter 6: "What the Men Think of It"

6.1: Thomas Walsh, derrickman. Empire State Building archive, 1930–1969, Avery Architectural & Fine Arts Library, Columbia University.

6.2: Thomas Walsh, derrickman. Courtesy of the George Eastman Museum.

6.3: Gus Comedeca, steam shovel operator. Empire State Building archive, 1930–1969, Avery Architectural & Fine Arts Library, Columbia University.

6.4: Gus Comedeca, steam shovel operator. Empire State Building archive, 1930–1969, Avery Architectural & Fine Arts Library, Columbia University.

6.5: Samuel Laginsky, glazier. Empire State Building archive, 1930–1969, Avery Architectural & Fine Arts Library, Columbia University.

6.6: Samuel Laginsky, glazier. Empire State Building archive, 1930–1969, Avery Architectural & Fine Arts Library, Columbia University.

6.7: Adam Bigelow, dampproofer. Courtesy of the George Eastman Museum.

6.8: Adam Bigelow, dampproofer. Empire State Building archive, 1930–1969, Avery Architectural & Fine Arts Library, Columbia University.

Chapter 7: "Look Him in the Eye"

7.1: Lewis Wickes Hine, photographer, around 1930. Courtesy of the George Eastman Museum.

7.2: Peter Madden. Courtesy of the George Eastman Museum.
7.3: Hine's handwritten note, "Look him in the eye." Courtesy of the George Eastman Museum.

Chapter 8: "The New Who's Who"

8.1: "The New Who's Who," by Will B. Johnstone (Oct. 18, 1930). Photo by the author.
8.2: "After All These Years," by Harry Haenigsen (Nov. 6, 1930). Photo by the author.
8.3: Louis Hummell, steamfitter, photographed by Hiram Myers. Empire State Building archive, 1930–1969, Avery Architectural & Fine Arts Library, Columbia University.
8.4: Thomas McWeeney, elevator constructor, photographed by Hiram Myers. Empire State Building archive, 1930–1969, Avery Architectural & Fine Arts Library, Columbia University.
8.5: Frank W. Pierson Jr., metal lather, photographed by Hiram Myers. Empire State Building archive, 1930–1969, Avery Architectural & Fine Arts Library, Columbia University.
8.6: Owen Scanlon, marble setter's helper, photographed by Hiram Myers. Empire State Building archive, 1930–1969, Avery Architectural & Fine Arts Library, Columbia University.
8.7: Owen Scanlon, marble setter's helper. Empire State Building archive, 1930–1969, Avery Architectural & Fine Arts Library, Columbia University.
8.8: Ferruccio Mariutto, terrazzo worker, photographed by Hiram Myers. Empire State Building archive, 1930–1969, Avery Architectural & Fine Arts Library, Columbia University.
8.9: Ferruccio Mariutto, terrazzo worker, photographed by Hiram Myers. Empire State Building archive, 1930–1969, Avery Architectural & Fine Arts Library, Columbia University.
8.10: Second Craftsmanship Award ceremony, February 11, 1931. "The Second Award on the Empire State Building, February 11, 1931," *Building Congress News*, March 1931, 5. New York Building Congress Records, WAG.167. Tamiment Library & Robert F. Wagner Labor Archives, New York University.
8.11: George R. Adams, painter and decorator. "The Second Award on the Empire State Building, February 11, 1931" (detail), *Building*

Congress News, March 1931, 5. New York Building Congress Records, WAG.167. Tamiment Library & Robert F. Wagner Labor Archives, New York University.

8.12: Unknown elevator constructor, photographed by Lewis Hine. Empire State Building archive, 1930–1969, Avery Architectural & Fine Arts Library, Columbia University.

8.13: William Deneen, elevator constructor's helper. "The Second Award on the Empire State Building, February 11, 1931" (detail), *Building Congress News*, March 1931, 5. New York Building Congress Records, WAG.167. Tamiment Library & Robert F. Wagner Labor Archives, New York University.

8.14: Frank J. Klein, plasterer (tentative). Empire State Building archive, 1930–1969, Avery Architectural & Fine Arts Library, Columbia University.

8.15: Pietro Vescovi, terrazzo worker's helper (tentative). Empire State Building archive, 1930–1969, Avery Architectural & Fine Arts Library, Columbia University.

8.16: Unidentified worker. Courtesy of the George Eastman Museum.

8.17: Unidentified worker. Empire State Building archive, 1930–1969, Avery Architectural & Fine Arts Library, Columbia University.

8.18: Unidentified worker. Empire State Building archive, 1930–1969, Avery Architectural & Fine Arts Library, Columbia University.

8.19: Unidentified worker. Empire State Building archive, 1930–1969, Avery Architectural & Fine Arts Library, Columbia University.

8.20: Unidentified worker. Empire State Building archive, 1930–1969, Avery Architectural & Fine Arts Library, Columbia University.

8.21: Unidentified worker. Empire State Building archive, 1930–1969, Avery Architectural & Fine Arts Library, Columbia University.

8.22: Unidentified worker. Empire State Building archive, 1930–1969, Avery Architectural & Fine Arts Library, Columbia University.

8.23: Unidentified worker. Empire State Building archive, 1930–1969, Avery Architectural & Fine Arts Library, Columbia University.

Chapter 9: The Sky Boy

9.1: Hine's photos on display in the Empire State Building, May 1931. Empire State Building archive, 1930–1969, Avery Architectural & Fine Arts Library, Columbia University.

9.2: Carl Percy Russell, "daring bird." Photo by the author.

9.3: Neil Doherty, "unsung hero of the air." Photo by the author.

9.4: Neil Doherty, ironworker. Courtesy of the George Eastman Museum.

9.5: Victor “Frenchy” Gosselin, ironworker. Empire State Building archive, 1930–1969, Avery Architectural & Fine Arts Library, Columbia University.

9.6: Hine at work, creating the iconic image. Empire State Building archive, 1930–1969, Avery Architectural & Fine Arts Library, Columbia University.

9.7: Buddy Turner, left, and Victor Gosselin. Courtesy of the George Eastman Museum.

9.8: The topping-out gang. Courtesy of the George Eastman Museum.

9.9: “Safer than a ride in a Pullman.” “Slook” or “Sluke” Ryerson, left, and Oscar Johnson. Courtesy of the George Eastman Museum.

9.10: “The Bolt Boss.” Dick McCarthy, ironworker. Empire State Building archive, 1930–1969, Avery Architectural & Fine Arts Library, Columbia University.

9.11: “The Bolt Boss.” Dick McCarthy, ironworker. Empire State Building archive, 1930–1969, Avery Architectural & Fine Arts Library, Columbia University.

9.12: *Icarus* or *The Sky Boy*. Courtesy of the George Eastman Museum.

9.13: *Icarus* or *The Sky Boy*. Courtesy of the George Eastman Museum.

9.14: Dick McCarthy, left, and the Sky Boy, right. Empire State Building archive, 1930–1969, Avery Architectural & Fine Arts Library, Columbia University.

9.15: Dick McCarthy, left, and the Sky Boy, right. Courtesy of the George Eastman Museum.

ACKNOWLEDGMENTS

The identifications and biographies presented here represent my best attempt to make sense of very fragmentary sources. My reconstructions must remain provisional and many, even if generally correct, undoubtedly contain errors. Some may be simply wrong or wildly inaccurate. I have found no way to avoid it. The process of uncovering the identities and personal details of men who appear in ninety-year-old photographs is archaeological, involving a vast amount of digging in the hope of unearthing a few, precious, if enigmatic fragments. As with more traditional forms of archaeology, there is always more buried than any one digger can find. New discoveries may come at any moment and may fundamentally alter my version of this history and so of these men's lives. And even the most seemingly obvious artifacts may be interpreted incorrectly. All errors are the responsibility of the author.

Any readers able to provide more information about the men mentioned here are encouraged to contact me.

I am profoundly grateful for the generous support of the John Simon Guggenheim Memorial Foundation for a 2016-2017 fellowship and to its president, Edward Hirsch, for his encouragement and example.

This project would not have been possible without the expertise and meticulous assistance of numerous archivists and archive staff, so many I cannot thank them all by name. My admiration and gratitude to:

At the Avery Architectural and Fine Arts Library, Columbia University: Nicole L. Richard, Janet Parks, Pamela Casey, and with particular appreciation to Shelley Hayreh, archivist and collections manager, for her truly above-and-beyond efforts in searching the Hine photos when the archive was unexpectedly closed. For assistance with image reproduction: Margaret Smithglass and Benjamin M. Read.

At the George Eastman Museum and Richard and Ronay Menschel Library: Ross Knaper, photo archivist, Rachael Andrews, Virginia Dodier, and Deborah Mohr. For image reproduction: Alice Wynd and Lauren Lean.

Special thanks to Carol Willis, founder and director of The Skyscraper Museum, not only for her assistance with the museum's invaluable collection of Empire State artifacts, but for her scholarship about the building, her acute critical eye, and for her friendship. At the Skyscraper Museum: Josh Vogel and Daniel J Borrero.

At New York University's Special Collections and the Tamiment Library and Robert F. Wagner Labor Archive: Sarah Moazeni, Michael Koncewicz, and Nicholas Martin, librarian for archival collections and reference services, NYU Special Collections, Bobst Library. For assistance with image reproduction: Lauren Holmes and Malia Guyer-Stevens.

At the J. Paul Getty Museum and Getty Research Institute, Reference Department and Research Library: Miriam Y. Katz, research associate for collections management, department of photographs, Rachel Matta, and Karen Hellman, assistant curator, department of photographs.

At the New York Public Library Photo Collection: Zulay Chang.

The staff of the New York Public Library Manuscripts Division and the Irma and Paul Milstein Division of United States History, Local History and Genealogy.

At the Brooklyn Public Library: Natiba Guy-Clement, manager of special collections.

At the Museum of Modern Art Library: Jennifer Tobias.

At the National Museum of American History: Peter Liebhold, curator, Division of Work and Industry.

The librarians, archivists, and staff at the Thomas J. Watson Library, Metropolitan Museum of Art, New York.

Beyond the archives, my heartfelt thanks to:

Anthony Malkin, chairman and CEO, Empire State Realty Trust, for his interest in the project, and Leslie Nelson, who provided an introduction.

Nina Rosenblum, for her gracious assistance guiding me through her research for *America and Lewis Hine* and for sharing her correspondence with Harold McClain.

Stephen Coles of the Letterform Archive, San Francisco, for help identifying the font used on the Craftsmanship Award plaque. As part of the restoration of the Empire State Building in 2007, Christian Schwartz and Paul Barnes created a custom typeface, based on this design. See: http://www.christianschwartz.com/esb.shtml.

Seth Bornstein, who introduced me to Andrew S. Hollweck, senior vice president, and Richard Anderson, president emeritus of the New York Building Congress.

Marilyn Harran, director of the Rodgers Center for Holocaust Education, Chapman University, for her many years of friendship and support.

Special honor to the late, legendary Leslie Robertson, who over several memorable lunches shared his unequalled experience, adventures, and insights into structural engineering.

Early on in my research, I had the privilege of visiting EverGreene Architectural Arts to learn about the restoration of the Empire State's lobby ceiling mural. Thank you to Emily Sottile, director of the Sacred Space Studio, and Bill Mensching, vice president, director of murals.

I am especially grateful to the descendants of Empire State workmen who were willing to share their recollections and family histories with me (and I apologize to the many people I contacted who shared a name but no family history with these men). Thank you to Audrey Romer and Sara McCloskey for George R. Adams; Judith Martens for her great-uncle Adam Bigelow; Andrew Deneen and Bill Deneen for recollections of William Deneen; Norbert Kowal for sharing his wife's research on Victor Gosselin; James J. Irons for memories of his grandfather, James Irons; Stuart H. Gollinger for Samuel Laginsky; James McManus, Ellen McManus, Daniel Madden, Theresa Madden Best for their remembrances of Peter Madden; Robin Mariutto for her moving tribute to her grandfather Ferruccio Mariutto; George McWeeney for his fond memories of Thomas McWeeney; Gail Lincoln for reminiscing about Carl Russell; Karen Tompkins for Charles E. Sexton; and Jim Vescovi for Antonio and Pietro (Peter) Vescovi.

Every day I feel inexpressible gratitude for my friends and my family, present and absent, named and unnamed: David Albert, Lauren Block, Stephen Block, Randy Briggs, Stephanie Cain, Jay Cantor, Cathrine de

Neergaard, Liza Doran, Alan Emtage, Rhonda Garelick, Alan Gerecke, Janice Gitterman, Michael Haviken, Rick Hilles, Carolyn Jackson, Joanne and Eliot Kaplan, Linda Karshan, Stephen Kirschner, Melanie Kranz, Ned and Tina Krutsky, Cynthia Kurtz, David Kurtz, Tom Le, Amanda Revere Lincoln, Bill and Sue Lincoln, Elaine J. McCarthy, Jim McCarthy, Peter Mendelsund, Nuria Mendoza, Daniel and Jocelyn Lockwood Meyers, Jessica Mihaly, Yvette Molina, Brant Murray, Zama Neff, Jim and Jeanette Petersen, Carl Pritzkat, Nancy Reisman, Michael Rhodes, Joshua-Michéle Ross, Celene Ryan, Kit Schulte, Anthony Sebok, Kathy Smith, Bianca Stigter, Tony Travostino, Jorge Daniel Torres de Veneciano.

Extra-special thanks to Dana Kurtz and Rob Mackenzie for their love, support, and genius for genealogy.

Malaga Baldi, for her tireless efforts shepherding me and this book through the years.

Steve Fisher at Independent Artists Group.

Katherine Seger and Adam Krasnoff, for their expert copyediting.

Finally, my enduring gratitude to Dan Simon, Stewart Cauley, Sofia DeSanto, Oona Holohan, Ruth Weiner, Rasheeda Saka, and the team at Seven Stories Press for their enthusiasm, professionalism, and their tremendous care in crafting this book.

AFTERWORD: ON THE QUESTION OF SOURCES

My research for *Men at Work* followed several well-trodden paths, though I hope from a different perspective than is typical, as well as several paths previously unexplored in this context. I have divided this examination of my sources and a consideration of the questions they pose into three sections, though these inevitably overlap: **The Empire State Building**, including its construction, history, cultural symbolism, and the symbolism of the skyscraper in general; **Lewis Wickes Hine**, including archival, biographical, and interpretive sources; and **The Men**, including the history of the New York Building Congress and the Certificates of Superior Craftsmanship, further discussion of those who died during construction and the manner of their deaths, and finally some tentative identifications and a brief exploration of the problem of identification in general.

Numerous physical archives and online databases underlie every aspect of the project:

- The Avery Architectural and Fine Arts Library (Columbia University, New York), specifically the Empire State Building archive, 1930–1969, which contains the largest collection of Lewis Hine's working prints for the Empire State Building project, as well as records from the architects Shreve, Lamb and Harmon, including several unorganized folders of photographs that proved invaluable to this book. (The Avery Library's "The Empire State Building Archive Finding Aid" is the essential starting point.) Of singular importance in this archive is the series of scrapbooks created either by or for Empire State Inc. from the vast number of newspaper, magazine, and trade journal articles, advertisements, and photographs clipped by the National Press Clipping Bureau (31 East Seventeenth Street and 48 West Twenty-Seventh Street), Luce's Press Clipping Bureau (100 Warren Street, New York), and perhaps other clipping services. These are hereafter referred to as the ESB Scrapbooks. The ESB Scrapbooks are themselves historical documents, illustrating the corporation's (and most probably Belle Moskowitz's) obsession with the building's public image. In addition, they constitute a unique and invaluable resource for understanding how journalists greeted the construction of the world's largest skyscraper. Where possible, I have provided the Scrapbook volume number in which I found my source, though changes in cataloguing over the years I consulted the Scrapbooks made this occasionally impossible.

- The George Eastman Museum and the Richard and Ronay Menschel Library in Rochester, New York, specifically the Lewis Wickes Hine papers, 1904–1940 (RRML.SC0029), which contains books, articles, manuscripts; the Lewis Wickes Hine scrapbook (RRML.SC0030); and the Eastman collection of Hine photographs, the second-largest collection of Hine's Empire State images. Many of these images are viewable online. (See the finding aid, "Guide to the Lewis Wickes Hine Papers.")

- The Tamiment Library and Robert F. Wagner Labor Archives of New York University's Special Collections (New York University, New York), which houses the New York Building Congress Records (WAG.167), as well as the records of numerous trade unions and the Building Trades Employers' Association (WAG.196).

- New York University Fales Library and Special Collections (New York University, New York), for the uncatalogued Nina Rosenblum Collection of Documentary Film and Video (MSS.558, particularly box 39, folder: "ALH Empire State Bldg") and the Walter and Naomi Rosenblum Collection of Photography and Photographic History (MSS.556). (A finding aid is also available for this collection, referenced by its call number.)

- The New York Public Library (NYPL) holds a small collection of Hine's Empire State Building images. Of particular relevance, see also the Judith Mara Gutman papers (MssCol 5982), particularly Series II.B. *Lewis W. Hine and the American Social Conscience* (1967), box 22, f. 1–8: Research Materials 1913–1941, and the Lewis Hine papers, ca. 1908–ca. 1921 (MssCol 1399). The NYPL's vast collection of historical magazines and newspapers was also a crucial resource, as was its collection of historical photographs of New York City. Much of this historic photographic documentation of the city is available in highly usable form through the independent website, OldNYC.org.

- The Skyscraper Museum, founded by architectural historian Carol Willis, is one of the best and most important resources for research into the Empire State Building. Carol Willis knows more about the building's history than anyone else, and the museum's archive holds two crucial sources, the in-house notebook created by Starrett Bros. and Eken and published as *Building the Empire State*, edited by Carol Willis (W. W. Norton, 1998). I refer to this hereafter as the Starrett's Notebook. In addition, the Skyscraper Museum holds a scrapbook in the form of a photo album created by Starrett Bros. and Eken entitled *Erection Views of Empire State Building*, documenting the construction work in extraordinary detail. For the purposes of identifying individuals involved in construction below the level of corporate directors, this scrapbook with its numerous annotated photographs is an unparalleled source. This scrapbook is accessible online via the Skyscraper Museum's website.

  The Skyscraper Museum refers to this resource as a scrapbook. To distinguish it from the ESB Scrapbooks at the Avery Library, I will refer to the Skyscraper Museum's document as the *Starrett's Photo Album*.

- For the genealogical information used throughout this book, I made extensive use of the National Archives, which houses most of the records I consulted, above all, the US census (https://www.archives.gov/research/census). Birth and death records, marriage certificates, military service records, and state census records are available online through numerous federal and state websites. Immigration records can be found through the website of the

Statue of Liberty–Ellis Island Foundation. Popular online interfaces to much of this material can be found through Ancestry.com and MyHeritage.com.

- For historical newspapers, magazines, trade journals, corporate reports, and telephone books, I consulted physical archives at the New York Public Library, the Brooklyn Public Library, New York University, Columbia University, and the New York Historical Society, as well as numerous online resources including Newspapers.com, the Internet Archive, HathiTrust Digital Library, and ProQuest Historical Newspapers. Additional digital resources for period newspapers and magazines that were decisive for my research included Chronicling America: Historic American Newspapers at the Library of Congress; *The New York Times*' TimesMachine; the Brooklyn Newsstand at the Brooklyn Public Library; New York Historic Newspapers at the Empire State Library Network; American Historical Newspapers Online at Cornell University. Also of particular utility has been FindaGrave.com and NYC Street Map from the New York City Department of City Planning.

THE EMPIRE STATE BUILDING

Any project about the Empire State Building begins with the many histories of skyscraper construction in the 1920s and 1930s in general and the Empire State Building in particular. These typically present a technical overview of the construction process and take what I call the "corporate view," focusing on the businessmen who conceived, financed, and managed construction. The best of these are: John Tauranac, *The Empire State Building: The Making of a Landmark* (Scribner, 1995); Jim Rasenberger, *High Steel: The Daring Men Who Built the World's Greatest Skyline* (HarperCollins, 2004); Neal Bascomb, *Higher: A Historic Race to the Sky and the Making of a City* (Doubleday, 2004). More popular studies of the Empire State Building, still containing useful information, include Theodore James, *The Empire State Building* (Harper & Row, 1975), and Jonathan Goldman, *The Empire State Building Book* (St. Martin's Press, 1980).

For treatments of the skyscraper as a symbol and the Empire State Building in particular as the fulfillment of America's self-image, see Thomas A. P. van Leeuwen, *The Skyward Trend of Thought* (MIT Press, 1988); Stanley Peter Andersen, "American Ikon: Response to the Skyscraper, 1875–1934" (PhD diss., University of Minnesota, 1960); Mark Kingwell, *Nearest Thing to Heaven: The Empire State Building and American Dreams* (Yale University Press, 2006); Rem Koolhaas, *Delirious New York: A Retroactive Manifesto for Manhattan* (Monacelli Press, 1978); and Ann Douglas, *Terrible Honesty: Mongrel Manhattan in the 1920s* (Farrar, Straus and Giroux, 1995).

Any deeper investigation of the history of the Empire State Building must begin with the in-house Notebook, cited above, created by an anonymous author in the office of Starrett Bros. and Eken and published as *Building the Empire State*, edited by Carol Willis (1998). Further exceptionally detailed documentation of the construction process is contained in the twelve-part series, "The Empire State Building," published in *The Architectural Forum* between June 1930 and July 1931. These include: Richmond Harold Shreve, "[I:] The Empire State Building Organization," 52, no. 6 (June 1930): 771–73, 787–88, and "II: The Window-Spandrel-Wall Detail and Its Relation to Building Progress," 53, no. 1 (July 1930): 98–104; J. L. Edwards, "III: The Structural Frame," 53, no. 2 (Aug. 1930): 241–46; Henry C. Meyer Jr., "IV: Heating and Ventilating," 53, no. 4 (Oct. 1930): 517–21; H. F. Richardson, "V: Electrical Equipment," 53, no. 5 (Nov. 1930): 639–44; Fred Brutschy, "V [misprint, really VI]: Plumbing," 53, no. 5 (Nov. 1930): 645–46; William Frederick Lamb, "VII: The General Design," 54, no. 1 (Jan. 1931): 1–8; Bassett Jones, "VIII. Elevators," 54, no. 1 (Jan. 1931): 95–99; Irwin Clavan, "IX: The Mooring Mast," 54, no. 2 (Feb. 1931): 229–34; John P. Carmody, "X: Field Organization and Methods," 54, no. 4 (Apr. 1931): 495–506; H. R. Dowswell, "XI: Materials of Construction," 54, no. 5 (May 1931): 625–32; and William Frederick Lamb, "XII: The Ground Floor Lobbies and Shops," 55, no. 1 (July 1931): 42–46.

Of great historical interest are the publications issued by Empire State Inc. to commemorate the opening. These include *Empire State: A History* (Publicity Associates, May 1, 1931) and *Empire State, a Pictorial Record of Its Construction* (Vernon Howe Bailey, W. E. Rudge, 1931). The first publication, which was widely reproduced and issued for sale at the observation deck gift shop, contains several photos by Lewis W. Hine. The second commemorative volume, published more exclusively in large format, features the somewhat misty architectural drawings of Vernon Howe

Bailey. Perhaps the divergent sensibilities of Belle Moskowitz and the officers and directors of Empire State Inc. could be read in the decisions regarding these illustrations.

The brothers Paul and William A. Starrett both published memoirs, although only Paul Starrett's later publication makes specific mention of the Empire State Building. Colonel William A. Starrett, *Skyscrapers and the Men Who Build Them* (Charles Scribner's Sons, 1928), is nevertheless a fascinating and highly detailed examination of the skyscraper construction process. Paul Starrett, *Changing the Skyline: An Autobiography* (McGraw-Hill, 1938), focuses more on the business of construction than its technical details.

The best resources about the significant figures on the corporate level are, for John Jakob Raskob, David Farber, *Everybody Ought to be Rich: The Life and Times of John J. Raskob, Capitalist* (Oxford University Press, 2013). John J. Raskob's papers are held at the Hagley Library, Wilmington, Delaware, and are accompanied by a useful finding aid.

For Alfred E. Smith, see Christopher M. Finan, *Alfred E. Smith: The Happy Warrior* (Hill and Wang, 2002) and Matthew and Hannah Josephson, *Al Smith: Hero of the Cities. A Political Portrait Drawing on the Papers of Frances Perkins* (Houghton Mifflin, 1969). Smith's papers are held in numerous archives. For his time as governor, see New York State Archives (Albany, NY), Governor Alfred E. Smith Central Subject and Correspondence Files, 1919–1920, 1923–1928. Some papers pertaining to his employment by Empire State Inc. may also be found at the Museum of the City of New York, Alfred E. Smith papers, 1886–1945 (activity #07638).

For Belle Lindner Israels Moskowitz, I relied on Elisabeth Israels Perry, *Belle Moskowitz: Feminine Politics and the Exercise of Power in the Age of Alfred E. Smith* (Oxford University Press, 1987). For more on Belle Moskowitz, see also Robert A. Caro, *The Power Broker: Robert Moses and the Fall of New York* (Alfred A. Knopf, 1974), and Oliver H. P. Garrett, "A Certain Person," Profiles, *The New Yorker*, October 9, 1926, 26–28. Belle Moskowitz's papers, along with a finding aid, are held at Connecticut College, Linda Lear Center for Special Collections and Archives, Belle Moskowitz papers 1883–1953 (MS.042, OCLC: 1155114429). Some of the collection is viewable online.

Other important figures, who play a small role here but were highly significant in the story of the Empire State's construction, include the structural engineer, Homer G. Balcom. See Richard G. Weingardt, "Homer Gage Balcom and the Empire State Building," *Leadership and Management* in *Engineering* 11, no. 2 (Apr. 2011): 209–18. For Aubrey Weymouth, chief engineer of Post & McCord, see William Engle, "Men and Steel," *New York World-Telegram*, April 7, 1931 [ESB Scrapbook 1.2 (42–82)].

Beyond this, one dives into the innumerable articles in contemporary newspapers, magazines, trade journals, and advertisements published during the 1920s about the then-new phenomenon of skyscraper construction. Among these, the five-article series published in *Fortune* magazine is undoubtedly the best. These articles were reissued by the American Institute of Steel Construction Inc. as *The Skyscraper from Fortune* (Mar. 1930, 2–35).

Journalism and Mythology

The Empire State Building has stood now for almost one hundred years, but what it stands for has changed perhaps unrecognizably over the course of that century. What its owners and builders imagined as they built it, and what its contemporary commentators believed as they witnessed it going up, have been no more enduring than any other newspaper headline. Perhaps this fluidity of cultural significance is demonstrated most dramatically by the fall of Alfred E. Smith himself from public consciousness. When the Empire State Building was constructed, it was believed former Governor Smith would be remembered as a man of biblical proportions, a man who "like King Solomon, paid tribute to the workers in stone and metal," and who "in his day and generation typified the heights to which American thought and industry had reached, in an age already opening out on vistas the most splendid in the history of the human race" ("The Empire State Building," editorial, *New York Enquirer*, May 10, 1931 [ESB Scrapbook 5.2 (1–40)]). Smith's forty-nine-word statement at the ceremonial laying of the Empire State's cornerstone on September 9, 1930, was compared with Abraham Lincoln's Gettysburg Address ("Day by Day with Governor Patterson," [source missing], Sept. 14, 1930 [ESB Scrapbook 1.1 (17–35)]). For this reason, Smith's thumbnail history of the site during this event is worth quoting. "Eighty years ago," he said, "a very short time when one stops to think, this land was part of a farm. More recently it was the site of one of the great hotels of the world, and soon it will be the location of the tallest structure ever built by man." Even into the 1960s, the comparison with Lincoln was noted as a commonplace.

(See Jordan A. Schwartz, "Al Smith in the Thirties," *New York History* 45, no. 4 [Oct. 1964]: 316–30, available on JSTOR.) Upon turning businessman following his disastrous defeat in the 1928 presidential election, Smith was compared to Cincinnatus, "who rose to the heights of Dictator in the Roman Empire . . . only to return quietly to his plow when his task was done" (Alfred Abelli, "Al Smith's No Business Novice," *Nation's Business: A General Magazine for Businessmen*, May 1930, 98–101).

It is impossible today to reproduce the extent to which Smith—and his signature brown derby—hung over the building like a talisman. Its monumental stature was understood merely as an echo of his even greater standing. "When the workmen put the last piece of steel in place in record time, they were so elated at their accomplishment that they wanted to celebrate it in some unique fashion. Carpenters stick a branch of a tree in the ridge of a house when they reach the highest point. The Smith workmen wanted to put a giant brown derby on top of the mooring mast when they finished the job. Smith said no" ("Ex-Governor Works 15 Hours a Day," *Brooklyn Daily Eagle*, Dec. 28, 1930, 55). Note that the men are called "Smith's workmen." This was not an isolated fantasy. Visiting the workers who constructed the mooring mast, James R. Ullman concluded his piece for the Brooklyn *Standard Union* with this elegiac hallucination: "By 3 o'clock they are on their way streetward and homeward. Then the jagged summit of the tallest building on earth will be as lonely, as far removed from the city's life, as the Sahara or the Himalayas. Only steel and wind and fading sunlight, and perhaps a symbolic brown derby, dropped on its topmost summit by some sentimental angels winging through the sky" ("How High is Up?," Dec. 4, 1930, 2).

Today, it would not surprise me if more people associate Lewis Hine's *The Sky Boy* with the Empire State Building than recognize Alfred E. Smith or know of his involvement in the building's construction. The fluctuations of historical memory, and so of any figure's perceived importance, are charted not by progress, but by the shifting valence of myths.

Already during its construction, the Empire State Building was mythological. While skyscraper construction is a supremely technical and technological undertaking, the reporting on skyscraper construction is not. These two opposing trends—the technological and the mythological—collide in almost every report, including those created by the builders themselves. In addition, there is an inherent sloppiness in recordkeeping the closer one looks and the harder one tries to pin down specifics. The result is an inexact, fuzzy kind of history, rather than the history of "facts."

The Fuzziness of Primary Sources

Empire State Inc.'s Scrapbooks at the Avery Library, and the Starrett Bros. and Eken's Notebook and Photo Album, both at the Skyscraper Museum, are without question the three most important archival sources for understanding the construction of the Empire State Building. Here I address some of the ambiguities of relying on these sources for the construction of history.

The clipping agencies that gathered the material for Empire State Inc.'s Scrapbooks were not always conscientious in annotating their sources. Often, they assumed a working knowledge of contemporary publications, which now renders some of their attributions cryptic or obscure. Today's sophisticated search engines may resolve some of these questions, but not all. Many clippings in the ESB Scrapbooks have become unique copies of vanished newspapers, magazines, and trade journals. Some of the sources I quote could not be traced back to their origin. Therefore, their citation is now "ESB Scrapbooks."

I was fortunate to consult these Scrapbooks numerous times over the course of more than a decade. During my first visit to the archive, the Scrapbooks were in their original bindings, complete with paper clips, rubber cement, and brittle cellophane tape. In later consultations, the Scrapbooks' creased, crumbling, oversize, black pages had been unbound and separated into twenty-three archival boxes. At the time of this writing (January 2025), deterioration has advanced so far that the Scrapbook pages are no longer accessible, pending extensive and expensive conservation. The newspaper and magazine stock was never meant to last a hundred years.

I hope the original pages will be preserved. Digitization can only hint at the handmade quality and pride of ownership evident in the collage-like physical artifact. The Scrapbooks present in one place a more or less chronological unfolding of the project as seen in the contemporary press, providing a running eyewitness account of the building's construction. In this sense, the Scrapbooks represent a profound time capsule of ideas, arguments, and fashionable and fanciful responses to the transformation of New York City by tall buildings. Taken individually, many of the clippings monotonously repeat the statistics concerning the project's size and voracious appetite for materials. Seen as a collection, the unifying undertone is an exhilaration at finding America at the forefront of a new, global civilization, with the skyscraper as its symbol.

As a resource for factual information, however, the articles collected in the Scrapbooks are problematic. Newspapers have a ring of authority and authenticity. But this authority frequently cannot be confirmed or is contradicted by other authoritative sources. In chapter 1, "The Named and the Unnamed," I illustrate the difficulty of relying on these primary sources to determine basic facts, in that context, the number of men who participated in construction. It's worth pursuing another dimension of this problem here.

On July 27, 1930, *The New York Times* published one of the most detailed accounts of construction, "Greatest Skyscraper Rises on a Clockwork Schedule," by C. G. Poore. "More than 3,000 men are daily at work. Going through the building one encounters them on all floors. Among them are 225 carpenters, 290 bricklayers, 384 brick laborers, 328 arch laborers, 107 derrick men. On the structural steel 285 men are working, while 249 other men are installing the elevators and 105 are doing electrical work. There are 182 plumbers, 194 heating and ventilating men, as well as many trade specialists, inspectors, checkers, foremen, clerks and water boys" (114). These figures are a peculiar kind of historical fact. Presuming the numbers were provided by the Starrett Bros.' timekeeper's office, which had the most precise data regarding the workforce at any given moment, they may be considered authoritative, but only for the single day on which Poore visited the site. The numbers would have been different the following day and every other day during construction.

Once again, the question *How many men worked on the Empire State Building?* is itself imprecise. One would have to specify *when*. A satisfactory answer to the question will therefore depend on what kind of answer one finds satisfying, whether general or precise, and then *how* general or *how* precise. Historical sources always set a limit to precision. To confirm Poore's answer, it would be necessary to corroborate his figures, and corroboration is now impossible. The nature of my questioning here necessarily bumped up against this limit at every turn.

Elsewhere, we can read many other authoritative figures. Richard Massock of the Associated Press cites 3,500 as the number of workers in his syndicated article, published variously as "Skyscraper Worker Eats

Cafe Lunch," *Democrat* (Leadville, CO), October 3, 1930; "Modern Building Methods Scrap Famous Old Hod," *Brooklyn Daily Eagle*, October 9, 1930, 5; and numerous other regional papers (ESB Scrapbook 2.2 [1–37]). The figure 4,500 was published in "Empire State Work Goes Ahead Rapidly," *New York Telegram*, June 6, 1930 (ESB Scrapbook 1.1 [1–16]); and the figure of 5,000 appears in "Sky Boys Who 'Rode the Ball' on Empire State," *The Literary Digest* 109, no. 8 (May 23, 1931): 30–32. Kenneth Andrews, in "At Thirty-Fourth and Fifth," *The Greensboro Record* (Greensboro, NC), October 26, 1930, 13, offers the range of 6,000–7,000 men practicing twenty-five to thirty trades. The number 7,000 is used in "Huge Quantities of Material for Empire State Building," *Journal of Commerce*, July 21, 1930 (ESB Scrapbook 1.1 [1–16]), as well as in "The High Place," *New Yorker*, November 22, 1930 (ESB Scrapbook 1.2 [42–82]). William Engle says 8,000 men and thirty trades, in "Men and Steel," *New York World-Telegram*, April 7, 1931 (ESB Scrapbook 1.2 [42–82]). Margaret Norris and Brenda Ueland, in "Riding the Girders," *Saturday Evening Post*, April 11, 1931, cite thirty-two trades. John Walker Harrington says sixty-seven trades in "Quarter Mile Climb to Summit of Building Efficiency," *Real Estate Magazine* 19, no. 8 (May 1931): 4–24 (ESB Scrapbook 5.2 [1–40]).

Although a definite number of men practicing a definite number of trades must have contributed to the building, those definite numbers are no longer determinable. This indeterminacy is now a historical fact. Therefore, when John Tauranac, for instance, writes, "There was specialist after specialist—sixty in all on the Empire State Building," he is estimating or rounding out, although he does not acknowledge this (*Making of a Landmark*, 179). This kind of "close enough" estimate is sufficient for a certain kind of historical writing. Nevertheless, it reproduces, compounds, and at the same time erases the fuzziness of contemporary journalistic accounts, presenting a satisfying answer with a ring of authority to a question that cannot, in fact, be answered authoritatively.

I find this loss of precision, the limit that sources set to precision, fascinating and worth noting, itself evidence of the inherent foaminess of historical events, which written history tends to clean up or ignore. In my view, erasing the fuzziness of sources is a kind of presentism, which makes the past seem more "immediate," when in truth "the past" is created by mediation. Unless we preserve a sense of this mediation, we are not writing history but a kind of historical fiction.

Occasionally, of course, this diffusion of sources enables a richer picture to emerge. Syndicated articles often appeared in different forms in different papers, edited according to the host paper's available space and editorial orientation. My quotations from Gilbert Swan, "Sidelights of New York," is a composite of two versions: the Saratoga Springs, New York, *Saratogian*, September 9, 1930 (ESB Scrapbook 1.1 [17–35]), and the New Jersey *Atlantic City Evening Union*, September 5, 1930 (ESB Scrapbook 1.1 [1–16]), which differ in length and some details.

One looks to archival sources to get as close as possible to a historical event. In the case of the Empire State Building, the Starrett's Photo Album at the Skyscraper Museum, together with the in-house Notebook, published as *Building the Empire State*, are the nearest thing to hearing the contractor think aloud about the project. Along with Empire State Inc.'s Scrapbooks, the Starrett's Photo Album and Notebook are historical documents in their own right, evidence of the corporate culture and mood during construction as well as of the contractor's narrative presuppositions. The information these documents provide is invaluable. And at the same time, like the Scrapbooks, the Starrett's documentation is riddled with small but significant inaccuracies if one delves beneath the surface. If precision is the goal, they cannot be relied on uncritically.

The Starrett's Photo Album contains a group photo of the field engineers, the men who used surveyors' theodolites to ensure the steel columns were plumb. The group photo includes the men's names, which is a remarkable level of detail and, in many cases, the only evidence of an individual's participation in the construction. This documentation enabled me to identify the surveyor seen in Lewis Hine's *Men at Work* with the caption, "Checking Up." According to the Starrett's Photo Album, his name is F. Hickey. But I could find no additional information about F. Hickey. It's possible my research was simply inadequate. It's also possible the caption in the Photo Album garbled his name. This is the case for a second field engineer, seen in the same group photo and identified there as Orville "Keyes." His name was really Orville Edward James *Keays*. The significance of this misspelling will depend on one's perspective, on the kind of historical answer one finds satisfying, and on how "authoritative" one considers primary sources. From a corporate perspective, relegated to an in-house memento, it's a minor clerical error. But historically, on the scale of the individual, it marks the boundary between recognition and obscurity.

Distinguishing these men as individuals has ramifications beyond simply establishing their historical role in the construction of the Empire State Building. Their separate identities also affect the interpretation of Lewis Hine's photographic practice and the use of his photographs as historical evidence. Hine photographed several of the field engineers named in the Starrett's Photo Album. A portrait of Orville Keays almost identical to the one of F. Hickey that Hine chose for *Men at Work* resides in the collection of Hine's photos at the Avery Library (Avery: 1971.003.00153). Another field engineer named in the Starrett's album, E. Peterson, appears in the same pose in a portrait held at the George Eastman Museum (GEM: 1985.0145.0005). These three images show Hine working to capture an idea. Only the individual depicted is different. With some additional clarification, the Starrett's Notebook restores their individuality. At the same time, recognizing them as individuals distinguishes Hine's *portraits* (of specific men) from his *work portraits* (of an idea or activity, using the worker as an illustration).

Misspellings are the cruel joke of primary sources. When newspapers included the names of the Craftsmanship Award winners, the names were frequently garbled. In one article, the New York *Evening World* turned Walsh into "Wals," Irons into "Irens," and Coons into "Orens." The following day, the same news item ran in the daily edition of *The World* and added "Kololff" for Kozloff to the errors ("Empire Building Workers Receive Golden Buttons," *Evening World* [New York], Oct. 8, 1930, and "Building Craftsmen Rewarded for Skill," *World* [New York], Oct. 9, 1930 [ESB Scrapbook 1.2 (42–82)]).

But misspellings do not always lead to obscurity. In numerous published articles, ironworker Neil Doherty's name is misspelled "Niel." The error propagated with syndication. One peculiarity of the present era of search engines, however, is that this misspelling facilitated locating numerous instances of the image. "Neil Doherty" is a very common name. "*Niel* Doherty" far less so. The image can be found in the Washington, DC, *Herald* (Sept. 20, 1930), *Boston Herald* (Oct. 5, 1930), Syracuse *Post-Standard* (Oct. 5, 1930), *Baltimore American* (Dec. 3, 1930), and elsewhere.

Just as inaccuracies, typos, or clerical errors at the source propagate with syndication, so they are absorbed into archives, databases, and other resources that any researcher must consult in order to pin down facts. In this way, the error becomes part of the historical record. The award-winning bellman, Thomas Walsh, shares his page in *Men at Work* with a hoisting engineer, anonymous in Hine's book, but identified on the back of

Hine's image of him at the George Eastman Museum. His name is Robert "Bob" Long (GEM: 1977.0167.0002; see *Men at Work* below the caption, "The hoist engineer controls the cable that lifts the load"). However, until recently, his name was incorrectly transcribed in the Eastman database as "Lang." (See also GEM: 1977.0167.0005, 1977.0167.0006, 1977.0167.0008, and Avery: 1971.0003.0086, 1971.003.00087.) In addition, a 1925 image by Hine, used to illustrate John Monk Saunders, "It's a Tough Job, but Somebody's Got to Swing It," *The American Magazine* 99 (June 1925): 44–47, 214–16, is included in the box of Hine's Empire State photos collected at the George Eastman Museum, where it is misidentified as belonging to that series (GEM: 1977.0160.0016).

Similarly, at the J. Paul Getty Museum, a famous Hine photograph of two workers completing the peak of the mooring mast, also included in *Men at Work* beneath the caption, "Finishing Up the Job," incorrectly identifies the men as Harold and Romie McClain. This identification is attributed to Naomi Rosenblum, based on Nina Rosenblum's correspondence with ironworker Harold McClain. However, either Naomi or Nina Rosenblum appears to have misread McClain's September 27, 1981, letter, in which he identifies the *derrick* that he and his brother installed and dismantled, not the men using it in the photo. He writes: "Note the men bolting up at story 102 are about thirty five or forty feet below the derrick. Thus the three connectors who rigged the derrick for removal became the highest in the world on a man made structure. They were Harold McClain, Romie McClain and Blackie Bavona [probably Anthony Bivona]" (Getty: object number 84.XM.470.4). Once again, whether this mistake in the institutional database that constitutes documented history is significant depends on one's perspective. Uncorrected, it has long outlived Harold McClain and will persist indefinitely. (For technical information about this final fifteen-ton guy derrick, positioned on the mooring mast at the "FF level," equivalent to the one-hundredth floor, see "Topping Out the Empire State Building," *Engineering News-Record* 106, no. 4 [Jan. 22, 1931]: 153–54.) Lewis Hine also photographed "Blackie" Bavona/Bivona, but garbled both his name and nickname, writing "Jo Bivana (Bladsie)" (GEM: 1977.0160.0009).

Harold McClain spells Victor "Frenchy" Gosselin's name "Goslin." Lewis Hine also frequently misspelled men's names in his handwritten notes on the backs of his photographs, for example, "Frenchy Geslin" (GEM: 1977.0160.0026). Hine's own name was not immune. His photos were published worldwide, and in the Austrian theater magazine *Die Bühne* he is "Levis W. Mine" (Paul Csernyei, "Empire State Building-New York," *Die Bühne* 8, no. 306 [June 1931]: 10–11). Hine's subsequent fame renders this mistake humorous, rather than existential, as a similar mistake would be for an otherwise unknown worker.

Mistakes like this are of many kinds and degrees. There are mistakes of memory that affect accurate citation. Hine's epigraph for *Men at Work* apparently does not come from the source he cites, William James, "The Moral Equivalent of War" (1910). Kate Sampsell-Willmann locates the origin of the quotation instead in James's 1899 essay, "What Makes Life Significant?" ("Lewis Hine, Ellis Island, and Pragmatism: Photographs as Lived Experience," *The Journal of the Gilded Age and Progressive Era* 7, no. 2 [Apr. 2008]: 221–52).

There are ambiguities created by conflicts in the documentation, which may affect fundamental issues of historical interpretation. Hine's work portrait of Thomas Walsh, bellman, in *Men at Work* next to the caption "The hoist engineer controls the cable that lifts the load," shows Walsh holding the two cords by which he signaled to the hoisting engineer how the derrick was to move. Perhaps this photo was staged or posed, as is often the case with Hine. (Note the work portrait of a riveter in *Men at Work*, under the heading "Riveting Gang." The rivets he drives are already rounded, and the riveting gun has no hose attached, no power source.) In the image of Thomas Walsh, what are we to make of the cords he holds? Did Walsh use bells? The Starrett's Notebook, as well as trade journal articles, suggest not or not only. It was traditional for these signals to be communicated by a bell or gong. However, on the Empire State, Frank H. Bedell, one of the electricians, invented a simultaneous light signal to provide additional information. According to several sources, a portable telephone was also installed between engineer and signalman. (See John P. Carmody, "Empire State Building X: Field Organization and Methods," *Architectural Forum*, 54 no. 4 [April 1931]: 495–506. For the attribution to Frank H. Bedell, see Willis, *Building the Empire State*, 87, report 24. For a far more detailed description of the operation of the innovative system, see *Safety Stories*, Bulletin no. 10 [Committee on Accident Prevention Building Trades Employers' Association, Jan. 1931]. See also "Planning and Control Permit Erection of 85 Stories of Steel in Six Months," *Engineering News-Record* 105, no. 8 [Aug. 21, 1930]: 280–84.) The bellman's use of bells is an obscure technicality, and yet uncertainty surrounding this detail affects the "authenticity" or "accuracy" not only of the depiction in Hine's photograph, but equally of the trade journal articles, and so the precise documentation of the Empire State's construction history and techniques. Did Hine pose Walsh with the cords because they were easier to see, although they were not used? Or is the question instead whether the innovative system was employed uniformly by all bellmen or only by some or only sometimes? Or maybe Walsh just preferred the older method? In other words, like so many other aspects of the Empire State Building's construction, the question *How did the bellman and the hoisting engineer communicate?* does not have a single, definitive answer.

And then there is deliberate mythmaking, as in Margaret Norris's article about the ironworker Paul Sommerville Rockhold, known as "Whitey" (Margaret Norris and Brenda Ueland, "Riding the Girders," *Saturday Evening Post*, Apr. 11, 1931, and Margaret Norris, *Heroes and Hazards: Talks with the Daredevils of To-Day; True Stories of the Careers of the Men Who Make Our Modern World Safe by Their Courage* (Macmillan, 1932). Checking up on primary sources may have multifarious effects. It may fix a person more specifically in the historical record, producing contradictions. Rockhold appears in the 1930 US census, age twenty-nine, a resident of 294 Lafayette Avenue, Brooklyn. The genealogical information there belies Norris's characterization of Rockhold's ancestry, confirming a pattern in her article of shaping figures to fit a cultural and ethnic ideal. At the same time, pursuing the record may add a degree of specificity, which helps to make the man more substantial than a blip in *The Saturday Evening Post*. Norris mentions Rockhold's Certificate of Superior Craftsmanship. According to the *Building Congress News*, he received it for work on the Hotel Governor Clinton at a ceremony held on July 17, 1929 ("New Honorary Craftsmen," Oct. 1929, 7–8).

Finally, diving into the substratum of historical documentation, we reach the level of pure, unverifiable cultural history, where truth is whatever a document says, if you're inclined to believe it. This kind of history is tantalizing and profoundly human. Several years prior to Norris's article, Rockhold had appeared in a pair of newspaper articles documenting his miraculous survival after a twelve-story fall at a building on Riverside Drive ("Worker Falls 7 Stories, Bounds 5 More; Lives," *Oakland Tribune*, Jan. 7, 1926, sec. B, p. 10, and "Tumbles 12 Stories; Lives," *Altoona Mirror* [Altoona, PA] Mar. 2, 1926, sec. II, p. 13). Both articles include photos of Rockhold in the hospital. From 1950–1969, Paul Sommerville Rockhold was an agent for the International Association of Bridge, Structural and Ornamental Iron Workers, Local 361, 89-19 Ninety-Seventh Avenue,

Ozone Park, New York. He died two days after his ninety-sixth birthday, on May 8, 1996, in Broward County, Florida.

Fun Facts

Perhaps we should refer to the frothiness of historical documentation as the level of "fun facts," a kind of history distinct from the search for accuracy and precision. It's what the world is mostly made of, and there is so much of it surrounding the construction of the Empire State Building that a small sample deserves a place here.

Paul "Whitey" Rockhold's deadpan response to his Craftsmanship Award, "I got a good feed out of it," likely refers to the ceremony on July 17, 1929. According to the *Building Congress News*, the exercises featured music by the orchestras of Rudy Vallée and Professor J. Scully, as well as a buffet luncheon for all workmen and guests. Such entertainments were uncommon at award ceremonies, but the Building Congress held an annual luncheon or dinner for all the year's honorary craftsmen. The event that winners of the Empire State's Craftsmanship Awards would have attended was held on April 10, 1931, at the Building Trades Employers' Association building on 2 Park Avenue. According to *The Brooklyn Daily Eagle*, 2,100 workers were invited ("Mechanics to Meet," Apr. 7, 1931, 27). According to the *Building Congress News*, two hundred honorary craftsmen attended. The article notes that "through the thoughtfulness of Charles Doyle, elevator constructor, a nine piece band composed of his son, Tom Doyle, and his Agawan Collegians entertained with popular music" ("Craftsmen From Fifty-four Buildings Attend Meetings," May 1931, 6). This was only one of several such celebrations, stratified by class, that helped to mark the completion of the Empire State Building. The owners, architects, and contractors held a dinner a week later, on April 16, 1931 (Empire State Inc., "Dinner in Commemoration of the Completion of the Empire State," Apr. 16, 1931; see Hagley Library Digital Archives ID: 08117074_empire_state). Several months earlier, on September 26, 1930, more than one hundred subcontractors hosted a luncheon in honor of the steel contractors, Post & McCord ("Laud Building Unity," *New York Times*, Sept. 27, 1930, 35). The construction foremen held a dinner-dance on November 21, 1930, at the Hotel Martinique in Manhattan (City Brevities, *New York Times*, Nov. 21, 1930, 20). And the architects, Shreve, Lamb, and

Harmon, were simultaneously honored and roasted, along with William Van Alen, designer of the Chrysler Building, and others, at the Beaux Arts Ball on January 21, 1931, where they appeared rather awkwardly in costumes modeled after their buildings ("A Beaux Arts Ball for Fiery Moderns," *New York Times*, Jan. 18, 1931, 81).

The architects were not alone in transforming skyscrapers into fashion. Gladys Parker, creator of the syndicated cartoon *Flapper Fanny* and author of the New York *Daily News*' weekly fashion feature, Femininities, drew a series of textile designs inspired by the Empire State Building, one of which she wore to the Beaux Arts Ball. (See "Towering with Chic." Femininities, by Gladys, [source missing (*Daily News*)], n.d. [ESB Scrapbook]. See also "'Flapper Fanny' Turns Stylist" *Danbury Times* [CT], Feb. 10, 1931, and "Flapper Fanny," *Brownsville Herald* [TX], Feb. 13, 1931, 5.) The designs were retailed by B. Altman & Co., the chief officer of which, Colonel Michael Friedsam, was one of the directors of Empire State Inc. ("Prints of Empire State Building Design," B. Altman & Co. advertisement, [source missing], [1931?] [ESB Scrapbook]).

Drawing history from contemporary sources may render the moment much looser and less unique than the subsequent canonization of the Empire State Building makes it seem. In most histories of the Empire State, much is made of the fact that, at the grand opening, President Herbert Hoover pressed a special button at the White House, which turned on the lights in the building in New York. But a similar theatrical opening was staged for the Woolworth Building in 1913, when President Woodrow Wilson "touched an electric button in the White House" to illuminate the fifty-five stories of that skyscraper ("World's Biggest Office Building Is Dedicated," *Brooklyn Times Union*, Apr. 25, 1913, 30). Coverage of the Woolworth Building prefigured much of the coverage of the Empire State. "Miracles of the Modern Skyscraper's Growth," from 1912, features an extended narrative from an ironworker, "a man who has been engaged in skyscraper construction for years" (*New York Sun*, Apr. 7, 1912, 52). No name is mentioned, but the article is illustrated by numerous photographs by Edwin Levick, showing ironworkers walking the beams and riding the ball, remarkably similar to Lewis Hine's Empire State Building images. Even Al Smith's cats were in a sense traditional. Kittens born in the Chrysler Building also served as ironworkers' mascots ("Threat of Kitten Litter for Every Floor Fills Empire State Janitors with Fear," *New*

York World-Telegram, May 29, 1931 [ESB Scrapbook 5.2], and "Kittens Born High Above Ground," *Brooklyn Daily Eagle*, Apr. 13, 1930, 5).

Revering the Empire State as a symbol of America in the 1930s also tends to obscure the fact that responses to it were not uniformly positive. Critic Douglas Haskell was not alone in finding the base of the building unsatisfying ("The Empire State Building," *Creative Art* 8, no. 4 [Apr. 1931]: 242–44; see also Douglas Haskell, "A Temple of Jehu," *The Nation* 132, no. 3438 [May 27, 1931]: 589–590). Talbot Faulkner Hamlin considered the street and avenue facades "a disappointment": "As is the case in so many high buildings, a soaring and carefully composed grandeur above disintegrates near ground level" ("The Prize-Winning Buildings of 1931," *The Architectural Record* 71, no. 1 [Jan. 1932]: 10–26). The building's most recognizable feature, its dirigible mooring mast, was also not universally admired. "Nothing could be stupider and sillier than this mast," sniffed Lewis Mumford ("Notes on Modern Architecture," *New Republic* 66, no. 850 [March18, 1931]: 119–22). And, despite the seriousness with which the architects (and I) treated the grand rendering of the building that decorates the lobby, the *San Pedro News-Pilot* placed it squarely in the context of folk and popular culture: "There is something reminiscent of a state fair exhibit about the picture, but although we looked for shocks of wheat and smoking factories in the background, all we saw were planetary rings, stars, and moons in the ceiling, like the marks cartoonists make when they mean 'Bam, glub, zowie!'" ("Broadway Echoes," May 14, 1931, 6).

The Empire State Building was always a part of popular culture, and much of its history takes place in this dimension, where questions of precision and accuracy play little role. The mooring mast may never have been seriously intended for dirigible docking, although the owners were serious enough to commission a study to determine its legality and to inquire with Navy officials about the requirements. (See Charles Pickett, "The Empire State Building Mooring Mast," *Air Law Review* [Brattleboro, VT] 2, no. 2 [Apr. 1931]: 130–52. The article was a revision of a memorandum prepared by the office of Messrs. Chadbourne, Stanchfield & Levy in January 1930 for Empire State Inc.) But while no dirigible ever moored there, other zeppelin-like objects did nuzzle the building. "Twenty-two huge, gayly-colored rubber balloons, in the shape of fantastic faces, miniature Zeppelins and comic strip characters set sail from West Thirty-fourth Street yesterday afternoon in a flurry of snow, at the conclusion of Macy's annual and most resplendent Thanksgiving Day parade. Buffeted by a strong wind, they soared around the towering Empire State Building and headed over the East River toward Brooklyn, Queens and the open sea. The finder of each one will find attached to it an order for $25 worth of merchandise at R. H. Macy & Co." ("Macy Balloons Head for Sea as Parade Finale," *New York Herald Tribune*, Nov. 28, 1930, 36). The balloons represented the entire Katzenjammer family. According to the *New York Herald Tribune*, they struck the building at the sixtieth floor. *The New York Times* said the seventieth floor, adding that Santa also arrived in a Zeppelin ("Santa Brings Snow for Macy's Parade," Nov. 28, 1930, 4).

Although it never received incoming dirigible passengers, the mooring mast began its career broadcasting outgoing news as soon as steelwork was completed, even before it was clad in its aluminum skin. "Results of the Governorship election, compiled from telegrams received over direct wires to *The New York Times*, will be flashed on Tuesday night from the world's highest building. A General Electric Company air beacon with a 34-inch light has been installed on the ninetieth floor of the Empire State Building and its rays may be observed over a wide area," announced *The New York Times*. The searchlight would swing up and down to the north if Roosevelt led the count and would shine steadily in the same direction if he were elected. The light would perform the same operation facing south to signal the lead or election of his opponent, Charles H. Tuttle. (See "Election Results Will Be Shown by Times Bulletins and Signals," *New York Times*, Nov. 4, 1930, 23. See also "Election Results Flashed by The Times from 90th Floor of Empire State Building 1,150 Feet Above Street," *New York Times*, Nov. 2, 1930, sec. N, p. 20.)

But perhaps contemporary sources serve their most significant function, beyond questions of accuracy or factuality, by reminding us that historical writing is a performance and that history struts across a stage.

> On a special series of sets designed by Arthur Knorr, coproducer and art director at the Capitol, and assisted by the Chester Hale Girls[,] Vincent Lopez and his orchestra, [*sic*] will tell the story of the rise of the Empire State Building in music, dance, and pantomime form on the Capitol stage for the week beginning Friday. Beginning with the barren site, working up through the various stages of crucible steel, molten metal and girders, pushing their way upward to form a new skyline for Manhattan, the production will end with a dirigible moving

across the stage and tying up to the mooring mast. Lopez will be featured along with George Jessel and Helen Kane.

("This Week at the Capitol," *News-Record* [New York], May 12, 1931 [ESB Scrapbook]; see also, Irene Thirer, "Laemmle Announces Film Lineup," *Daily News* [New York], May 11, 1931, 120).

LEWIS WICKES HINE

As far as I have been able to determine, only one scholar has recognized that Lewis W. Hine specifically photographed the winners of Certificates of Superior Craftsmanship. See Ezra Shales, "Corporate Craft: Constructing the Empire State Building," *The Journal of Modern Craft* 4, no. 2 (2011): 119–45, DOI: 10.2752/174967811X13050332209206. Shales follows a very similar path of research to that conducted here, employing many of the same sources. However, he does not follow his conclusion to a specific identification of individual men beyond those already identified by Hine in his notes on the working prints housed at the Avery Library and those identified in Empire State Inc.'s in-house newsletter, *Empire Statements*. Shales also seems to believe that the Craftsmanship Awards were sincere appreciations of craftsmanship. For my contrasting interpretation, see chapter 5, "Splendid Ideals."

A conceptually similar, and often more successful and detailed attempt to trace the subjects of Lewis Hine's photographs can be found at "The Lewis Hine Project." Created by Joe Manning, the blog, *Mornings on Maple Street*, is dedicated to identifying the children in Hine's child labor photographs from the 1910s.

Regarding the Empire State photographs, most scholars write as if the decision to photograph men of different trades was an expression of Hine's fascination with the construction process, not his specific assignment to photograph Craftsmanship Award winners. Timothy J. Duerden, in a typical example, contends, "Hine came to understand very quickly that it would not do to just stand on the streets below and take pictures of the building progressing skyward; he had to actually join the Sky Boys and the other workers in their labors as they ascended toward the heavens. Hine, therefore, photographed all aspects of the building's construction, from the steelworkers and riveters leading the way upward . . . to those other tradesmen, such as the bricklayers and carpenters, following up from below" (*Lewis Hine: Photographer and American Progressive* [McFarland, 2018], 144).

This highlights one reason critics have failed to notice the pattern in Hine's Empire State worker portraits: the preference for seeing Hine as an independent artist, not a working photographer who also happened to be a photographer of genius. In retrospect, Hine's genius overwhelms the facts of his daily work and in this way, strangely, the appreciation of his work distorts the history of its production.

The artistic appreciation of Hine's work may also conceal another, entirely commercial motivation for him to have suppressed the names of individuals and to stress instead his photographs' abstract, conceptual content. To survive as a freelance photographer, Hine licensed his images for general use, in essence, as "stock" photography. In this context, a general designation, "worker," may have been more attractive to potential clients than the specific, "Peter Madden, asbestos worker." Indeed, Hine arranged his catalogs by these generic descriptions. Under the heading "Men Workers at Work," Hine's 1921 catalog of photos for publication included "Bindery, Brewery, Buttons, Candy, Cannery, Cigars, Cotton mill, Furs, Glass, Pottery, Tailoring, Ice-cream, Steel mill: casting. Steel mill: emery wheel. Steel mill: handling hot iron. Steel mill: puddler. Steel mill: rolling steel. Steel mill: wash-up of men. Steel mill: steam hammer." Under the heading "construction work," Hine offers: "Derrick. Dump carts. Pick and shovel. Sledge hammer. Steam drill. Steam shovel. Swinging ladder" (Lewis Hine, "Social and Industrial Photographs, Hine Photo Company, 27 Grant Avenue, Yonkers, N.Y.," New York Public Library, Lewis Hine papers, ca. 1908–ca. 1921 [MssCol 1399]).

The essential contemporary sources about Lewis Hine, his work portraits, and his job at the Empire State Building are "Treating Labor Artistically," *The Literary Digest* 67, no. 10 (December 4, 1920): 32–34; "He Photo-Interprets Big Labor: Camera Studies of Men at Work by Lewis W. Hine," *The Mentor*, September 1926, 42–43 Hester Donaldson Jenkins, "Man and the Skyscraper," *The Commercial Photographer* 6, no. 11 (Aug. 1931): 634–36; Elizabeth McCausland, "Lewis Hine: Portrait of a Photographer (1938)," *History of Photography* 16, no. 2 (Summer 1992): 102–4; Beaumont Newhall, "Lewis W. Hine," *Magazine of Art* 31, no. 11 (Nov. 1938): 637; Robert W. Marks, "Portrait of Lewis Hine: His Name Is Little Known, but His

Pictures Are Etched in the Conscience of the Nation," *Coronet*, February 1939, 147–57.

Critical sources about Hine are voluminous. Those I engaged with most often included Judith Mara Gutman's *Lewis W. Hine and the American Social Conscience* (Walker, 1967), which I believe offers the clearest critical impression of Hine's personality and practice; *America & Lewis Hine: Photographs 1904–1940*, forward by Walter Rosenblum, biographical notes by Naomi Rosenblum, essay by Alan Trachtenberg (Aperture, 1977); Kate Sampsell-Willmann, *Lewis Hine as Social Critic* (University Press of Mississippi, 2009); Timothy J. Duerden, *Lewis Hine: Photographer and American Progressive* (McFarland, 2018). The critical essays I found most useful, in addition to those cited below, in the section, "Interpretations of Hine and His Photography," included Melissa Dabakis, "The Individual vs. the Collective: Images of the American Worker in the 1920s," *IA. The Journal of the Society for Industrial Archeology* 12, no. 2 (1986): 51–62; Judith Mara Gutman, "The Worker and the Machine," *Afterimage* 17, no. 2 (Sept. 1989): 13–15; and C. Zoe Smith, "An Alternative View of the 30s: Hine's and Bourke-White's Industrial Photos," *Journalism Quarterly* 60, no. 2 (June 1983): 305–10.

For insight into Hine's personality and his sense of himself as a photographer, no source is better than his letters, collected in *Photo Story: Selected Letters and Photographs of Lewis W. Hine*, edited by Daile Kaplan (Smithsonian Institution Press, 1992). Unfortunately, there are numerous errors in the introduction and notes to this volume of Hine's letters. Archival sources for the same letters can be found in the Lewis Wickes Hine papers at George Eastman Museum, "Lewis Hine. Letters Photocopied from Social History Archives, Univ. of Minn. ALibraries [*sic*]" and in the Judith Mara Gutman papers (New York Public Library [MssCol 5982]).

Hine's photographs began appearing in Paul and Arthur Kellogg's journal—variously named *Charities and The Commons* (1905–1909); *The Survey* (1909–1921); and *The Survey Graphic* (1921–1952)—beginning in 1907. His work studies of workers, craftsmen, and craftswomen, appeared in numerous issues beginning in 1921. See, among others, "The Railroaders: Work Portraits," *Survey Graphic* 47 (Oct. 29, 1921): 159–66; "Power Makers: Work Portraits," *Survey Graphic* 47 (Dec. 31, 1921): 511–18; "The Man on the Job: Work Portraits," *Survey Graphic* 47 (Mar. 25, 1922): 991–96.

Hine's Empire State photos appeared in the photo story "Up from the City Streets," *Survey Graphic* 65 (Jan. 1, 1931): 361–65. Hine published twenty-eight Empire State photos in his 1932 book, *Men at Work: Photographic Studies of Modern Men and Machines* (Macmillan, 1932). A handy, inexpensive reprint is available, Lewis W. Hine, *Men at Work*, second edition with a supplement of eighteen related photos (Dover, 1995). For a more extensive collection of Hine's Empire State images, see Freddy Langer, editor, *Lewis W. Hine: The Empire State Building* (Prestel-Verlag, 1998). For a representative sample of Hine's career work from the George Eastman Museum collection, including a facsimile of *Men at Work*, see *Lewis Hine: From the Collections of George Eastman House, International Museum of Photography and Film* (DAP/Distributed Art Publishers, 2014).

Prints of Hine's Empire State images not included in the Avery Library and George Eastman Museum collections are scattered among numerous archives, museums, libraries, and in private collections around the world. In this context, the question of "authentic" representations of the workmen's voices is echoed in the problem of authentic Lewis Hine prints. In the 1990s, a controversy or a scandal erupted in the world of art collectors regarding prints of Hine's works. A complaint was lodged against Walter Rosenblum, a leading Hine scholar, the first curator of his archive, and Hine's friend and student in his last years, alleging that photographs sold by Rosenblum, purportedly printed by Hine himself, had in fact been made many years after his death. A settlement was reached in August 2001. (See Ralph Blumenthal, "The F.B.I. Investigates Complaints About Lewis Hine Prints," *New York Times*, Aug. 16, 2001, sec. E, p. 1, and Richard B. Woodward, "Too Much of a Good Thing," *The Atlantic*, June 2003, 67–76.)

Hine's only published writing about the Empire State Building project is Lewis Hine, "Up Goes the Skyscraper," *Young Wings*, February 1934, 4–5. For a list of Hine's essays and articles, as well as his photographic publications, and a survey of work about Hine up to 1977, see Naomi Rosenblum, *America & Lewis Hine*, 138–42. For the history of *The Survey Graphic*, see Caroline A. Lanza, "'Truth Plus Publicity': Paul U. Kellogg and Hybrid Practice, 1902–1937" (PhD diss., University of Washington, 2016).

Interpretations of Hine and His Photography

Each of the critical studies about Lewis Hine that I cite, enormously useful in situating him in the currents of early twentieth-century thought and social practice, approaches Hine as a thinker who conveys ideas through photographs. As a result, the critics themselves tend to think about Hine's images, rather than look carefully at them. Kate Sampsell-Willmann is typical in turning the men in Hine's photos into symbols of work in the abstract: "Indeed, the skywalkers were visually perfect images of the masculine work ethic, pictured by Hine the imperfect messenger, the product of their labor a Jacob's ladder. Be he Icarus, the sky boy, or the foundation man, each man at work represented a character in a grand morality play, the denouement of which was the salvation of work and society itself" (*Lewis Hine as Social Critic*, 208–209). Beyond this preference for conceptualizing Hine's work, one of my primary contentions is that art historians haven't really known what to do with Hine as a person, finding him too negligible a character to have authored such powerful, enduring photographs. Thus Alan Trachtenberg, who eliminates the workers from Hine's photos by considering them representations of "work itself," pursues this pattern by eliminating Hine from the photographic process: "Hine participates in the making of the tower by serving as its faithful reflection—its self-consciousness, one might say. It is as if the making of the tower, an epitome of the constructive potential of labor, photographs itself" ("Ever—the Human Document," in Rosenblum, 135).

Much of the "mythological" interpretation of Hine's images demonstrates this desire to discern a "greater" source of power in the photographs than Lewis Hine himself. Alexander Nemerov, by contrast, attributes godlike powers to Hine in *Soulmaker: The Times of Lewis Hine* (Princeton University Press, 2016). Nevertheless, he equally avoids looking at the individuals in Hine's images by presuming that "each of the workmen he [Hine] photographed was a kind of self-portrait as Hine mulled, and invented, what his own heroism had been" (168). Of the interpretive works that fantasize about Hine's photographs, none is more elaborate than Nemerov's.

Critiques of Hine as a thinker using photography to convey a social message tend to focus on his alleged failure to uphold an anti-corporate stance. George Dimock is most explicit, asserting that "following the war, Hine's role changed from social reformer to corporate apologist" ("Children of the Mills: Re-Reading Lewis Hine's Child-Labour Photographs," *Oxford Art Journal* 16, no. 2 [1993]: 37–54). An alternative view of Hine's shift in the 1920s and 1930s from social reform toward "work portraits" can be found in Domenica M. Barbuto, PhD, and Martha M. Kreisel, "'To Keep the Present and Future in Touch with the Past'—Lewis Wickes Hine," *Behavioral & Social Sciences Librarian* 13, no. 1 (1994):

11–38 (published online Oct. 18, 2008). They write, "Unlike the child labor photographs which emphasized the repression of the factory system, Hine's work portraits seem to celebrate the industrial process and the significant role workers play." Patricia Pace, while disagreeing with Dimock, nevertheless reasserts his criticism. For her, in the work portraits, Hine had resolved "the difficult anxieties of the industrial age by linking the natural male body with the machine" ("Staging Childhood: Lewis Hine's Photographs of Child Labor," *The Lion and the Unicorn* 26, no. 3 [Sept. 2002]: 324–52). And Peter Seixas, in "Lewis Hine: From 'Social' to 'Interpretive' Photographer," *American Quarterly* 39, no. 3 (Autumn 1987): 381–409, writes: "Whereas the prewar Hine had been delivering a challenge to the employers of child labor and the managers responsible for the deplorable accident rates in the Pittsburgh mills, he now offered himself for hire to employers." Seixas leaves it unclear how Hine was supposed to survive as a freelance photographer without employers.

Regarding Hine's employment at the Empire State Building, I have asserted that Belle Moskowitz is the most likely source. But this remains an open question. Did Hine know his Hastings-on-Hudson neighbor, architect Richmond Shreve? It's possible that, prior to his employment by Empire State Inc., Hine was aware that some of his neighbors were involved in the project. He would certainly have known after he was hired. (See "Hine's Photos of 'Empire' to Be Shown Here; Shreve, Balcom and Andres Helping in Erection of World's Tallest Building," *Hastings News*, Aug. 15, 1930 [ESB Scrapbook 1.1 (17–35)].) Although I dispute the notion that the commission came through Shreve, it's not impossible that Hine knew him or others in the architect's circle socially through his wife, Sara Rich Hine. On March 20, 1930, the same week that steelwork on the Empire State began, *The New York Times*' Suburban Social Notes included this item: "Mrs. Lewis Hine of Hastings entertained the Hastings Literature Club at her home" (Mar. 20, 1930, 36). Timothy J. Duerden further notes that Shreve and Hine's homes were near to each other (143). For the attribution of Belle Moskowitz as the source of Hine's employment, see Jim Rasenberger, "The 'Sky Boys,'" (*New York Times*, Apr. 23, 2006) and Elisabeth Israels Perry, *Belle Moskowitz: Feminine Politics and the Exercise of Power in the Age of Alfred E. Smith* (208). Rasenberger's claim is unsubstantiated. Perry points to Judith Mara Gutman as her source, but no evidence is cited in Gutman's text (Gutman, 58). See also John Tauranac, who notes Hine's sociological background, but not his yearslong connections to Belle Moskowitz (282). Duerden remarks on the numerous, progressive connections between Hine and Moskowitz, including their work at settlement houses and at Ethical Culture, but blandly concludes these "would surely have led to their paths crossing once in a while" (143). Ezra Shales identifies Belle Moskowitz's son, Josef Israels II, as Hine's employer, citing Tauranac (135). That Moskowitz and Israels employed Hine is well documented and, several years after the fact, Hine referred to "Joe" Israels as "my mentor on [the] Empire State job" (letter to Berenice Abbott and Elizabeth McCausland, Sept. 30, 1938, in Kaplan, *Photo Story*, 121). But this still leaves unresolved the question of how Hine came to be employed.

A question I do not address in the text, but which deserves to be mentioned, concerns Hine's ideas for *Men at Work*. It is often believed that Hine conceived of his book as being for children. Kate Sampsell-Willmann explicitly claims: "*Men at Work* was intended as a Children's book" (*Lewis Hine as Social Critic*, 168). Alexander Nemerov calls it "a book for child readers" (167). This contention is based on Hine's letter to Paul Kellogg (Sept. 8, 1932) requesting a review of the book in *The Survey Graphic*, in which Hine says: "It was built as a picture book for children, from the adolescent up, and even we blasé adults can get a good deal from it, I hope" (Kaplan, *Photo Story*, 48; cf. Sampsell-Willmann, *Lewis Hine as Social Critic*, 187). But a book for children "from the adolescent up" pretty much excludes *children*, per se, and in his 1909 article, "Social Photography: How the Camera May Help in Social Uplift," Hine refers to adults as "us older children." This leaves open the question of whether Hine was himself being playful. Further, it provides an additional example of how an impression of Hine's personality influences the interpretation of his words. (See Lewis Hine, "Social Photography: How the Camera May Help in Social Uplift," in *Proceedings of the National Conference of Charities and Correction at the Thirty-Sixth Annual Session Held in the City of Buffalo, New York, June 9–16, 1909*, ed. Alexander Johnson [Press of Fort Wayne, 1909], 355–59.)

In his letters, Hine comes across as quite playful, as well as modest, erudite, passionate, and occasionally arch. Interpreting Hine's personality as revealed in his private writings may also affect how we interpret his descriptions of his experience at the Empire State Building. In my view, Hine had a teacher's sensitivity to the specific needs of his audience. The "thrills" he describes to young readers in *Young Wings* may have been more dangerous than he lets on there, when explicitly addressing young readers. On December 10, 1930, Hine gave a talk at the Hastings-on-Hudson Rotary Club. A local paper reported:

> Lewis W. Hine, photographer of Locust Hill, almost lost his life when a plank gave way while he was walking 60 stories above the ground on the new Empire State Building, he revealed before the Rotary Club at its luncheon at Farragut Inn yesterday. Mr. Hine, a former Rotarian, declared the 'safety gang' had not anchored the plank and as he stepped on it the board began to 'give,' but that his other foot, which came down immediately, righted the plank again. A steel worker nearby told Mr. Hine that he almost fainted when he saw the local man step on the plank, he said.
>
> ("Photographer Tells of Skyscraper Thrill," *Statesman* [or *Herald?*] [Yonkers, NY], Dec. 10, 1930 [ESB Scrapbook 2 (1–37)]; for *Young Wings*, see New York Public Library, Judith Mara Gutman papers [MssCol 5982], Series II.B. *Lewis W. Hine and the American Social Conscience* [1967] box 22, folder 2: "Writings Lewis Hine National Research Project 1937").

Hine's modesty frequently led him to conceal his own feelings about his work. Therefore, it's worth noting when he refers to himself. Regarding Hine's ride in a basket to photograph the completion of the mooring mast, see the image of "Sluke" Ryerson and Oscar Johnson, now held at the George Eastman Museum, which shows the basket itself (GEM: 1977.0160.0038 and here on page 219). The only comment in which Hine refers to himself in all the surviving documentation is scribbled on the back of another image, also housed at the George Eastman Museum, showing the derrick that lofted this basket, the same derrick installed by the McClain brothers and "Blackie" Bavona/Bivona (GEM: 1977.0162.0001). Hine writes there, perhaps with some pride: "The very derrick which swung Hine out."

Hine's photographs of daring steelworkers, of course, remain central to his popularity. The term "Skyboy" or "Sky Boy" has become generic when referring to these images. Most commonly, it is used today to designate Hine's portrait of Victor Gosselin riding the hoisting ball. But Hine himself used the title for a different photo, published as a frontispiece to *Men at Work*, which I discuss in chapter 9, "The Sky Boy," although Hine also gave that photo the title Icarus in other contexts. Hine was still referring to the photo as "Icarus" in May 1931 ("Sky Boys Who 'Rode the Ball' on Empire State," *The Literary Digest* 109, no. 8 [May 23, 1931]: 30–32). In that article, Hine comments, "The name was suggested by the fact that the figure expresses the sense of flight." Nevertheless, to my ear, *Sky Boy* is a far superior title, considering that in the myth, Icarus flies too close to the sun on his waxen wings and plummets back to earth. Despite his frequent playfulness, there is no reason to believe Hine wished to be ironic about the ironworkers' audacious skyward climb. Instead, the title *Icarus* may again show Hine employing "grand" mythological language, without fully considering its implications. But *The Sky Boy* itself becomes a myth. Completing the circle, an idealized drawing of Hine's portrait of Frenchy Gosselin was used as the cover for an actual children's book, *Sky Boys: How They Built the Empire State Building*, by Deborah Hopkinson, illustrated by James E. Ransome (Dragonfly Books, 2012).

Another phrase often associated with Hine's photographic practice is the "human document." It's not clear when or where Hine began to use this phrase to describe his own motivations. Interestingly, however, the editors of *Life* magazine also used the phrase to denote the surprising humanity of otherwise alien lives in a note to the premier issue in 1936. In this instance, however, the editors were not referring to Lewis Hine but to Margaret Bourke-White. Describing her photograph of the newly constructed Fort Peck Dam in Montana, featured on *Life*'s first cover, they wrote, "What the Editors expected—for use in some later issue—were construction pictures as only Bourke-White can take them. What the Editors got was a human document of American frontier life which, to them at least, was a revelation" ("Introduction to This First Issue of *Life*," *Life* 1, no. 1 [Nov. 23, 1936]: 3).

Finally, whatever Hine's attraction to machines and modern industrial processes, his abiding concern remained the people he encountered. Throughout his career, Hine chose to photograph his human subjects frontally, often looking at the camera. Variations on the phrase "look him in the eye" thus recur frequently in the critical reception of his work.

In captioning his photo of Peter Madden, discussed in chapter 7, "'Look Him in the Eye,'" with this phrase, it is possible that Hine was alluding to Walt Whitman's poem, "Mannahatta": "The mechanics of the city, the masters, well form'd, / beautiful-faced, looking you straight in the eyes."

Hine's preference for eye contact characterizes his whole career, as many critics have noted. See especially Alan Trachtenberg's observation regarding the Ellis Island portraits:

> He [Hine] learned how to achieve a certain physical distance, corresponding to a psychological distance, that allowed for a

> free interaction between the eyes of the subject and the camera eye. Put another way, he allowed his subjects room for *their* self-expression. This is something that cannot be taught, cannot be reduced to rules. As much as in any other aspect of his style, Hine's own character expresses itself in where he places himself *vis-à-vis* his subject. The camera set down before the subject opens a place, creates a scene in which the subject can stand forth and the camera can do its work of recording.
>
> ("Ever—the Human Document," in Naomi Rosenblum, *America & Lewis Hine*, 125).

See also Kate Sampsell-Willmann: "Although the subject may have felt like they were staring into a black anonymous lens . . . , from Hine's perspective, he was looking them straight in the eye, squarely and without flinching" ("Lewis Hine, Ellis Island, and Pragmatism," 228).

THE MEN

The literature regarding "workers" in general on the Empire State Building is vast. The literature about specific individuals is by contrast exceedingly scanty. Victor Gosselin was featured in John Cushman Fistere's profile, "No Timid Man Could Hold This Job," *The American Magazine* 111, no. 6 (June 1931): 80–81, 146, in the column Interesting People. This profile is reproduced almost verbatim in Jim Rasenberger's *High Steel* (205–207). Other workers appear in Edmund M. Littell, "Men Wanted," *The American Magazine* 109, no. 4 (Apr. 1930): 46–51, 115–17; "Sky Boys Who 'Rode the Ball' on Empire State," *The Literary Digest* 109, no. 8 (May 23, 1931): 30–32; Margaret Norris and Brenda Ueland, "Riding the Girders," *Saturday Evening Post*, April 11, 1931, 14, 98, 101–2; and Margaret Norris, *Heroes and Hazards* (Macmillan, 1932). See also Lowell Thomas, *Men of Danger* (Frederick A. Stokes, 1936).

While the men themselves have rarely been considered as historical subjects, many aspects of their work and even their attire have been subject to extensive examination. For a fascinating deep dive into the history of the work shirt, see Bryan Shettig, "A Brief History of the Work Shirt

1886–1930" and "A Brief History of the Work Shirt, Part 2: 1930–1940," *The Rite Stuff* (blog), *The Rite Stuff* (Nov. 8, 2021).

Information about the Certificates of Superior Craftsmanship and the New York Building Congress's Committee on Recognition of Craftsmanship comes from the archives of the New York Building Congress (NYBC) at the Tamiment and Robert F. Wagner Labor Archives, New York University (WAG.167). In addition to unpublished reports and documents, the archive holds the NYBC's official publication, the *Building Congress News*, which changed its name in July 1931 to *New York Building Congress News*. My interpretation of the history and symbolic significance of the Certificates of Superior Craftsmanship is based almost entirely on writings by William Orr Ludlow, who chaired the NYBC's Committee on Recognition of Craftsmanship from its inception in 1925 until 1940. Belief that the recognition of craftsmanship should be "spiritual" and not monetary was a central tenet of all statements by members of the committee and those who spoke at award ceremonies. Nevertheless, this belief was not universally held beyond the confines of the NYBC. John Jakob Raskob, lead financier on the Empire State Building and a pioneer in both installment buying and employee stock plans, understood the question of the worker's "interest" quite differently than Ludlow: "Unless a manager or worker has an interest—a financial interest—in what he does, he will hardly develop his capability. He is not content to see all the money he makes going to someone else." Raskob goes on to say, "Together with money he must have complete responsibility in his own sphere. He must be more than a cog" (quoted in Farber, *Everybody Ought to Be Rich*, 190).

The design of the Craftsmanship Award button was updated in 1929 through a competition, curated by William Van Alen, at the Beaux-Arts Institute of Design. The winner was Ray Wever, a student at the institute (William O. Ludlow, "Report of the Committee on Recognition of Craftsmanship," *Building Congress News*, April 1930, 6). While the award's utility in furthering the careers of its winners may be ambiguous, it was considered a legal guarantee of competence. In December 1931, the *New York Building Congress News* reported that a Certificate of Superior Craftsmanship had been recognized in the New York State Supreme Court as evidence of "expert witness" status ("Supreme Court Recognizes Craftsmanship Certificate," *New York Building Congress News*, Dec. 1931, 8). Although I have cast doubt on their authenticity, the *Building Congress News* frequently published blurbs of praise for the awards from workmen (see "Report of Committee on Recognition of Craftsmanship," *Building Congress News*, Jan. 1928, 8, and "Report of Committee on Recognition of Craftsmanship," *Building Congress News*, May 1928, 6). Another fun fact: The gold button awarded to Empire State Craftsman entitled them to free entry to the building's observation deck ("Craftsmen from Fifty-Four Buildings Attend Meetings," *Building Congress News*, May 1931, 6).

I have concentrated here on the question, *Who were the men?* But there is a parallel question of importance concerning those who worked on the Empire State Building, largely unaddressed, *Who weren't the men?* In the first case, they weren't women. The only two women mentioned in the Starrett's Notebook and Photo Album are the nurse, C. Lynch, about whom I could find nothing further, and Elizabeth Eager, who died as a result of falling debris (see below for more about Elizabeth Eager). Among the materials suppliers for the building, Ann Anzel appears to have been the only woman. She ran the Specialty Manufacturing Company, which provided all the building's mirrors ("Women in Business 'Happiest in World,'" *Brooklyn Daily Eagle*, Aug. 31, 1931, 16). They were not Black Americans. During construction, the Colored Mechanics Association complained to former Governor Alfred E. Smith that no "negro mechanics" were employed on the construction of the Empire State Building ("Al Smith Recognizes Fight of Mechanics," *The Chicago Defender*, Oct. 18, 1930, 10). For a history of labor union discrimination, see Marc Karson, *American Labor Unions and Politics, 1900–1918* (Southern Illinois University Press, 1958). See also Herbert Hill, "The Problem of Race in American Labor History," *Reviews in American History* 24, no. 2 (June 1996): 189–208. For a historical perspective, see Charles H. Wesley, "Organized Labor and the Negro" (1939), Howard University Faculty Reprints, paper 213 (https://dh.howard.edu/reprints/213).

The celebration of Kahnawake Mohawks in construction begins with Joseph Mitchell, "The Mohawks in High Steel," *The New Yorker*, September 17, 1949, 38–52, reprinted in Edmund Wilson, *Apologies to the Iroquois* (Farrar, Straus & Cudahy, 1960). Kahnawake Mohawks were recognized as an independent nation in 1926 and were singled out again as a distinct nation with the right to work in the US in 1940. A 1940 *New York Times* editorial, "Our Indian Colony," mentioned that approximately three hundred "Indian" ironworkers lived in Brooklyn and the Bronx. "If a structural steel worker requires superior physical coordination, the Iroquois stock has it. They are a superior race in many ways" (May 20, 1940, 13). For an excellent discussion of how the figure of the "Indian" was assimilated into twentieth-century modernism, while retaining the traditional ethnographic clichés of wildness, nomadic life, and authenticity, see Fiona Green, "'The Iroquois on the Girders': Poetry, Modernity, and the Indian Ironworker," *Critical Quarterly* 55, no. 2 (July 10, 2013): 2–25. For a history of Mohawk ironworkers from the perspective of the workers themselves, see Richard Hill, *Skywalkers: A History of Indian Ironworkers* (Woodland Indian Cultural Educational Centre, 1987), 29. Hill's book contains a comprehensive bibliography of essays and articles concerning the Kahnawake ironworkers.

In ironworker Harold McClain's conversations with documentary filmmaker Nina Rosenblum, he stated that Victor Gosselin was Mohawk (personal communication, Jan. 25, 2020).

Regarding construction workers' attitudes toward the Craftsmanship Awards, I claim that the men's voices were not recorded. But this does not necessarily mean the men were never invited to speak. According to a *New York Times* report, coincidentally published on May 1, 1931, the day of the Empire State Building's grand opening, seventeen men received Certificates of Superior Craftsmanship for work on the Paramount Annex, 521 West Forty-Third Street. At that ceremony, held on April 30, 1931, "most of them made brief acceptance speeches" ("Mechanics Get Awards: Paramount Annex Called Evidence of Faith in Future," 55). As far as I have been able to determine, the winners' speeches were not recorded.

Questions of Identification

Hine's handwritten notes on the backs of his Empire State photos contain many names that I was unable to connect with faces. These prints appear sometimes to have served as Hine's notepads. On the back of an image of Victor Gosselin, now held at the George Eastman Museum, Hine records Frenchy's name (though he spells it "Geslin"), an address, along with numerous other names. Among these are Harry Stetler, foreman, and "Red-Derrickman" (GEM: 1977:0160:0026). "Red" the derrickman is mentioned in other notations, making a tentative visual identification possible. I believe he appears in three photos included in *Men at Work*, most strikingly the one captioned "A derrick man moves up to the next floor." According to Hine's notes, "Red" may have been a policeman in Brooklyn (GEM: 1977.0165.0084). In one image, titled "Derrick gang noon hour," Red sits in the center of his gang (GEM: 1977.0164.0005). I was unable to locate "Harry" Stetler, but Horace A. Stetler, born in Pennsylvania in 1896, is well represented in the genealogical databases. His draft registration card from April 1942 confirms that he worked for Harris Structural Steel, which appears to have supplied men to Post & McCord to erect the Empire State's structural frame. (On the same photo of Frenchy, Hine scribbled "Harris Struct Steel" beneath Gosselin's name.) According to the 1930 census, Horace Stetler lived in Ozone Park, Queens, New York, with his wife and their two-year-old son.

On another photograph of Victor Gosselin, seen in *Men at Work* to the right of the caption, "As the building pushes skyward the connectors stay aloft," Hine writes, "'Frenchy,' our Modern Tarzan, and his buddy take a ride on the ball." The "buddy" who rides the ball with Frenchy was identified by Harold McClain as Buddy Turner. Turner is featured in a series of Hine photos (see Avery 1971.003.00137, 1971.003.00138, 1971.003.00139; GEM: 1985.0156.0004). On the back of yet another print showing Frenchy and this man rigging the derrick, Hine has written "Buddie Turner" with an address, as well as another name, "Curley/D. Stuart?," and the address "2033 Lemoine Ave., Ft. Lee, N.J." (GEM: 1977.0157:0030). Census records identify two brothers, both ironworkers, living with their parents at this address in Fort Lee, New Jersey: James P. and Daniel B. Stuart. Both men were born in Alabama. It was common for ironworkers to be known by nicknames. Daniel appears to be "Curley," as noted on the back of Hine's photo. It is possible the other was "Alabama," the man mentioned in Margaret Norris and Brenda Ueland's article, "Riding the Girders," published in *The Saturday Evening Post* (Apr. 11, 1931). Hine's note creates some confusion, however, since it's unclear whether he means to identify Buddy Turner or Curley Stuart in the photo. I am inclined to believe it's Buddy Turner, following Harold McClain.

Harold McClain also identified "Sluke" (or "Slook") Ryerson, who appears in numerous Hine images documenting the completion of steelwork on the mooring mast (GEM: 1977.0164.0012; Getty Images: 3199736). The name "Sluke" also appears in Hine's handwriting on the back of another photo, the portrait of an unidentified worker (included here on page 191), along with several other names: "Wolff (Asst. Sup); Al Turner (Asst. Sup); Jim Trainer (Boss Rivet); Lowman (Post & McCord)" (GEM: 1977.0154.0024). Sluke stands with a man identified as John Lowman in a portrait in the *Starrett's Photo Album* (89). In his book *Men of Danger*, Lowell Thomas refers to "Sam Lowman" as a steel foreman on the Empire State job (32–33). Perhaps this is the same person and Thomas got the first name wrong. Dick McCarthy also appears on the same page of the Starrett's Photo

Album, standing with a man identified as John Lowman of Post & McCord. Confusingly, however, the two John Lowmans identified by the Starretts on this page are not the same person. According to Harold McClain's identifications, the man standing with Sluke Ryerson in the Starrett's Album may be the assistant superintendent Al Turner, also referred to in Hine's note.

Finally, in an unusually clear-cut case, Hine's photographs of stone-rigger Charles Nelson are marked with his name and address and the note "Stone Rigger 71 years old and active" (GEM 1977:0154:0029; see also GEM: 1977:0154:0028, 1977:0154:0030; Avery 1971.003.00184, 1971.003.00185, 1971.003.00186). The initials "C. N." are clearly visible on the bib of Nelson's overalls.

The Dead

I can document eight fatalities during construction of the Empire State Building, though a few open questions remain. This ambiguity is not peculiar to the Empire State Building. The Chrysler Building was celebrated for the absence of any fatalities during its construction ("No Loss of Life Marked in Chrysler Building Construction," *Brooklyn Citizen*, Jan. 19, 1930, 5). But other published reports claim one death (William Engle, "Men and Steel," *New York World-Telegram*, Apr. 7, 1931 [ESB Scrapbook 1.2 (42–82)]).

The eight Empire State fatalities include the six workmen listed in the Starrett's Notebook—laborers Giuseppi Tedeschi and Luis De Dominichi, ironworker Reuben Brown, and carpenters Sigus [Peder Joachim] Andreasen, Frank Sullivan, and Albert Carlsen—in addition to passerby Elizabeth Eager and the suicide, carpenter Finn Egeland.

Most histories of the Empire State Building take at face value the letter submitted by Starrett Bros. and Eken to the Committee on Accident Prevention of the Building Trades Employers' Association of the City of New York on November 7, 1930, which acknowledges five fatalities ("Only Five Killed at Empire State," *New York Sun*, Nov. 8, 1930 [ESB Scrapbook 1.2]). The Starrett letter was written in response to a request for clarification from the Building Trades Employers' Association, which had met on October 9, 1930, by coincidence one day after the first Craftsmanship Award ceremony, to discuss rumors of a high death toll. These rumors can be found in numerous sources. A letter to the editor of *The Brooklyn Daily Eagle* from Pete Haigney on August 5, 1930, stated that thirty-eight men had been killed and two hundred injured (19). As mentioned in the text, the Communist paper *The Daily Worker* alleged that 128 men had died, seventeen on a single day ("The Empire State Building," May 28, 1931, 4), with an earlier article claiming "over one hundred men seriously injured, crippled for life" ("Conceal Death of Carpenter in Al Smith's New Building," Dec. 10, 1930, 2). I could find no records for the number of men injured.

The Starrett's Notebook includes the names and dates of six worker fatalities, in addition to the passerby Elizabeth Eager (Willis, report 76, p. 167). More recent histories of the Empire State rely on these numbers, though, again, the published figures differ depending on how each author counts. Mark Kingwell cites seven dead (*Nearest Thing to Heaven*, 9) and Geraldine B. Wagner, who also bases her number on the Starrett Notebook, claims six (*Thirteen Months to Go: The Creation of the Empire State Building* [Thunder Bay Press, 2003], 129).

A close examination of the sources provides additional detail concerning these fatalities, sometimes contradictory, highlighting as well several inaccuracies in the Starrett's Notebook. As shown in the text, the Starretts misstate Peder Joachim Andreasen's name. In addition, the Notebook refers to Elizabeth "Eagher," while her death certificate and other genealogical documents spell her name "Eager."

An obituary for Peder Joachim Andreasen appeared in the Brooklyn *Standard Union*, July 16, 1930, 16. An account of his death was published in the Troy, New York *Observer*: "Losing his balance while working on the thirty-second floor of the Empire State Building, [. . .] a carpenter, fell down a shaft to the sub-basement, 35 floors below, and was killed" ("Long Plunge to Death," July 20, 1930 [ESB Scrapbook 1]).

Sources contain conflicting reports concerning carpenter Frank Sullivan's death. In one account, "Sullivan was struck by an arm of a hoisting machine which had become loosened from its mooring. The accident occurred on the 24th floor. Sullivan was killed almost instantly" ("Carpenter Killed While Working in Empire Building," *Home News* [New York], July 30, 1930 [ESB Scrapbook 1.2 (1–41)]). In another, "Leaning out at the twenty-fourth floor to repair a material hoist, Frank Sullivan, 34, [. . .] a carpenter, was crushed to death by a descending car on the Empire State Building" ("Lift Kills Carpenter," *Journal* [New York], July 31, 1930 [ESB Scrapbook 1.2]). Frank Sullivan had received a Certificate of Superior Craftsmanship for work on "Private Dwellings, 70–71st Streets" in August 1929 ("New Honorary Craftsmen," *Building Congress News*, Nov. 1929, 8).

An incidental reference in Lowell Thomas's *Men of Danger* may describe ironworker Reuben Brown's death:

> "They get so used to it they forget there is any danger," explained the official at the Structural Steel Board of Trade. "We had a case of a man who was standing on the edge of a beam where it was temporarily bolted to the column. About twenty floors up. Absolutely nothing for him to steady himself with, of course. He saw a bolt in the column right under him, down a couple of feet, that needed driving in. He just leaned over and swung his maul at it. Well—the weight of the maul naturally carried him off his balance, and shot him clear across Fifth Avenue. He just hadn't thought, that was all." (42)

This same source adds an open question to the problem of counting the dead. Lowell Thomas quotes R. B. Thomas, counsel for the Structural Steel Board of Trade, whose office "records all accidents in the trade, from scratches on the fingers to fatal falls." According to his account, "there were only two iron workers killed in all the time the Empire State Building was being erected" (37). However, I could find no confirmation of a second ironworker's death.

Competing motivations may explain some ambiguity surrounding the number and circumstances of deaths. Starrett Bros. and Eken naturally wished to emphasize the safety measures taken at the site and their effectiveness. Workers' rights organizations, by contrast, wished to highlight lapses and failures. These competing agendas color accounts of carpenter Albert Carlsen or Carlson's death, which occurred on December 10, a month after the Starretts published their letter claiming five deaths. *The Daily Worker* alleged the Starretts attempted to conceal this death, which indeed received less attention than other fatalities ("Conceal Death of Carpenter," Dec. 10, 1930, 2). For Albert Carlsen's death, see "Rising Hoist Kills Carpenter," *World* (New York), December 10, 1930. This article, which spells his name "Carlson," gives his home address as 130 Seventy-Third Street, Brooklyn.

Numerous sources reported Finn Egeland's death, though his name was sometimes spelled Egland. His fall from the building was apparently witnessed by passersby ("Death Plunge Seen by 5th Ave. Crowd," *American*

[Askov, MN?], Apr. 7, 1931 [ESB Scrapbook 1.2]). Some accounts state he was at work: "Finn Egeland, 30, was killed the other day when he fell from the 78th floor of the Empire State Building, New York. Mr. Egeland had work to do at one of the windows and suddenly lost his balance; his body was whirled through space to the roof of an adjoining building where he was found dead. He had come from Kristiansand, Norway, about ten years ago, and had followed the trade of a carpenter" ("Fell from 78th Floor," *American* [Askov, MN], Apr. 23, 1931 [ESB Scrapbook 5]). Contrast this with *The New York Times*:

> A carpenter's helper who formerly had worked on the Empire State Building returned to the structure yesterday morning, presumably in search of employment, and jumped or fell to his death from a window on the seventy-eighth floor, his body falling fifty-seven stories to the roof of the 21st floor extending from the main tower. The body was taken to the West 30th street station and was not identified until later in the day at the city morgue as F. Egland, 30 years old, of 761 44th St. Brooklyn, by Henry Genell, a carpenter who had worked previously with Egland. Genell recalled that Egland had arrived at the building before 8 o'clock and had said he was looking for work. Egland appeared to be despondent, according to Genell. Egland had a wife and one child. The police were inclined to regard the case as suicide.
>
> ("Carpenter's Death at Empire State Building Believed to Be Suicide," Apr. 7, 1931 [ESB Scrapbook 1.2])

The Daily Worker carried another account of the incident: "We asked the workers still on construction to tell us the story of the worker who had committed suicide several weeks ago. We were told that he had been fired and came back two weeks later, despondent, and asked the foreman to give him back his former job. Needless to say he was refused. Poverty and despair overwhelming him, he jumped from the seventy-second floor of the building." According to this article, "the Empire State workers are sullen and morose because of the secrecy which has accompanied the murder of their comrades" (Francine Schneeberg, "48 Killed on Empire

Building," May 13, 1931, 1). Further accounts of Egeland's death can be found in: "Tallest Building Has First Suicide," *Record* (East Grand Forks, MN), April 17, 1931 (ESB Scrapbook 4 [1–31]); "Man Falls From Tallest Building," *New York Sun*, April 6, 1931; "Plunge Kills Man at Empire Tower," *New York Telegram*, April 6, 1931; and "Death Fall at Empire State," *Journal* [location missing], April 6, 1931 (all in ESB Scrapbook 1.2 [42–82]).

Best Guesses

Finally, the identities of currently anonymous workers, especially Craftsmanship Award winners photographed by Lewis Hine, remain the most troubling unanswered questions in this history. Although some of these men could be detected in the historical record, I could not discover enough information to feel confident of the biographies or to connect their biographies to images. These are my best guesses for a few of the remaining workmen.

John Connolly: There are too many John Connollys to count. Yet roofers are less common. According to the 1930 census, a forty-six-year-old roofer named John Connolly lived in Brooklyn, with his wife Alice, and eight children, ages two to fourteen. He was born in Northern Ireland on March 8, 1879. On his 1942 draft registration card, John Joseph Connolly, now age sixty-three and living at 112 Calyer Street, Brooklyn, named his employer, the Tuttle Roofing Company, which still exists today. The company is listed in the Starrett's Daily Job Report. On August 14, 1930, the company had two foremen and six helpers at work placing temporary felt covering over finished floors in the basement and on the fourteenth and fifteenth floors. Perhaps John Connolly was among them. Although I have not been able to connect this man's biography to his image, you can buy a digital print of the New York Building Congress Certificate of Superior Craftsmanship awarded to John Connolly, roofer, for work on the Empire State Building from Alamy.com, an online stock image vendor (image ID: M008BN).

Joseph Leffert: In 1930, a thirty-one-year-old New York native Joseph Leffert, "Helper" in the "Tile" industry, was a roomer in a house on East 142nd Street in the Bronx. If this is the right man, he served in the Army from August 29, 1942, until April 2, 1943. His enlistment classification indicated "Semiskilled construction occupations," and the document states he is "separated with no dependents." The Department of Veterans Affairs lists his death on September 9, 1973.

R. Maddalena: The tile setter R. Maddalena is distinguished as the only man whose full name was not included on the Craftsmanship Awards plaque. It has been impossible to isolate him in the historical record. In the 1930 census, a Romano *Maddelena*, tile setter, is living on Union Street in Jackson, Michigan. This man is forty-one years old, owns his house, and arrived in the United States from Italy in 1912. Ellis Island has the manifest for his arrival aboard the *Mauretania*. He was born in Fanna, north of Venice, in the area famous for its stone and tile work. His profession is "mosaic worker." Several other men named *Maddelena* were also tile setters, but none that I could find named Maddalena. Much more information is available for the tile itself, because its manufacturer, William F. Kenny, was a close friend of Alfred E. Smith and a principal backer of Smith's 1928 presidential campaign. An article published in a local New Jersey paper in August 1930 describes the tile company and its innovative manufacturing process noting that "practically all the tile which is produced in the plant is shipped to New York City, to be used in the construction of the new Empire State Building" ("Oil Now Used as Fuel for Kilns In Brick Plant," [source missing] [New Brunswick, NJ], Aug. 17, 1930 [ESB Scrapbook 1.1 (17–35)]). For more on Al Smith's connection to William F. Kenny, see also "McCooey at Brick Plant," *Brooklyn Times Union*, July 2, 1930, 4. Kenny hosted Smith for a birthday dinner on December 30, 1930 ("Friends Force Smith to Observe Birthday," *New York Times*, Dec. 31, 1930, 4).

William L. Moran: In 1930 a forty-eight-year-old William Moran, steamfitter, lived in Brooklyn, on Marion Street, with his wife of twenty years. Both were born in New York, as were their parents. In 1940, a different William Moran, steamfitter, lived in Linwood, Pennsylvania, south of Philadelphia. This man is sixty-nine years old, unmarried, with a lodger in the house. There are also many other William Morans.

John E. O'Connor, plumber, is another man whose name, rather than identifying him, tends instead to render him anonymous. But perhaps this is him: In 1930, a John O'Connor, age thirty-four, lived with his wife and their three young daughters on Bergen Street, Brooklyn. He was a plumber, born in New York to south Irish immigrant parents. Either he or a different man with the same name won another Craftsmanship Award as a steamfitter's helper for work on the Walker-Lispenard Building on October 20, 1931 ("New Honorary Craftsmen," *New York Building Congress*

News, Jan. 1932, 12). And either he or another man with the same name died at the Veterans Administration Center in Kecoughtan, Virginia, on December 6, 1955. The plumbing installation for the Empire State was performed by J. L. Murphy Inc., then located at 340 East Forty-Fourth Street, New York (Willis, *Building the Empire State*, report 61, p. 150).

Gino Santoni also proved impossible to discern in the historical record. Cement masons were frequently Italian. But I could find no Santonis. Is his name misspelled on the bronze plaque? Several Eugenio *Santinis* arrived in the United States from various points in Italy, including Naples, Genoa, and Turin, in 1902, 1906, 1912, 1913, and 1914. But perhaps Gino Santoni was not Italian. In 1905, a *Eugene* Santini is living in what appears to be a small Hungarian colony in Pohatcong Township, New Jersey. He is listed with more than fifteen census pages of other Hungarians, fifty names per page. This Eugene Santini was born in April 1879, arrived in the United States in 1902, and worked at a cement mill. Based on little more than a hunch, my guess for the visual identification of Gino Santoni/Santini centers on the two men, seen here on page 191, top left, and 192, top. Hine often used backgrounds to hint at his subject's profession. Both men are sitting by piles of lumber. The men are seated outside, since the lumber for concrete formwork on floor arches was hoisted by the steel derricks (Willis, *Building the Empire State*, report 33, p. 105).

The marble setter Louis Shane Jr. may be fixed in the historical record. Louis Joseph Shane was born on March 22, 1877, according to his World War I draft registration card. He grew up in Brooklyn, where his family first appears in the 1880 census. There are seven children in the household, including Louis, the youngest. His parents were born in Baden, Austria, and both emigrated to the US as teenagers. By 1900, Louis, age twenty-three, is already a marble setter. And by 1915, he lives with his wife and their four sons. Louis's 1917 draft registration card states that he is employed by John H. Shipway & Bro., Bolton, Warren County, New York, in the Finger Lakes region of upstate New York. At the time, John H. Shipway & Bro. was one of the premier marble suppliers in the country. After this, however, it becomes unclear which Louis Joseph Shane was employed at the Empire State Building, since his oldest son, also named Louis Shane, born in 1906, was also a marble cutter. The elder Louis Shane died on February 21, 1944. The younger, a Navy veteran of World War II, died in 1956.

Clifford Smith may offer a final illustration of the vagaries of identification, even with extensive representation in the databases. A well-documented man who may or may not be the correct Clifford Smith was born in Portland, Oregon, on October 9, 1900, and died of cancer a few days after his seventy-fourth birthday on October 12, 1974. A 1918 application for a Seaman's Protection Certificate lists his profession as shipbuilder and includes a photograph of the eighteen-year-old man looking confidently at the camera. But the image does not closely resemble any of Hine's portraits taken twelve or thirteen years later. An application for a military burial in 1974 states that he served in the Navy during World War I as an electrician's mate, third class. After the war, he used this training to become a professional electrician. He appears in the 1930 census as Clifford A. Smith, living on Sixty-Eighth Street in Queens with his wife Gertrud and their young son. By 1940, however, this Clifford Smith had divorced, remarried, and moved to California, where he worked at the Mare Island Naval Shipyard. By 1950, he had relocated to Woodland, Washington, where he and his second wife operated the Lakeside Motel at 272 Pacific Highway. Ten years later, he was elected Woodland's justice of the peace. He subsequently served as the Woodland Municipal Police Court judge until his death in 1974. His photo appears in the newspapers, but, again, the older man pictured does not closely resemble any of Hine's portraits from forty years earlier. This Clifford Smith had several grandchildren, children of his son with his first wife. However, after the divorce around 1933 and his relocation to the West Coast, it seems he had no contact with them. His granddaughter had no photographs of him and did not know of his second marriage, his subsequent career, or any connection to the Empire State Building. If this is the right man, his Certificate of Superior Craftsmanship for work on the Empire State Building was, as for so many of the award winners, just a passing episode in a long, eventful, and otherwise ordinary life.

BIBLIOGRAPHY

Abelli, Alfred. "Al Smith's No Business Novice." *Nation's Business: A General Magazine for Businessmen*, May 1930, 98–101.

Alden, Alice. "Beauty in Skyscraper Construction." [Source missing], n.d. Empire State Scrapbook 2 (1–37), p. 11. Avery Architectural & Fine Arts Library, Columbia University.

Altoona Mirror (Altoona, PA). "Tumbles 12 Stories; Lives [Paul Rockhold]." March 2, 1926, sec. 2, p. 13.

American [Askov, MN?]. "Death Plunge Seen by 5th Ave. Crowd." April 7, 1931. Empire State Scrapbook 1.2. Avery Architectural & Fine Arts Library, Columbia University.

American (Askov, MN). "Fell from 78th Floor." April 23, 1931.

Andersen, Stanley Peter. "American Ikon: Response to the Skyscraper, 1875–1934." PhD diss., University of Minnesota, 1960.

Andrews, Kenneth. "At Thirty-Fourth and Fifth." *News-Record* (Greensboro, NC), October 26, 1930, 13.

———. "Building the World's Tallest." [Source missing], November 7, 1930. Empire State Scrapbook 2.2 (1–37), p. 17. Avery Architectural & Fine Arts Library, Columbia University.

Angola (NY) Record. "Back-Pats." November 28, 1929, 4.

Bailey, Vernon Howe. *Empire State, a Pictorial Record of Its Construction*. W. E. Rudge, 1931.

The Baltimore Sun. "Victor Gosselin [Obituary]." August 28, 1943, 11.

The Baltimore Sun. "The Week's News [Victor Gosselin]." August 29, 1943, 3.

B. Altman & Co. "Prints of Empire State Building Design," [date and source missing (1931?)] Empire State Scrapbook. Avery Architectural & Fine Arts Library, Columbia University.

Barbuto, Domenica M., and Martha M. Kreisel. "'To Keep the Present and Future in Touch with the Past'—Lewis Wickes Hine." *Behavioral & Social Sciences Librarian* 13, no. 1 (1994): 11–38. https://doi.org/10.1300/J103v13n01_02.

Bascomb, Neal. *Higher: A Historic Race to the Sky and the Making of a City*. Doubleday, 2004.

Berry, Romeyn. "State and Tioga." [Source missing], n.d. Empire State Scrapbook 6 (1–36), p. 22. Avery Architectural & Fine Arts Library, Columbia University.

Blau, Eleanor. "A Photographer of Immigrants Is Remembered." *New York Times*, September 27, 1984. http://www.nytimes.com/1984/09/27/arts/a-photographer-of-immigrants-is-remembered.html.

Blumenthal, Ralph. "The F.B.I. Investigates Complaints about Lewis Hine Prints." *New York Times*, August 16, 2001, sec. E, p. 1.

Bragdon, Claude. "Architecture in the United States III: The Skyscraper." *The Architectural Record* 25, no. 2 (August 1909): 85–96.

———. "The Shelton Hotel, New York." *The Architectural Record* 58, no. 1 (July 1925): 1–18.

Brooklyn Citizen. "No Loss of Life Marked in Chrysler Building Construction." January 19, 1930, 5.

Brooklyn Daily Eagle. "By the Way [Michael Tierney]." July 9, 1934, 13.

Brooklyn Daily Eagle. "Death Announcement [Frank A. Moeglin]." May 25, 1934.

Brooklyn Daily Eagle. "Empire State Building Opens." May 1, 1931, 2.

Brooklyn Daily Eagle. "Ex-Governor Works 15 Hours a Day." December 28, 1930, 55.

Brooklyn Daily Eagle. "George Robert Adams [Obituary]." March 25, 1949, 23.

Brooklyn Daily Eagle. "Hardware Demand Is Only Moderate." February 11, 1931, 38.

Brooklyn Daily Eagle. "Injured Workmen Sue for $100,000." October 8, 1936, 2.

Brooklyn Daily Eagle. "Kittens Born High Above Ground." April 13, 1930, 5.

Brooklyn Daily Eagle. "Mechanics to Meet." April 7, 1931, 27.

Brooklyn Daily Eagle. "Obituary [Frank A. Moeglin]." November 14, 1934, 31.

Brooklyn Daily Eagle. "Owen Scanlon Dies from Auto Injuries." August 6, 1936, 3.

Brooklyn Daily Eagle. "Raskob Rents Office on the 80th Floor." May 3, 1931, 2.

Brooklyn Daily Eagle. "Rockefeller Lauds Workmen Employed on New Building." June 15, 1930, 44.

Brooklyn Daily Eagle. "Structural Steel Board Declines Al Smith Aid." April 9, 1930, 2.

Brooklyn Daily Eagle. "To Reward Workmen for Craftsmanship." February 1, 1927, 28.

Brooklyn Daily Eagle. "Victor Scores Again with Newest Radio [Advertisement]." October 9, 1930, 4.

Brooklyn Daily Eagle. "Women in Business 'Happiest in World.'" August 31, 1931, 16.

Brooklyn Times Union. "McCooey at Brick Plant." July 2, 1930, 4.

Brooklyn Times Union. "Mrs. Moskowitz' Passing Is Shock to Many Leaders." January 3, 1933, 2.

Brooklyn Times Union. "Selassie Ready to Offer Peace Plan of His Own." December 21, 1935, 2.

Brooklyn Times Union. "World's Biggest Office Building Is Dedicated." April 25, 1913, 30.

Brown, Joseph. "Building Trades Pay." *Brooklyn Daily Eagle*, August 7, 1931, 14.

Brownsville (TX) Herald. "Flapper Fanny." February 13, 1931, 5.

Brutschy, Fred. "The Empire State Building V [misprint, really VI]: Plumbing." *Architectural Forum* 53, no. 5 (November 1930): 645–46.

Building Age. "'Let This Man Do It' Said the Architect." June 1927. WAG.167, box 5, folder 21. Tamiment Library & Robert F. Wagner Labor Archives, New York University.

Building Congress News. "Business Leaders Encourage Men at Craftsmanship Awards." March 1931, 5.

Building Congress News. "Eight Hundred Workmen Witness Chrysler Award." February 1930, 4.

Building Congress News. "Growth of Craftsmanship Should Be Encouraged—Smith." July 1930, 7.

Building Congress News. "Impressive Craftsmanship Award to Men on 40 Wall Street." December 1929, 5–6.

Building Congress News. "New Honorary Craftsmen." October 1929, 7-8.

Building Congress News. "New Honorary Craftsmen." November 1929, 8.

Building Congress News. "Supreme Court Recognizes Craftsmanship Certificate." December 1931, 8.

Building Congress News. "Two Thousand Witness Empire State Building Award." November 1930, 5.

Bulletin (Providence, RI). "200-Foot Mooring Mast for Airships Completed." November 22, 1930. Empire State Scrapbook 2 (1–37), p. 21. Avery Architectural & Fine Arts Library, Columbia University.

Butcher, Harold. "Tallest Building on Earth." *London Daily Herald*, December 11, 1931. Empire State Scrapbook 5.2 (97–123), p. 114. Avery Architectural & Fine Arts Library, Columbia University.

Byck, S. S. "The Southeast Corner." *Brooklyn Times Union*, May 4, 1931, 1.

Carmody, John P. "The Empire State Building X: Field Operations and Methods." *Architectural Forum* 54, no. 4 (April 1931): 495–506.

Caro, Robert A. *The Power Broker: Robert Moses and the Fall of New York*. Alfred A. Knopf, 1974.

The Chicago Defender. "Al Smith Recognizes Fight of Mechanics." October 18, 1930, 10.

Christian Science Monitor. "Tattoo of Riveter's Hammer Quiets Along Line of New York's Skyscrapers." March 2, 1931. Empire State Scrapbook 4 (1–31), p. 2. Avery Architectural & Fine Arts Library, Columbia University.

Chronicle (Milford, DE). "L.D. Cault Company [Advertisement]." November 27, 1931. Empire State Scrapbook 12 (1–30), p. 13. Avery Architectural & Fine Arts Library, Columbia University.

Clavan, Irwin. "The Empire State Building IX: The Mooring Mast." *Architectural Forum* 54, no. 2 (February 1931): 229–34.

Clune, Henry W. "Seen and Heard." *Democrat and Chronicle*, June 16, 1931, 15.

Columbia Missourian. "What Others Say: Honoring Craftsmen." October 21, 1930, 8.

Committee on Accident Prevention Building Trades Employers' Association. *Safety Stories*. Bulletin 10. Committee on Accident Prevention Building Trades Employers' Association, January 1931.

Contracting Stone Setters Association and the Journeyman Stone Masons and Setters Union. "Contract," 1930. Building Trades Employers' Association, WAG.196, box 8, folder 22. Tamiment Library & Robert F. Wagner Labor Archives, New York University.

Courier (Buffalo, NY). "Wrecking Gotham Buildings Is Favorite Outdoor Sport." August 18, 1930. Empire State Scrapbook 1.1 (17–35). Avery Architectural & Fine Arts Library, Columbia University.

Crane, Hart. *The Bridge*. Liveright, 1970.

Cruger, George. "Lewis Hine." *Arts in Virginia* 16, no. 1 (Fall 1975): 16–40.

Csernyei, Paul. "Empire State Building-New York." *Die Bühne* (Vienna, Austria) 8, no. 306 (June 1931): 10–11.

Dabakis, Melissa. "The Individual vs. the Collective: Images of the American Worker in the 1920s." *The Journal of the Society for Industrial Archeology* 12, no. 2 (1986): 51–62.

Daily Boston Globe. "Airship Landing 1225 Feet Above Fifth Avenue." December 7, 1930, sec. D, p. 2.

Daily Mail (London). "Mankind's Tallest Structure Nears Completion." February 1, 1931. Atlantic Edition. Empire State Scrapbook 3 (1–19), p. 17. Avery Architectural & Fine Arts Library, Columbia University.

Daily Worker. "Conceal Death of Carpenter in Al Smith's New Building." December 10, 1930, 2.

Daily Worker. "The Empire State Building." May 28, 1931, 4.

Daily Worker. "Firing out of Town Workers Is AFL Plan." August 5, 1930, 2.

Daily Worker. "If Blood Be the Price." May 21, 1931, 4.

Distributed Art Publishers. *Lewis Hine: From the Collections of George Eastman House, International Museum of Photography and Film*. DAP, 2014.

di Donato, Pietro. *Christ in Concrete*. Signet Classics, 1993.

Dimock, George. "Children of the Mills: Re-Reading Lewis Hine's Child-Labour Photographs." *Oxford Art Journal* 16, no. 2 (1993): 37–54.

Douglas, Ann. *Terrible Honesty: Mongrel Manhattan in the 1920s*. Farrar, Straus & Giroux, 1995.

Dowswell, H. R. "The Empire State Building XI: Materials of Construction." *Architectural Forum* 54, no. 5 (May 1931): 625–32.

Duerden, Timothy J. *Lewis Hine: Photographer and American Progressive*. McFarland, 2018.

Edwards, J. L. "The Empire State Building III: The Structural Frame." *Architectural Forum* 53, no. 2 (August 1930): 241–46.

Eken, Andrew J. "Beyond the Skyline." *Building Congress News*, May 1930, 6.

Eliot, T. S. *Selected Poems*. Ecco, 1967.

Emerson, Ralph Waldo. "American Civilization." *The Atlantic Monthly*, April 1862.

Empire State Inc. "Dinner in Commemoration of the Completion of the Empire State." April 16, 1931. Hagley Library Digital Archives. Object ID: 08117074_empire_state.

Engle, William. "Men and Steel." *New York World-Telegram*, April 7, 1931. Empire State Scrapbook 1.2 (42–82), p. 63. Avery Architectural & Fine Arts Library, Columbia University.

Esposito, Michael D. "The Travails of Pietro di Donato." In "Between Margin and Mainstream." *Melus* 7, no. 2 (Summer 1980): 47–60.

Evening World (New York, NY). "Empire Building Workers Receive Golden Buttons." October 8, 1930.

Farber, David. *Everybody Ought to Be Rich: The Life and Times of John J. Raskob, Capitalist.* Oxford University Press, 2013.

Finan, Christopher M. *Alfred E. Smith: The Happy Warrior.* Hill and Wang, 2002.

Fistere, John Cushman. "No Timid Man Could Hold This Job," Interesting People: "'Frenchy'—Victor Gosselin." *The American Magazine* 111, no. 6 (June 1931): 80–81, 146.

Fitz Gerald, J. G. "Construction Leader Declares Industry Will Follow Construction Upturn." *News* (Detroit, MI), November 2, 1930. Empire State Scrapbook 2 (1–37), p.16. Avery Architectural & Fine Arts Library, Columbia University.

Fortune. "The Skyscraper from *Fortune.*" Reprint, American Institute of Steel Construction Inc., March 1930, 2–35.

Frigidaire Corp. "Man's Greatest Gesture Skyward [Advertisement]." *Brooklyn Daily Eagle*, April 1, 1931, 11.

Garrett, Oliver H. P. "A Certain Person [Belle Moskowitz]." Profiles. *New Yorker*, October 9, 1926, 26–28.

"The Gist of It [Hiram Myers]." *Survey Graphic* 62, no. 11 (September 1, 1929): 547.

Glass Digest. "Glass and the World's Largest Building." June 1931. Empire State Scrapbook 5.2 (41-74). Avery Architectural & Fine Arts Library, Columbia University.

Glass, J. P. "Foremost Americans [Homer Balcom]." *Standard Union* (Brooklyn), March 28, 1931, 7.

Glens Falls Times. "New York Excavator Dreams of Large Underground Vault." October 7, 1942, 7.

Goldman, Jonathan. *The Empire State Building Book.* St. Martin's Press, 1980.

Gray, Christopher. "Streetscapes/The Henry Hudson Hotel, 353 West 57th Street; From Women's Clubhouse to WNET to $75 a Night." *New York Times*, January 4, 1998, sec. 11, p. 5.

"Greater Building Heights and What They Mean to the Art." *Engineering News-Record* 106, no. 8 (February 19, 1931): 306.

Green, Fiona. "'The Iroquois on the Girders': Poetry, Modernity, and the Indian Ironworker." *Critical Quarterly* 55, no. 2 (July 10, 2013): 2–25.

Griffiths, Ivor. "The Wonder Building of the World." *Sunday Express*, February 3, 1931. Empire State Scrapbook 3 (1–19), p. 18. Avery Architectural & Fine Arts Library, Columbia University.

Grossutti, Javier. "Emigration From Friuli Venezia Giulia towards the United States." N.d. http://www.ammer-fvg.org/_Data/Contenuti/Allegati/eng/EN_storia_USA_Grossutti.pdf.

———. "Italian Mosaicists and Terrazzo Workers in New York City. Estimating the Size, Characteristic and Structure of a High-Skill Building Trade." October 24, 2007. https://italianacademy.columbia.edu/sites/default/files/content/paper_fa07_Grossutti_0.pdf.

Gutman, Judith Mara. Judith Mara Gutman Papers. MssCol 5982. Series II.B. *Lewis W. Hine and the American Social Conscience* (1967), box 22 f. 1-8: "Research Materials 1913–1941," folder 5: "Lewis Hine Writings Correspondence 1934–1941." New York Public Library.

———. *Lewis W. Hine, 1874–1940: Two Perspectives.* ICP Library of Photographers, vol. 4. Grossman Publishers, 1974.

———. *Lewis W. Hine and the American Social Conscience.* Walker, 1967.

———. "The Worker and the Machine," *Afterimage* 17, no. 2 (September 1989): 13–15.

Haenigsen, Harry. "After All These Years [Cartoon]." *Citizen* [location missing], November 6, 1930. Empire State Scrapbook 10. Avery Architectural & Fine Arts Library, Columbia University.

Haigney, Pete. Letter to the editor. *Brooklyn Daily Eagle*, August 5, 1930, 19.

Hamlin, Talbot Faulkner. "The Prize-Winning Buildings of 1931." *The Architectural Record* 71, no. 1 (January 1932): 10–26.

Harrington, John Walker. "Quarter Mile Climb to Summit of Building Efficiency." *Real Estate Magazine* 19 no. 8 (May 1931): 4, 24. Empire State Scrapbook 5.2 (1–40), p. 1. Avery Architectural & Fine Arts Library, Columbia University.

Haskell, Douglas. "The Empire State Building." *Creative Art* 8, no. 4 (April 1931): 242–44.

———. "A Temple of Jehu." *The Nation* 132, no. 3438 (May 27, 1931): 598–90.

Haskin, Frederic J. "The House That Al Built." *Courier* (Elgin, IL), November 3, 1931. Empire State Scrapbook 13 (1–25), p. 10. Avery Architectural & Fine Arts Library, Columbia University.

Hastings (NY) News. "Hine's Photos of 'Empire' to Be Shown Here; Shreve, Balcom and Andres Helping in Erection of World's Tallest Building." August 15, 1930. Empire State Scrapbook 1.1 (17–35). Avery Architectural & Fine Arts Library, Columbia University.

Haverstraw-Rockland County (NY) Times. "[Charles E. Sexton]." October 18, 1930, 3.

Heaton, Maurice. "Who Is the Craftsman?" *Arts Education Today*, 1–7, 10. Bureau of Publications, Teachers College, Columbia University, 1938.

Hill, Edwin C. "The World's Greatest Lighthouse Will Radiate Beams That Can Be Seen by Mariners 50 Miles at Sea." *Democrat Press* (Lyons, NY), May 6, 1931. Empire State Scrapbook 4 (1–31), p. 24. Avery Architectural & Fine Arts Library, Columbia University.

Hill, Herbert. "The Problem of Race in American Labor History." *Reviews in American History* 24, no. 2 (June 1996): 189–208.

Hill, Richard. *Skywalkers: A History of Indian Ironworkers.* Woodland Indian Cultural Educational Centre, 1987.

Hine, Lewis Wickes. Empire State Building Archive, 1930–1969. The Avery Architectural and Fine Arts Library, Columbia University.

———. "Fifty Years of Preparation." John Simon Guggenheim Memorial Foundation Application, [1939?]. Lewis Hine Collection, MSS. 251-340 & Roy Stryker, box 5 of 5, folder 324. George Eastman Museum.

———. "Hands: Work Portraits." *Survey Graphic* 49 (February 1, 1923): 559–65.

———. "Harbor Workers: Work Portraits." *Survey Graphic*, February 25, 1921, 851–58.

———. "Industrial Training for Deaf Mutes: A Practical School Where an Opportunity Is Furnished for Them to Become Desirable, Self-Supporting Citizens." *The Craftsman* 13, no. 4 (January 1908): 400–408.

———. "Learning to Be Citizens: A School Where Boys and Girls of All Creeds, Races and Classes of Society Work Together." *The Craftsman* 9, no. 6 (March 1906): 774–88.

———. "Lewis Hine. Letters Photocopied from Social History Archives, Univ. of Minn. ALibraries [*sic*]." N.d. George Eastman Museum.

———. Lewis Hine Papers, ca. 1908–ca. 1921. MssCol 1399, New York Public Library.

———. Lewis Wickes Hine Papers, 1904–1940. RRML.SC0029. The George Eastman Museum and the Richard and Ronay Menschel Library.

———. Lewis Wickes Hine Scrapbook (RRML.SC0030) The George Eastman Museum and the Richard and Ronay Menschel Library.

———. "The Man on the Job: Work Portraits." *Survey Graphic* 47 (March 25, 1921): 991–96.

———. *Men at Work: Photographic Studies of Modern Men and Machines*. First edition. Macmillan Company, 1932.

———. *Men at Work: Photographic Studies of Modern Men and Machines*. Second edition with a supplement of eighteen related photos. Dover, 1995.

———. "Power Makers; Work Portraits by Lewis Hine: Photographs Taken in the Power Plants of the Pennsylvania System." *Survey Graphic* 47 (December 31, 1921): 511–18.

———. "The Railroaders: Work Portraits." *Survey Graphic* 47 (October 29, 1921): 159–66.

———. "Social and Industrial Photographs" [undated catalogue]. Hine Photo Company, 27 Grant Avenue, Yonkers, N.Y. New York Public Library: Lewis Hine Papers, ca. 1908-ca. 1921. MssCol 1399.

———. "Social Photography: How the Camera May Help in Social Uplift." In *Proceedings of the National Conference of Charities and Correction at the Thirty-Sixth Annual Session Held in the City of Buffalo, New York, June 9–16, 1909*, edited by Alexander Johnson. Press of Fort Wayne, 1909, 355–59.

———. "Suggestions for a Preliminary Photographic Survey for the Tennessee Valley Authority." N.d. Judith Mara Gutman papers. MssCol 5982. Series II.B. *Lewis W. Hine and the American Social Conscience* (1967), box 22 f. 1-8: "Research Materials 1913–1941," folder 5: "Lewis Hine Writings Correspondence 1934–1941." New York Public Library.

———. "Up from the City Streets." *Survey Graphic* 65 (January 1, 1931): 361–65.

———. "Up Goes the Skyscraper." *Young Wings*, February 1934, 4–5.

Hine, Lewis Wickes (attributed). *Tenement*. N.d. Photograph. Art Institute of Chicago. Object ID: 99738/Tenement.

Hoffman, Charles W. "Report by the Committee of the National Probation Association." *Journal of the American Institute of Criminal Law and Criminology* 8, no. 5 (January 1918): 745–48.

Home News (New York). "Carpenter Killed While Working in Empire Building." July 30, 1930. Empire State Scrapbook 1.2 (1–41), p. 32. Avery Architectural & Fine Arts Library, Columbia University.

Home News (New York). "Strange Bugs and Freak Snowstorms Met by Bronx Riveter atop Empire State Tower." November 9, 1930. Empire State Scrapbook 1.2. Avery Architectural & Fine Arts Library, Columbia University.

Hopkinson, Deborah. *Sky Boys: How They Built the Empire State Building*. Dragonfly Books, 2012.

How the Empire State Building Grew. Otis Elevator Company Press, 1931.

"How the World's Tallest Building Handles Its Drainage." *The Plumbers and Heating Contractors Trade Journal*, November 15, 1930, 17–19.

James, Theodore. *The Empire State Building*. Harper & Row, 1975.

Jenkins, Hester Donaldson. "Man and the Skyscraper." *The Commercial Photographer* 6, no. 11 (August 1931): 634–36. Lewis Hine Collection, folder 58. George Eastman Museum.

Jenkins, Sandra Giles. "The National Society of Craftsmen, New York, New York (1906–1920) & the New York Society of Craftsmen (1920–1957): A Craft Continuum from the Arts and Crafts Movement to the Studio Craft Movement." Master's thesis, The Smithsonian Associates and Corcoran College of Art & Design, 2009.

Jim, Bernard L. "'Wrecking the Joint': The Razing of City Hotels in the First Half of the 20th Century." In "The American Hotel." *The Journal of Decorative and Propaganda Arts* 25 (2005): 288–315.

Johnstone, Will B. "The New Who's Who [Cartoon]." *Herald* [location missing], October 18, 1930. Empire State Scrapbook 3. Avery Architectural & Fine Arts Library, Columbia University.

Jones, Bassett. "The Empire State Building VIII: Elevators." *Architectural Forum* 54, no. 1 (January 1931): 95–99.

Josephson, Matthew, and Hannah Josephson. *Al Smith: Hero of the Cities. A Political Portrait Drawing on the Papers of Frances Perkins*. Houghton Mifflin Company, 1969.

Journal (New York). "Lift Kills Carpenter." July 31, 1930. Empire State Scrapbook 1.2. Avery Architectural & Fine Arts Library, Columbia University.

Journal [location missing (New York?)]. "Death Fall at Empire State," April 6, 1931. Empire State Scrapbook 1.2 (42–82). Avery Architectural & Fine Arts Library, Columbia University.

Journal of Commerce. "Huge Quantities of Material for Empire State Building." July 21, 1930. Empire State Scrapbook 1.1 (1–16). Avery Architectural & Fine Arts Library, Columbia University.

Kaplan, Daile, ed. *Photo Story: Selected Letters and Photographs of Lewis W. Hine*. Smithsonian Institution Press, 1992.

Karson, Marc. *American Labor Unions and Politics, 1900–1918*. Southern Illinois University Press, 1958.

Kingwell, Mark. *Nearest Thing to Heaven: The Empire State Building and American Dreams*. Yale University Press, 2006.

Kohn, Robert D. "The New York Building Congress, 1921–1931." *Building Congress News*, May 1931, 3.
Koolhaas, Rem. *Delirious New York: A Retroactive Manifesto for Manhattan.* Monacelli Press, 1978.
Lamb, William Frederick. "The Empire State Building VII: The General Design." *Architectural Forum* 54, no. 1 (January 1931): 1–8.
———. "The Empire State Building XII: The Ground Floor Lobbies and Shops." *Architectural Forum* 55, no. 1 (July 1931): 42–46.
Landmarks Preservation Commission. "The Empire State Building." May 19, 1981. Designation list 143. LP 2000. http://s-media.nyc.gov/agencies/lpc/lp/2000.pdf.
Langer, Freddy, ed. *Lewis W. Hine: The Empire State Building.* Prestel-Verlag, 1998.
Lanza, Caroline A. "'Truth Plus Publicity': Paul U. Kellogg and Hybrid Practice, 1902–1937." PhD diss., University of Washington, 2016.
Lemen, Richard A., and Philip J. Landrigan. "Toward an Asbestos Ban in the United States." *International Journal of Environmental Research and Public Health* 14, no. 11 (2017): 1302. https://doi.org/doi: 10.3390/ijerph14111302.
Lesser, Margaret. "Young Wings: Magazine of The Junior Literary Guild." February 1934. Lewis Hine Collection, box 4, folder 222. George Eastman Museum.
Life Magazine. "Introduction to This First Issue of *Life.*" November 23, 1936, 3.
The Literary Digest. "Sky Boys Who 'Rode the Ball' on Empire State." 109 no. 8, May 23, 1931, 30–32.
The Literary Digest. "Treating Labor Artistically." 67, no. 10 (December 4, 1920): 32-34.
Littell, Edmund M. "Men Wanted." *The American Magazine* 109, no. 4 (April 1930): 46–51, 115–17.
Los Angeles Times. "Pen Points." November 9, 1930, sec. A, p. 4.
Low, Frances. "'A Chase Up into the Sky.'" *American Heritage* 9, issue 6 (October 1968): 14–21, 80.
Ludlow, William Orr. "New York Building Congress: Recognition of Craftsmanship," 1929. WAG.167, box 5, folder 22. Tamiment Library & Robert F. Wagner Labor Archives, New York University.
———. *Recognition of Craftsmanship: How It Is Put into Effect,* [1927]. WAG.167, box 5, folder 20. Tamiment Library & Robert F. Wagner Labor Archives, New York University.
———. "Report of Committee on Recognition of Craftsmanship." *Building Congress News*, January 1928, 8.
________. "Report of Committee on Recognition of Craftsmanship." *Building Congress News*, May 1928, 6.
________. "Report of the Committee on Recognition of Craftsmanship." *Building Congress News*, April 1930, 5-6.
———. *What Is a Good Craftsman?* New York Building Congress, [1928]. WAG.167, box 5, folder 23. Tamiment Library & Robert F. Wagner Labor Archives, New York University.
Madden, Joseph. "Bungalow." Unpublished manuscript, n.d. Courtesy of Terry Madden Best.

Manning, Joe. "The Lewis Hine Project." *Mornings on Maple Street* (blog). https://morningsonmaplestreet.com/lewis-hine-project-index-of-stories/lewis-hine-project.

Marks, Robert W. "Portrait of Lewis Hine: His Name Is Little Known, but His Pictures Are Etched in the Conscience of the Nation." *Coronet*, February 1939, 147–57.

Massock, Richard. "Skyscraper Worker Eats Cafe Lunch." *Democrat* (Leadville, CO), October 3, 1930. Empire State Scrapbook 2.2 (1–37). Avery Architectural & Fine Arts Library, Columbia University.

———. "Modern Building Methods Scrap Famous Old Hod." *Brooklyn Daily Eagle*, October 9, 1930, 5.

McCausland, Elizabeth. "Lewis Hine: Portrait of a Photographer (1938)." *History of Photography* 16, no. 2 (Summer 1992): 102–4.

McIntyre, O. O. "102-Story Blunder May Yet Prove Out." *Hays City (KS) News*, November 19, 1931. Empire State Scrapbook 11 (1–25), p. 18. Avery Architectural & Fine Arts Library, Columbia University.

McManus, James. *Positively Fifth Street: Murderers, Cheetahs, and Binion's World Series of Poker*. Picador, 2004.

The Mentor. "He Photo-Interprets Big Labor: Camera Studies of Men at Work by Lewis Hine." September 1926, 42–43. Judith Mara Gutman papers. MssCol 5982. Series II.B. *Lewis W. Hine and the American Social Conscience* (1967), box 22, f. 1–8: "Research Materials 1913–1941," folder 4: "Lewis Hine Writings 1935–1937." New York Public Library.

Merewether, E. R. A. "The Occurrence of Pulmonary Fibrosis and Other Pulmonary Affections in Asbestos Workers." *Journal of Industrial Hygiene* 12 (1930): 239–57.

Meyer, Henry C., Jr. "The Empire State Building IV: Heating and Ventilating." *Architectural Forum* 53, no. 4 (October 1930): 517–21.

Mitchell, Joseph. "The Mohawks in High Steel." In *Apologies to the Iroquois*, edited by Edmund Wilson. Farrar, Straus & Cudahy, 1960.

Morison, Roderick. "Mankind's Tallest Structure Nears Completion." *London Daily Mail Atlantic Edition*, Febrary 1, 1931. Empire State Scrapbook 3 (1-19). Avery Architectural & Fine Arts Library, Columbia University.

Moskowitz, Belle. "The Way of the Girl." *The Survey* 22 (July 3, 1909): 486–96.

Moskowitz, Mrs. Henry. "Cave Drawings in the Empire State." *New Republic* 67, no. 861 (June 3, 1931): 75.

Mumford, Lewis. "Notes on Modern Architecture." *New Republic* 66, no. 850 (March 18, 1931): 119–22.

National Bellas Hess Catalogue. "The Work Shirt That Helped to Build the World's Highest Building." N.d. Empire State Scrapbook 1.2. Avery Architectural & Fine Arts Library, Columbia University.

Nemerov, Alexander. *Soulmaker: The Times of Lewis Hine*. Princeton University Press, 2016.

New York Building Congress. "Committee on Recognition of Craftsmanship," September 15, 1925. WAG.167, box 5, folder 17. Tamiment Library & Robert F. Wagner Labor Archives, New York University.

New York Building Congress. New York Building Congress Records (WAG.167). The Tamiment Library and Robert F. Wagner Labor Archives of New York University's Special Collections.

New York Building Congress News. "Craftsmen From Fifty-Four Buildings Attend Meetings." May 1931, 6.

New York Building Congress News. "New Honorary Craftsmen." January 1932, 12.

New York Enquirer. "Daring Bird Perches 'Mid Forest of Steel [Carl Russell] [Photograph]." September 30, 1930. Empire State Scrapbook. Avery Architectural & Fine Arts Library, Columbia University.

New York Enquirer. "The Empire State Building." May 10, 1931. Empire State Scrapbook 5.2 (1–40), p. 22. Avery Architectural & Fine Arts Library, Columbia University.

New York Herald Tribune. "Empire State Mechanics Rewarded for Good Work: Sixteen Get Craftsmanship Certificates and Medals." February 12, 1931, 34.

New York Herald Tribune. "Macy Balloons Head for Sea as Parade Finale." November 28, 1930, 36.

New York Herald Tribune. "Wreckers Plan Strike, Menacing Radio City Work." March 30, 1931, 15.

New York Sun. "Keeping Skyscrapers Rainproof." April 4, 1931. Empire State Scrapbook 1.2. Avery Architectural & Fine Arts Library, Columbia University.

New York Sun. "Man Falls from Tallest Building." April 6, 1931. Empire State Scrapbook 1.2 (42–82), p. 64. Avery Architectural & Fine Arts Library, Columbia University.

New York Sun. "Miracles of the Modern Skyscraper's Growth." April 7, 1912, 52.

New York Sun. "Only Five Killed at Empire State." November 8, 1930. Empire State Scrapbook 1.2. Avery Architectural & Fine Arts Library, Columbia University.

New York Sun. "Plastering Contract Let on Empire State Building." July 3, 1930. Empire State Scrapbook 1.2 (1–41), p. 29. Avery Architectural & Fine Arts Library, Columbia University.

New York Telegram. "Empire State Work Goes Ahead Rapidly." June 6, 1930. Empire State Scrapbook 1.1 (1–16). Avery Architectural & Fine Arts Library, Columbia University.

New York Telegram. "Plunge Kills Man at Empire Tower." April 6, 1931. Empire State Scrapbook 1.2 (42–82), p. 64. Avery Architectural & Fine Arts Library, Columbia University.

New York Times. "Artisans Value Awards for Labor." April 8, 1928, sec. RE, p. 1.

New York Times. "Baker, Smith & Co. [Advertisement]." May 5, 1865.

New York Times. "A Beaux Arts Ball for Fiery Moderns." January 18, 1931, 81.

New York Times. "Big Sunday Crowd Sees Empire Tower." May 3, 1931, 13.

New York Times. "Breadline Meals to Be Regulated." February 12, 1931, 2.

New York Times. "Building in Excelsis." May 1, 1931, 24.

New York Times. "Building Men Press Non-Resident Ban." August 4, 1930, 5.

New York Times. City Brevities. November 21, 1930, 20.

New York Times. "Column to Support 5,000 Tons on Empire State Building." January 10, 1930, 42.

New York Times. "Election Results Flashed by The Times from 90th Floor of Empire State Building 1,150 Feet Above Street." November 2, 1930, sec. N, p. 20.
New York Times. "Election Results Will Be Shown by Times Bulletins and Signals." November 4, 1930, 23.
New York Times. "Empire State Tower, Tallest in World, Is Opened by Hoover." May 2, 1931, 1.
New York Times. "Excavation Finished for Smith Building." March 6, 1930, 42.
New York Times. "Friends Force Smith to Observe Birthday." December 31, 1930, 4.
New York Times. "Honoring Craftsmanship." May 31, 1930, 6.
New York Times. "Honoring Craftsmen." October 10, 1930, 22.
New York Times. "Ironworkers Free in Contempt Case." July 16, 1930, 33.
New York Times. "Ironworkers Row Up Here Tomorrow." June 1, 1930, 56.
New York Times. "Jacob Volk Dies from Pneumonia." March 16, 1929, 13.
New York Times. "Killed in 57-Story Fall: Carpenter's Death at Empire State Building Believed to Be Suicide." April 7, 1931, 18.
New York Times. "Labor Men Indicted in Racketeer Case." April 16, 1931, 15.
New York Times. "Laud Building Unity." September 27, 1930, 35.
New York Times. "Mechanics Get Awards: Paramount Annex Called Evidence of Faith in Future." May 1, 1931, 55.
New York Times. "Mechanics Hear Chrysler." January 21, 1930, 45.
New York Times. "$1,000,000 a Year to See City from Tower." June 6, 1931, 9.
New York Times. "1,000 Wreckers to Return to Jobs; New Wage Agreement Signed by Some." April 4, 1926, 6.
New York Times. "Our Indian Colony." May 20, 1940, 13.
New York Times. "Relics Discovered in Wall St. Digging." January 18, 1931, 16.
New York Times. "Santa Brings Snow for Macy's Parade." November 28, 1930, 4.
New York Times. "Schwab Foresees Record Prosperity." October 25, 1930, 10.
New York Times. "Smith Acts to Bring Peace to Iron Trade Here." March 28, 1930, 1.
New York Times. "Smith as a Laborer Helps Honor Workers; Adopts Role to Speak in Place of Union Leader at Building Exercises." February 12, 1931, 14. Empire State Scrapbook 3 (20–36), p. 23. Avery Architectural & Fine Arts Library, Columbia University.
New York Times. "Smith Has Laryngitis." April 3, 1931, 19.
New York Times. "Smith Helps to Honor His Building Workers." October 9, 1930, 11.
New York Times. "Smith Lays Stone for Tallest Tower." September 10, 1930, 27.
New York Times. "Smith to Honor Workers." October 8, 1930, 52.
New York Times. "Smith to Make Awards." February 8, 1931, 50.
New York Times. "Speeding up the Elevator for Our Taller Skyscrapers." April 5, 1931, 126.
New York Times. "Steel Union Ready to End Long Fight." April 10, 1930, 17.
New York Times. "Steel Union Seeks $3,500,000 Damage." November 21, 1930, 25.
New York Times. "Steel Workers Get Open Shop Notice." March 9, 1931, 43.
New York Times. "Stocks Go Higher; Public Buying Again." February 11, 1931, 1.
New York Times. "Strike of Wreckers Ends in Compromise." April 9, 1931, 3.
New York Times. Suburban Social Notes. March 20, 1930, 36.

New York Times. Topics of the Times. November 28, 1930, 17.

New York Times. "200 House Wreckers Strike for 'Safety.'" February 15, 1930, 3.

New York Times. What Is Going On This Week. April 26, 1931, sec. N, p. 20.

New York Times. "Wreckers Strike on 45 Buildings." April 2, 1931, 11.

New York World-Telegram. "Threat of Kitten Litter for Every Floor Fills Empire State Janitors with Fear." May 29, 1931. Empire State Scrapbook 5.2. Avery Architectural & Fine Arts Library, Columbia University.

New Yorker. "Empire State [Advertisement]." April 11, 1931, 35.

New Yorker. "The High Place." November 22, 1930, 19. Empire State Scrapbook 1.2 (42–82), p. 76. Avery Architectural & Fine Arts Library, Columbia University.

Newcombe, John Timberman. "The Footprint of the Twentieth Century: American Skyscrapers and Modernist Poems." *Modernism/Modernity* 10, no. 1 (January 2003): 97–125.

Newhall, Beaumont. "Lewis W. Hine." *Magazine of Art* 31, no. 11 (November 1938): 637.

News-Record (New York). "This Week at the Capitol." May 12, 1931. Empire State Scrapbook. Avery Architectural & Fine Arts Library, Columbia University.

Norris, Margaret. *Heroes and Hazards: Talks with the Daredevils of To-Day; True Stories of the Careers of the Men Who Make Our Modern World Safe by Their Courage*. Macmillan, 1932.

Norris, Margaret, and Brenda Ueland. "Riding the Girders." *Saturday Evening Post*, April 11, 1931, 14, 98, 101–2.

Oakland Tribune. "Worker Falls 7 Stories, Bounds 5 More; Lives [Paul Rockhold]." January 7, 1926, sec. B, p. 10.

"Observations by Old-Timer." *Printers' Ink Monthly* 22, no. 6 (June 1931): 60.

Observer (Troy, NY). "Long Plunge to Death." July 20, 1930. Empire State Scrapbook 1. Avery Architectural & Fine Arts Library, Columbia University.

Pace, Patricia. "Staging Childhood: Lewis Hine's Photographs of Child Labor." *The Lion and the Unicorn* 26, no. 3 (September 2002): 324–52.

Panzer, Mary. *Lewis Hine*. 55. Phaidon, 2002.

Parker, Gladys. "Towering with Chic." Femininities, by Gladys. [Source missing (*Daily News*)], n.d., Empire State Scrapbook. Avery Architectural & Fine Arts Library, Columbia University.

Parry, Albert. "Artists of Wrecking." *Esquire*, April 1, 1936, 92–96.

Patriot (Princeton, NJ). "Gloom." October 30, 1930. Empire State Scrapbook 2 (1–37), p. 23. Avery Architectural & Fine Arts Library, Columbia University.

Perry, Elisabeth Israels. *Belle Moskowitz: Feminine Politics and the Exercise of Power in the Age of Alfred E. Smith*. Oxford University Press, 1987.

Pickett, Charles. "The Empire State Building Mooring Mast." *Air Law Review* 2, no. 2 (April 1931): 130–52.

Pierpont, Claudia Roth. "The Silver Spire." *New Yorker*, November 18, 2002, 74–81.

Piper, Jean. "Man Who Erected World's Highest Building Has Features and Face of an Artist." *Brooklyn Daily Eagle*, April 23, 1925, 87.

"Planning and Control Permit Erection of 85 Stories of Steel in Six Months." *Engineering News-Record* 105, no. 8 (August 21, 1930): 280–84.

Poole, Ernest. "Cowboys of the Sky." *Everybody's Magazine* 19, no. 5 (November 1908): 641-653.

Poore, Charles G. "Books of the Times." *New York Times*, September 15, 1939, 27.

———. "Greatest Skyscraper Rises on a Clockwork Schedule." *New York Times*, July 27, 1930, 114.

Post-Currier (Camden, New Jersey). "John Rusciani, Retired Cement, Concrete Worker, Dies." August 14, 1985, 48.

Poughkeepsie Eagle-News. "Empire State Briefs." August 7, 1936, 6.

Poughkeepsie Eagle-News. "Man Dies After Crash on Tongue Mountain." August 6, 1936, 2.

Poughkeepsie Eagle-News. "Worker Killed in 10 Foot Fall. Glazier's Skull Fractured as Window Frame Drops at Wingdale Hospital." October 20, 1932, 1.

Press (Albany, NY). "Free Woodpile Established for N.Y.'s Unemployed." November 23, 1930. Empire State Scrapbook 2 (1–37), p. 21. Avery Architectural & Fine Arts Library, Columbia University.

Publicity Associates. *Empire State: A History*. Publicity Associates, 1931.

Publicity Associates, *Empire Statements* vol. 1, nos. 1-6, n.d. Empire State Scrapbook1.2 (42-82). Avery Architectural & Fine Arts Library, Columbia University.

Rasenberger, Jim. *High Steel: The Daring Men Who Built the World's Greatest Skyline*. HarperCollins, 2004.

———. "The Sky Boys." *New York Times*, April 23, 2006, section 14, p. 9.

Record (East Grand Forks, MN). "Tallest Building Has First Suicide." April 17, 1931. Empire State Scrapbook 4 (1–31), p. 26. Avery Architectural & Fine Arts Library, Columbia University.

Register (Ossining, NY). "Organized Labor Fights to Keep Local Jobs for Residents of the State." August 15, 1930. Empire State Scrapbook 1.1 (17–35), p. 24. Avery Architectural & Fine Arts Library, Columbia University.

Richardson, H. F. "The Empire State Building V: Electrical Equipment." *Architectural Forum* 53, no. 5 (November 1930): 639–44.

Richmond (VA) Palladium and Sun-Telegram. "Metal Workers to Get Charter." June 1, 1916, 7.

Roberts, Sam. "100 Years of Grandeur: The Birth of Grand Central Terminal." *New York Times*, January 18, 2013.

Rosenblum, Naomi. *America & Lewis Hine: Photographs 1904–1940*. Forward by Walter Rosenblum, biographical notes by Naomi Rosenblum, essay by Alan Trachtenberg. Aperture Inc., 1977.

Rosenblum, Nina. Nina Rosenblum Collection of Documentary Film and Video. MSS 558, box 39, folder: "ALH Empire State Bldg." New York University Special Collections.

Rosenblum, Nina, and D. V. Allentuck, dirs. *America and Lewis Hine*. Documentary. Daedalus Productions Inc., 1984.

Rosenblum, Walter and Naomi. Walter and Naomi Rosenblum Collection of Photography and Photographic History. MSS.556. New York University Fales Library and Special Collections.

Russell, John (Jack). "A Biography of John (Jack) Russell: His 20th Century." Unpublished manuscript, n.d. Courtesy of Gail Lincoln.

Sak, Charlie "Chic." "Al Smith's 102-Story Building Gives 'Chic' Stiff Neck and Idea." *The Times* [location missing], July 23, 1930. Empire State Scrapbook 1.1 (1–16). Avery Architectural & Fine Arts Library, Columbia University.

Salerno, Jacqueline Michela. "Zone of Uncomfortable Beauty: Lewis W. Hine's Window on the World and The Empire State Building." Master's thesis, Syracuse University, 1999.

Sampsell-Willmann, Kate. *Lewis Hine as Social Critic*. University Press of Mississippi, 2009.

———. "Lewis Hine, Ellis Island, and Pragmatism: Photographs as Lived Experience." *The Journal of the Gilded Age and Progressive Era* 7, no. 2 (April 2008): 221–52.

San Pedro (CA) News-Pilot. "Broadway Echoes." May 14, 1931, 6.

Saunders, John Monk. "It's a Tough Job, but Somebody's Got to Swing It." *The American Magazine* 99 (June 1925), 44–47, 214–16.

Schleier, Merrill. *The Skyscraper in American Art, 1890–1931*. Da Capo Press, 1986.

Schneeberg, Francine. "48 Killed on Empire Building." *Daily Worker*, May 13, 1931, 1.

Schwartz, Daniel. "New Wrecking Technique Speeds Up Building of Skyscrapers." *New York Times*, July 5, 1931, 95.

Schwartz, Jordan A. "Al Smith in the Thirties." *New York History* 45, no. 4 (October 1964): 316–30.

Seabrook, William. "American Comrades: Red, White, and Jew—They Were Enemies in Russia, but Here They Are Brothers." *The American Magazine*, December 1937, 48–49, 141–51.

Seixas, Peter. "Lewis Hine: From 'Social' to "Interpretive' Photography." *American Quarterly* 39, no. 3 (Autumn 1987): 381–409.

Shales, Ezra. "Corporate Craft: Constructing the Empire State Building." *The Journal of Modern Craft* 4, no. 2 (2011): 119–45. https://doi.org/DOI: 10.2752/174967811X13050332209206.

Shepard, Joan. "The Last Ironworker." *New York Daily News*, September 27, 1984, 97.

Shettig, Bryan. "A Brief History of the Work Shirt 1886–1930," *The Rite Stuff* (blog), The Rite Stuff, November 8, 2021. https://the-rite-stuff.com/blogs/news/the-evolution-of-the-work-shirt.

———. "A Brief History of the Work Shirt, Part 2: 1930–1940." *The Rite Stuff* (blog), The Rite Stuff, November 8, 2021. https://the-rite-stuff.com/blogs/news/a-brief-history-of-the-work-shirt-1930-1940.

Shreve, Richmond Harold. "[I] The Empire State Building Organization." *Architectural Forum* 52, no. 6 (June 1930): 771–73, 787–88.

———. "The Empire State Building II: The Window-Spandrel-Wall Detail and Its Relation to Building Progress." *Architectural Forum* 53, no. 1 (July 1930): 98–104.

Smith, C. Zoe. "An Alternative View of the 30s: Hine's and Bourke-White's Industrial Photos." *Journalism Quarterly* 60, no. 2 (June 1983): 305–10.

[Source missing]. "Day by Day with Governor Patterson." September 14, 1930, Empire State Scrapbook 1.1 (17–35), p. 28. Avery Architectural & Fine Arts Library, Columbia University.

[Source missing]. "He Knows How. He Is Not Afraid [Neil Doherty] [Photograph]." October 5, 1930. Empire State Scrapbook. Avery Architectural & Fine Arts Library, Columbia University.

[Source missing]. "Oil Now Used as Fuel for Kilns in Brick Plant." August 17, 1930. Empire State Scrapbook 1.1 (17–35). Avery Architectural & Fine Arts Library, Columbia University.

[Source missing]. "Stock Market off 40 Billion from 1929 Peak." N.d. Empire State Scrapbook 3 (1–19), p. 9. Avery Architectural & Fine Arts Library, Columbia University.

Sparling, Earl. "Pinnacle of Stone and Steel Reared by Man Far Above the World Gives Petters Fog and Others Place to Scratch Initials for $1." *New York World-Telegram*, May 6, 1931, sec. 2, p. 28.

St. Louis Post-Dispatch. "Last Survivor Recalls Work on Empire State Building." November 19, 1984, 7.

Standard Union (Brooklyn). "Building War on Contracts Is Threatened." March 31, 1931, 6.

Standard Union (Brooklyn). "Peace Looms in Iron Trade after 25 Years." April 10, 1930, 1.

Standard Union (Brooklyn). "Peder Joachim Andreasen [Obituary]." July 16, 1930, 16.

Standard Union (Brooklyn). "Smith Dodges Girls' Kisses on Short Visit to Washington." December 13, 1929, 25.

Standard Union (Brooklyn). "Smith Offers to Mediate in Building War." March 28, 1930, 4.

Standard Union (Brooklyn). "Smith to Hold Another Steel Parley Friday." April 3, 1930, 5.

Standard Union (Brooklyn). "Steel Workers End Strife Lasting Quarter Century." May 13, 1930, 2.

Staten Island Advance (Staten Island, NY). "John Rusciani, 91, Organized Union Local." August 14, 1985, 15.

Starrett Bros. and Eken, *Erection Views of Empire State Building*: A Photograph Album Compiled by Starrett Brothers and Eken Incorporated (1929-1931, unpublished). Call number: 2002.05. Skyscraper Museum.

Starrett, Paul. *Changing the Skyline: An Autobiography*. McGraw-Hill, 1938.

Starrett, William Aiken. *Skyscrapers and the Men Who Build Them*. Charles Scribner's Sons, 1928.

Statesman [or *Herald?*] (Yonkers, NY). "Photographer Tells of Skyscraper Thrill." December 10, 1930. Empire State Scrapbook 2 (1–37). Avery Architectural & Fine Arts Library, Columbia University.

Steinhilber, Walter. "42 Men Killed Constructing the New Empire State Building [Drawing]." *The New Masses*, June 1931, 9.

Stern, Philip Van Doren. *The World's Most Famous Building: Its Genesis and Tradition*. Margail, 1964.

Stern, Robert A. M., Gregory Gilmartin, and Thomas Mellins. *New York 1930: Architecture and Urbanism Between the Two World Wars*. Rizzoli International, 1987.

Structural Gypsum Corporation. "Over 100,000 Bags of Plaster Will Be Used in the Empire State Building [Advertisement]." *Pencil Points* 10 (1930).

Sutton, Philip. "The Woolworth Building: The Cathedral of Commerce." *NYPL Blog*, April 22, 2013.

Swan, Gilbert. "Sidelights of New York." *Evening Union* (Atlantic City, NJ), September 5, 1930. Empire State Scrapbook 1.1 (1–16). Avery Architectural & Fine Arts Library, Columbia University.

———. "Sidelights of New York." *Saratogian* (Saratoga, NY), September 9, 1930. Empire State Scrapbook 1.1 (17–35). Avery Architectural & Fine Arts Library, Columbia University.

Swezey, K. M. "Robot Elevators to Serve 85,000 in Greatest Building." *Popular Science Monthly*, April 1931, 44–45, 151.

Tauranac, John. *The Empire State Building: The Making of a Landmark*. Scribner, 1995.

Thirer, Irene. "Laemmle Announces Film Lineup." *Daily News* (New York), May 11, 1931, 120.

Thomas, Gordon, and Max Morgan-Witts. *The Day the Bubble Burst: A Social History of the Wall Street Crash of 1929*. Doubleday, 1979.

Thomas, Lowell. *Men of Danger*. Frederick A. Stokes, 1936.

Times (Danbury, CT). "'Flapper Fannie' Turns Stylist." February 10, 1931.

"Topping Out the Empire State Building." *Engineering News-Record* 106, no. 4 (January 22, 1931): 153–54.

Trachtenberg, Alan. "Ever—the Human Document." In *America & Lewis Hine: Photographs 1904–1940*, Forward by Walter Rosenblum, biographical notes by Naomi Rosenblum, essay by Alan Trachtenberg. Aperture Inc., 1977.

Trumbull, Walter. "Manhattan Days and Nights." *Journal* (Louisville, KY), May 15, 1931. Empire State Scrapbook 4 (1–31), p. 9. Avery Architectural & Fine Arts Library, Columbia University.

Turkel, Studs. *Working*. New Press, 2004.

Ullman, James R. "How High Is Up?" *Standard Union* (Brooklyn), December 4, 1930, 2.

van Leeuwen, Thomas A. P. *The Skyward Trend of Thought*. MIT Press, 1988.

Wagner, Geraldine B. *Thirteen Months to Go: The Creation of the Empire State Building*. Thunder Bay Press, 2003.

The Washington Post. "Wide Recognition for Building Men Held to Aid Trade." April 8, 1928, sec. R, p. 3.

Weeks, Linton. "The 1940 Census: 72-Year-Old Secrets Revealed." NPR, April 2, 2012.

Weingardt, Richard. "Homer Gage Balcom and the Empire State Building." *Leadership and Management in Engineering* 11, no. 2 (April 2011): 209–18.

Wesley, Charles H. "Organized Labor and the Negro." Paper 213. Howard University Faculty Reprints, 1939. https://dh.howard.edu/reprints/213.

White, E. B. "Destructionist [Jacob Volk]." *New Yorker*, March 15, 1929. https://www.newyorker.com/magazine/1929/03/23/destructionist.

Willis, Carol, ed. *Building the Empire State*. W. W. Norton, 1998.

———. *Form Follows Finance: Skyscrapers and Skylines in New York and Chicago*. Princeton Architectural Press, 1997.

———. "Skyscraper Utopias: Visionary Urbanism in the 1920s." In *Imagining Tomorrow: History, Technology, and the American Future*, edited by J. J. Corn. MIT Press, 1986.

Wilson, Edmund, ed. *Apologies to the Iroquois*. Farrar, Straus & Cudahy, 1960.

Wilson, Edmund. "Progress and Poverty." *New Republic* 67, no. 859 (May 20, 1931): 13–14.

Woodward, Richard B. "Too Much of a Good Thing." *The Atlantic*, June 2003, 67–76.

World (New York). "Building Craftsmen Rewarded for Skill." October 9, 1930. Empire State Scrapbook 1.2 (42–82), p. 68. Avery Architectural & Fine Arts Library, Columbia University.

World (New York). "Empire State Building Crafts to Be Honored." July 28, 1930. Empire State Scrapbook 1.1 (17–35). Avery Architectural & Fine Arts Library, Columbia University.

World (New York). "Rising Hoist Kills Carpenter." December 10, 1930. Empire State Scrapbook. Avery Architectural & Fine Arts Library, Columbia University.

Youtz, Philip N. *Sounding Stones of Architecture*. W. W. Norton, 1929.

Zismer, Gustav. "Old Waldorf's Interior in Ruin: Wreckers Peel Murals from Ceilings, While Debris Rumbles Down Chute." [Source missing], 1930. Empire State Scrapbook 1.2 (1–41), p. 21. Avery Architectural & Fine Arts Library, Columbia University.

INDEX

GLENN KURTZ is the author of *Three Minutes in Poland: Discovering a Lost World in a 1938 Family Film* (FSG, 2014), which was named a "Best Book of 2014" by *The New Yorker*, *The Boston Globe*, and National Public Radio. Based on his book, the documentary film, *Three Minutes: A Lengthening*, was directed by Bianca Stigter, co-produced by Steve McQueen, and narrated by Helena Bonham Carter. After premiering at the Venice Film Festival in 2021, the film was named an official selection of the Sundance Film Festival and received the inaugural Yad Vashem Award for Outstanding Holocaust Documentary. Kurtz is also the author of *Practicing: A Musician's Return to Music* (Knopf, 2007) and the recipient of a 2016-2017 Guggenheim Fellowship. A native New Yorker, he lives with his family in San Francisco.